RESTORATIVE JUSTICE AND LIVED RELIGION

RELIGION AND SOCIAL TRANSFORMATION

General Editors: Anthony B. Pinn and Stacey M. Floyd-Thomas

Prophetic Activism: Progressive Religious Justice Movements in Contemporary America
Helene Slessarev-Jamir

All You That Labor: Religion and Ethics in the Living Wage Movement
C. Melissa Snarr

Blacks and Whites in Christian America: How Racial Discrimination Shapes Religious Convictions
James E. Shelton and Michael O. Emerson

Pillars of Cloud and Fire: The Politics of Exodus in African American Biblical Interpretation
Herbert Robinson Marbury

American Secularism: Cultural Contours of Nonreligious Belief Systems
Joseph O. Baker and Buster G. Smith

Religion and Progressive Activism: New Stories about Faith and Politics
Edited by Ruth Braunstein, Todd Nicholas Fuist, and Rhys H. Williams

"Jesus Saved an Ex-Con": Political Activism and Redemption after Incarceration
Edward Orozco Flores

Solidarity and Defiant Spirituality: Africana Lessons on Religion, Racism, and Ending Gender Violence
Traci C. West

After the Protests Are Heard: Enacting Civic Engagement and Social Transformation
Sharon D. Welch

Ecopiety: Green Media and the Dilemma of Environmental Virtue
Sarah McFarland Taylor

Catholic Activism Today: Individual Transformation and the Struggle for Social Justice
Maureen K. Day

Religion, Race, and COVID-19: Confronting White Supremacy in the Pandemic
Stacey M. Floyd-Thomas

Networking the Black Church: Digital Black Christians and Hip Hop
Erika D. Gault

The Contemporary Black Church: The New Dynamics of African American Religion
Jason E. Shelton

White Property, Black Trespass: The Religion of Mass Criminalization
Andrew Krinks

Restorative Justice and Lived Religion: Transforming Mass Incarceration in Chicago
Jason A. Springs

Restorative Justice and Lived Religion

Transforming Mass Incarceration in Chicago

Jason A. Springs

NEW YORK UNIVERSITY PRESS
New York

NEW YORK UNIVERSITY PRESS
New York
www.nyupress.org

© 2024 by New York University
All rights reserved

Please contact the Library of Congress for Cataloging-in-Publication data.
ISBN: 9781479823772 (hardback)
ISBN: 9781479823789 (paperback)
ISBN: 9781479823819 (library ebook)
ISBN: 9781479823796 (consumer ebook)

This book is printed on acid-free paper, and its binding materials are chosen for strength and durability. We strive to use environmentally responsible suppliers and materials to the greatest extent possible in publishing our books.

Manufactured in the United States of America

10 9 8 7 6 5 4 3 2 1

Also available as an ebook

In memory of Ora Schub,
warrior for peace,

and with gratitude
to Susan Sharpe,

my first teachers in restorative justice,

and to the young people at PBMR and Circles and Ciphers,
who continue to be

Demanding everything is as ineffective as demanding nothing, because it obscures what that struggle looks like on a daily basis. It can also be demoralizing because when the goal is everything, it is impossible to measure the small but important steps forward that are the wellspring of the movement.

Keeanga-Yamahtta Taylor,
From #BlackLivesMatter to Black Liberation

CONTENTS

Introduction	1
1. South Africa to South Side: What Is Restorative Justice?	21
2. Resurrection in Back of the Yards: The Past Inhabiting the Present	28
3. Pillars and Circles	40
4. The Power of a Credible Messenger	53
5. Restorative Justice and the New Jim Crow	63
6. Restorative Justice *Is* "Transformative Justice": How Restorative Justice Transforms Structural and Cultural Violence	74
7. Restorative Justice with a Hammer? Beyond a "Damage-Centric" Account of Trauma and Care	87
8. What Does "Spiritual" Get You That "Trauma" Does Not? Accompaniment as Spiritual and Critical Praxis	101
9. But Is It *Really* "Justice"? The Power and Impact of Restorative Justice Ethics	117
10. Peacemaking Circles as Ethical Practice	125
11. Justice That Heals and Transforms: Accountability, Forgiveness, and Nondomination	130
12. #LaquanMcDonald: Resistance and Compromise in Lawndale	152
13. Can Policing Be Restorative Too? Critical Praxis and the Dilemma of "Restorative Policing"	166
14. The Price of a Powerful Slogan Is a Concrete, Constructive Alternative: Transformation beyond the "Abolition versus Reform" Dichotomy	181

15. Everyday Religion in Unexpected Places: Restorative Justice through Lenses of Lived Religion   191

Conclusion: *How* to "Change It All": Small but Important Steps toward a Transformational Social Movement   203

Acknowledgments   211

Notes   213

Index   247

About the Author   259

Introduction

The United States incarcerates more of its citizens than any other country in the world. We have long been recognized for our excessive imprisonment of poor people, but recent decades have also exposed savage inequalities in the treatment of our Black and Brown fellow citizens. This has led activists to identify the US prison-industrial complex as a caste system that discriminates based on race and ethnicity. If this discrimination is systemic, rather than a matter of bad acts by individuals, then nothing short of a transformational social movement will alter the prison-industrial complex and its hyper-incarceration of Latino/as, African Americans, and poor people of all colors across the United States.

The US prison system as it exists is based around the idea that when people have committed crimes (however ambiguous or minor), the correct response is *punishment*. This book examines another possible approach: that instead of focusing on punishment, or even on rehabilitation, our society could practice what scholars and activists call "restorative justice." It explores how restorative justice practices and initiatives can challenge and transform the structurally racist features of the US justice system's culture of retribution. It makes the case that restorative justice's transformative power depends on understanding its often implicit, yet nonetheless frequently controversial, ethical and religious dynamics.

A central contention of this book is that a holistic approach to restorative justice can be a theory of justice, and form concrete justice practices, only because it fosters moral and spiritual forms of association between people. This approach is "holistic" because it rejects the view that restorative justice is mainly a "tool in a tool kit" that might help to mediate individual or group conflicts. Instead, it recognizes that restorative justice is a framework, a way to help envision and cultivate an integrated restorative approach to individual agency, life together in community, and society more broadly. When we think of it in this way, we can see restorative justice embodied in a range of purposeful ethical practices reflecting dynamics of lived, "everyday" moral and spiritual sensibilities.

These dynamics are "moral" in that they are characterized by mutual recognition, reciprocal respect, critical empathy, compassion, and care. Accountability for destructive conflict, in this approach, aims to repair harms, address needs, and heal. This concept of accountability strives to honor the dignity and promote the flourishing of all the people involved in a given circumstance and context.

To speak of "spiritual" dynamics of restorative justice may strike some readers as strange. This book argues that the term "spiritual" conveys frequently overlooked aspects of restorative justice. That term also names, simultaneously, a dimension of the crisis that restorative justice addresses in the United States. Indeed, neglecting to attend to the spiritual dimensions of both our societal malady and our response is to misunderstand, misdiagnose, and invite inadequate responses.

From the perspective of a holistic approach to restorative justice, US mass incarceration is, at its heart, a spiritual crisis—a crisis of meaning, value, and identity that expresses itself in a number of ways. For example, the crisis calls into question the identity or character (the *ethos*, or the spirit of the culture) of the United States as it has been, as it currently is, and as it can become and *is* becoming. This crisis is caused by the deep historical devaluing, dehumanizing, and domination of minority, marginalized, and poor people and communities of all colors. US mass incarceration is a *spiritual* crisis of meaning and value, further, in that it is an extractive enterprise. It plunders and diverts value from the communities it harms in the forms of actual monetary wealth. But, just as importantly, it drains and diverts social value, individual and community self-worth, and symbolic significance. It decimates so-called social capital—the networks of relationships that nurture and enable individuals and promote communal prosperity. This crisis is spiritual, relationally speaking, in that US mass incarceration destroys the relationships and broader communal bonds that people depend on for their well-being and flourishing as whole persons.

Most encompassing, the crisis of mass incarceration is spiritual in that it directly bears upon our shared societal identity—the "soul of America," as Martin Luther King Jr. described it in the context of the civil rights movement. Historically, policing and incarceration have been key instruments for enforcing racialized social control throughout US society. In effect, they continue to be. And so we must ask, regarding consequences of policing and mass incarceration, will the present-day United States continue to be a society inspired by, and beholden to, the ghosts of its White supremacist past?[1]

The relational dynamics of restorative justice practices, holistically understood, are *spiritual* in that they respond to these spiritual dimensions of the crisis of US mass incarceration. The practices aim to cultivate relationships that recognize and nurture mutual interdependence among neighbors, community members, and fellow citizens. These dynamics promote individual agency and self-reliance, but do so by fostering acknowledgment of and a just response to each person's indebtedness to the relationships and communities that are integral to their well-being and flourishing.[2] They facilitate forms of intentional meaning making. They cultivate individual self-worth and shared community value. They help develop forms of individual and collective agency. They fortify community resources that cut against the shaming, silencing, and scapegoating, meaninglessness and despair (nihilism), community fragmentation, and marginalization perpetrated by the racist and classist structural and cultural violence of the US prison-industrial complex.

The cultivation of mutual recognition, reciprocal respect, empathy, compassion, and care, exhibit the moral dimensions of a holistic account of restorative justice. Amplified individual agency and self-reliance that is interwoven with the co-creation of interdependent community through practices of meaning-making, repair, and healing, exhibit its spiritual dynamics.

Such moral and spiritual dynamics, importantly, do not necessarily identify with any particular religious tradition or with any explicitly religious set of commitments. In other words, a person does not need to identify as generally "religious" or identify with a particular religious tradition or specific commitments to find value in the moral and spiritual dynamics of the forms of association that restorative justice engenders. Indeed, many of the practitioners and community members we will encounter in the coming chapters describe the dynamics of restorative justice as "spiritual," but in an explicitly *non*religious sense. At the same time, for some practitioners, the "spirituality" they identify or associate with restorative justice practices may come from or coexist peacefully and in collaboration with explicitly religious traditions and commitments.[3]

To fully understand this holistic restorative justice and its potentially transformational effects, this book examines and assesses the moral and spiritual dynamics of the distinctive forms of human association out of which the values and practices of restorative justice emerge. In the final chapters it uses the category of "lived" religion to illuminate the moral and spiritual dynamics reflected in holistic restorative practices, understandings, and initiatives. These facilitate, I argue, informal, everyday, but nonetheless powerful forms of *critical praxis* that can aid in transforming the systemic injustices of the US prison-industrial complex.

As I use it in this book, *critical praxis* refers to both a given set of practices and an ensuing reflection that feeds back into and refines those practices in the wake of new experiences and applications. Critical praxis works for the fullest possible understanding of some state of affairs in order to challenge and transform the causes and conditions of injustice and violence that persist there. Its purpose is to bring about more just and peaceful conditions. What I describe as the moral and spiritual critical praxis of restorative justice often occurs informally and unconventionally. It occurs, nonetheless, and is a pivotal component of a holistic vision of restorative justice. When people engage in this critical praxis together, they embody a restorative vision of justice, bringing it alive in the world and enabling them to transform the violence perpetuated by racialized systemic injustice.

What Is Restorative Justice?

"Restorative justice" names both a philosophical-ethical framework and a range of community-based and victim/survivor-centered practices of justice, healing, and peacebuilding. It has been implemented widely in international contexts, often informing "truth and reconciliation" efforts in the wake of violent conflict. For example, truth and reconciliation commissions have responded to contemporary and historical genocidal events and repressive regimes in South Africa, Peru, Morocco, and Canada, among numerous others, aiming to uncover what individuals and communities have done and to bring about community healing and repair rather than locking up or executing offenders.[4]

In North America, "restorative justice" typically names a range of small-scale measures that "divert" alleged wrongdoers from a standard path of arrest, trial, and prison by funneling them into "alternative justice" programs (such as victim-offender mediation). These aim to repair harms caused to the victims, the wider community, and even those who caused the harm. And yet, when deployed as diversionary mechanisms within the US justice system, restorative justice initiatives often fail to address the structural and cultural violence that we find throughout the justice system itself. Such forms of violence include the criminalization of people and communities of color, racially biased and brutal policing, and the marginalization and arbitrary treatment of poor people of all colors. This violence creates shame, stigma, and fragmentation in local communities.

As opposed to these diversionary approaches, can a more holistic approach to restorative justice ethics and practices transform structural violence? I argue that it can. But in order to avoid being hastily dismissed by critics as idealistic and wishful thinking, such prescriptions for restorative justice need to be complemented by accounts of it as it is actually practiced in local communities beset by violence. Careful attention to these on-the-ground practices demonstrates that they interweave care and compassion with strenuous ethical practices of relationship building, accountability, and restorative community cultivation. It is the distinctive integration of these practices that opens up the transformational potential of an altogether different account of justice. This holistic account of restorative justice blunts accusations that it is merely soft, naive, or wishful thinking, a version of justice that ultimately lets wrongdoers off the hook.

To offer a convincing account of this approach, in this book I describe the distinctive ways that on-the-ground practitioners think about restorative justice—and the distinctive things they intend to achieve through it. I also examine how the normative features of restorative justice, what I call its moral and spiritual dynamics, facilitate the construction of a different form of justice. These dynamics enable people to implement justice practices in ways that resist the forms of violence characteristic of the US prison-industrial complex, and even potentially transform them.

To examine this potential, we will journey to one "ground zero" where the structural and cultural violence of the US prison-industrial complex has severely harmed particular neighborhoods and local communities. The South and West Sides of Chicago have been devastated by policing and mass incarceration. But religious and community-based restorative justice initiatives and practices have had a healing effect on these places. These local, neighborhood people and community-led initiatives are constructively transforming conflict to restore their city. And they are fashioning practices of justice that critically engage and transform structures and cultures of violence, government policy, and law.

The result is an emerging citywide collaborative network of restorative justice community initiatives that work alongside the justice processes, institutions, and culture of mass incarceration. Through points of ad hoc, strategic, and resistant engagement with the current system, they also have the potential to challenge and transform it. If mass incarceration (and specifically the war on drugs) operates, in Michelle Alexander's terminology, as the New Jim Crow,[5] then Chicago's restorative justice network offers a model for developing transformational and sustainable social movements to change that system. Chicago offers a concrete example of the types of practices and initiatives that are necessary to shift the entrenched dynamics of structural violence that fuel the prison-industrial complex across the United States.

The Structure and Claims of This Book

Chapter 1 goes into more depth on two key questions this book seeks to answer: What is restorative justice? And how might it respond to structural forms of violence? Here I set the parameters for restorative justice interventions and alternatives that could effectively combat the violence manifest in the US prison-industrial complex. Chapter 1 begins by examining a case study of restorative justice that is widely recognized as successful and remains highly influential around the world—South Africa's Truth and Reconciliation Commission (TRC). This case is commonly cited by US restorative justice practitioners as an exemplary and transformative response to violence.[6] In reality, the TRC has had mixed results in South Africa, especially in addressing structural violence. I discuss this case in order to identify and define the central values and practices of restorative justice, but also to show that the "portability" of restorative justice from one context to the next is not straightforward. Considering an international example helps to cast into stark relief the distinctive challenges and forms of violence inherent in US hyper-incarceration.

Chapter 2 brings us back to the United States, and specifically to a community center, the Precious Blood Ministry of Reconciliation, located in a South Side Chicago neighborhood called Back of the Yards. Back of the Yards and many communities like it are frequently caricatured and stigmatized as inner-city "ganglands" and "ghettos." This chapter pushes beneath the surface appearance of the present day to show how deep dynamics of structural and cultural violence from the past assert themselves in contemporary forms of conflict. At the same time, this neighborhood is not simply a site of various forms of violence. It also has a long history as a place where numerous groups and communities have struggled for justice and achieved transformational change. These are powerfully instructive episodes that also frame its present-day context. This chapter enters into this location, seeking to understand how the living spirit of its past makes it a site for resistance to violence and struggle for justice in the present.

Chapters 3 and 4 further explore how other people and practitioners in Back of the Yards conceive of and implement restorative justice practices there. The range of initiatives includes peacemaking circles, trauma-informed accompaniment, urban farming, arts and performance, mentoring, tutoring, craft and skill training, carpentry apprenticeship and construction for neighbors, and legal support. I argue that despite challenges, these initiatives work collectively to form an expansive, holistic restorative justice response to the stigmatizing, community-fragmenting, and social movement-denuding acids of locally prevalent forms of violence. They are exemplary practices and community networks of care and healing that build relationships, repair and transform communities, and strive to cultivate a sustainable social ecology that integrates justice and peace.

Chapter 5 describes the distinctive forms of structural and cultural violence that restorative justice must address in these contexts. It asks, for example, What is the New Jim Crow? How does it manifest and perpetuate structural violence through policing and mass incarceration in ways that especially target people of color? Michelle Alexander's groundbreaking book on this subject gestures to restorative justice as an indispensable approach to countering the methods and effects of US mass incarceration.[7] Others have expanded on this proposal, prescribing restorative justice to address the direct violence experienced by communities that have borne the brunt of New Jim Crow policies.[8] Any such efforts to apply restorative justice to these contexts, they argue, depends on the willingness of others to cultivate care and compassion for the groups of people and communities who have been broadly criminalized in the war on drugs, "tough on crime" policies, and policing practices. These insights are correct and indispensable. Yet their proponents are sometimes portrayed as merely using restorative justice to "hate the crime, but love the criminal." This does not adequately account for its power and transformational effectiveness in practice. Moreover, there are risks in yoking restorative justice ethics and practices to what may *appear* to be an idealistic call for a "kinder, gentler" approach to people and communities suffering from violence. Chapter 5 pushes beyond such criticisms.

In chapter 6 I address concerns raised by those who claim that restorative justice can work only at the level of healing harms related to interpersonal conflicts. These critics claim that restorative justice is not able to address the structural and cultural violence that helped create the contexts in which these interpersonal relationships exist. But I make the case that intervening in and transforming structural and cultural violence and systemic injustices is, in fact, intrinsic to a holistic restorative justice. Illumination of, resistance to, and transformation of systemic injustice do not occur after, separately from, or as adjuncts to the cultivation of relationships that are healthy and just. Rather, these occur *in and through* the cultivation of such relationships and the ensuing self-sufficiency that flows from restorative justice practices. Restorative justice does not merely take back power from the criminal justice system, but also explores the structures and distributions of power that identify certain actions as "violence" and "crime" in the first place. In this way, it creates possibilities for awareness, resistance, self-transformation, and structural change. This is especially true for those who develop critical consciousness for purposes of resisting the forms of oppression that they confront and must resist. But restorative justice practices also open up avenues for critical awareness and action for people who are beneficiaries of oppressive structures and conditions. In learning how to become the kinds of people who can recognize, learn from, and aid others' work of self-liberation, beneficiaries of oppression can learn how to liberate themselves.[9]

Chapter 7 focuses on how the popular discourse of "trauma" has had a considerable effect on restorative justice. On the one hand, trauma discourse has importantly expanded practitioners' understandings of the nature and character of the harms caused by destructive conflict and violence. At the same time, there is a genuine risk of trauma discourse overriding the normative vision of restorative justice and turning it into a therapeutic model for addressing harm. I argue, however, that restorative justice can be *justice*—and not therapy by other means—so long as its relational (and thus, moral and spiritual) dynamics remain its point of orientation and purpose. The tools and understandings from trauma discourse can then provide indispensable supplementary support.

Chapter 8 makes the case that "restorative accompaniment"—a central pillar of restorative justice as it is conceived at Precious Blood and in related restorative justice hubs across Chicago—is coherently "spiritual" and also can serve as a mode of "critical praxis" in order to transform structural and cultural violence. These both occur through what practitioners there call the "co-creation of community." Chapter 9 then argues that restorative justice comprises a distinctive account of *justice* rather than merely a process of interpersonal relational repair and healing in response to trauma or harm. It is justice in the classic sense of each person being owed, and receiving, what is due to them.[10] I offer an account of the relational dynamics of this conception of justice and show how its origins relate to the lived and everyday religious and ethical motivations of the practitioners and initiatives I observed.

In chapter 10 I move forward the ethical groundwork for my case that restorative justice is, indeed, justice. Here I discuss peacemaking circles as ethical practices. Contrary to those who see peacemaking circles as glib cultural mimicking of "indigenous folkways," or dismiss them as so-called New Age self-help, peacemaking circles are painstaking normative practices of relational justice. They develop a long tradition of community-based, relational justice and peacebuilding. Understanding this is crucial to making explicit the kinds of care, focus, and effort such a practice requires. It also makes explicit the kinds of durable, compassionate communities of accountability and healing that emerge from such practices of justice.

Chapter 11 returns again to the Precious Blood Ministry of Reconciliation in Back of the Yards to examine a different set of stories there—stories told from the perspectives of those who caused harm and their families. This chapter adds narrative substance to the condensed, abstract ethical exposition of chapter 10. Here we see in the daily lives of neighborhood people how restorative justice circles, as ethical practices, tap into and build up the relational dynamics of justice. They provide platforms and catalysts for critical praxis and facilitate organized efforts to change and transform the conditions of oppression inflicted on people directly ensnared in the criminal justice system and their families. This chapter continues my account of restorative justice ethics—a rejoinder to those who claim that restorative justice simply gives wrongdoers a pass or compels people who have experienced harm to forgive those who have harmed them. Further, despite common assumptions by those who view restorative justice as an exclusively theological or religious-tradition-specific enterprise, I argue that it need not be linked with formal concepts of forgiveness or reconciliation.

One never simply "takes back power" in the process of transforming a system. Nor is "imagining alternatives" sufficient. Transformation occurs by way of complex processes of resistance and critical negotiation with realities that already exist. Chapter 12 thus takes up the question, What are the risks of close interaction with the criminal justice system? How likely is it that restorative justice practices and initiatives will be captured and assimilated into a violent system that would protect and preserve itself through processes that only *appear* to alter its surface-level operations? To answer these questions, I examine how people implement restorative justice practices in North Lawndale, a neighborhood on the West Side of Chicago. Specifically, I investigate the alternative "restorative justice court" that some people who come into contact with the system can opt to enter. The Lawndale court works in tandem with the Cook County justice system, prompting the question, Do formal cooperation and/or collaboration with the contemporary criminal justice system (such as police and judges) place restorative justice initiatives at risk of becoming a new form by which previous structural injustices are perpetuated (a process that sociologists refer to as "preservation through transformation")? There are many possibilities for failure along these lines, but I argue that it is indeed possible for restorative justice to respond at the levels of system and structure to this complex state of affairs.

Chicago is notorious for police brutality and abuse of force. Nationally recognized scandals in Chicago policing, such as the murder of Laquan McDonald in 2014 and its subsequent cover-up, suggest that systemic corruption is present throughout the policing system.[11] Chapter 13 acknowledges and grapples with the depth and severity of the ways that policing and police abuse of force manifest the New Jim Crow in Chicago communities. However, it also documents and assesses several police initiatives that are using restorative justice practices to reform and revitalize community policing in Chicago neighborhoods. Is it possible for law enforcement to reform itself in line with restorative justice in ways that do not merely preserve oppressive dynamics? Some police and judges cooperate with restorative justice initiatives to address the destructiveness of the current system and to attend to the harms the police themselves have suffered while working in violent neighborhoods. As challenging as it may be, police participation in community-based restorative justice initiatives and practices can begin to repair relationships that have become toxic. Yet these processes are obstructed by the depth and pervasiveness of the corruption from which the Chicago Police Department currently suffers. Systemic transformation is required.

The final two chapters explore in greater depth what I identify as the moral, spiritual, and "lived religious" dynamics of restorative justice. In what ways can holistic models of restorative justice ethics and practices be thought of as "religious"? Moreover, what difference do such religious dynamics make in transforming structural violence? As we will see, many neighborhood people and practitioners disavow formal connections to established "religion" in their restorative justice practices. Many of the same stakeholders, nonetheless, describe the relational, community-formative, and community-sustaining work of restorative justice as "spiritual." What do they mean when they describe their work in this way? And how do such terms help us understand the transformational potential of their practices?

Based on my observations across the South and West Sides of Chicago, I argue that the moral and spiritual dynamics of the practices of restorative justice can be best understood through analytical lenses of lived or everyday religious sensibilities. These are practices of creating and renewing community, cultivating accountability, and mutual caretaking among individual members. They are dignity-affirming practices of collaborative resilience through shared meaning making. People in restorative justice communities implement these practices together. In doing so they embody a relational account of justice that orients their commitments and purposes, and illuminates, cultivates, repairs, and strengthens the webs that hold them together. I argue that the moral and spiritual resonances of these practices can drive and sustain the resistant capacities of restorative justice. Moreover, they do so in ways that can cut to the roots of, and transform, systemic injustices and forms of structural and cultural violence present in the prison-industrial complex.

Examining how restorative justice ethics and practices reflect various religious dimensions of commitment, self-understanding, relationality, and motivations responds to a high-stakes question at the heart of both the prison abolition and restorative justice movements: What does it mean to resist mass incarceration in ways that can concretely challenge and transform its causes and conditions, rather than merely reconfiguring its surface-level features while (however inadvertently) perpetuating the deeper forms of violence it effects, on the one hand, or railing against the system with utopian claims to "abolish it all now," on the other?

Developing an account of the ways that restorative justice reflects sensibilities illuminated by categories of everyday or lived religion, I argue, makes them available as modes of critical praxis through which resistance to and transformation of structural injustices become possible. In terms of scholarly discourse, this analysis dislodges restorative justice from its placement within a dichotomous framing of "the secular" versus "the religious." This avoids portraying the everyday religious dimensions of restorative justice as a vague "spirituality" that provides moral camouflage for the systemic injustices of mass incarceration.

Studying Restorative Justice through Critical Participatory Action Research

This book addresses several audiences.[12] Its account of the relational ethics at the heart of restorative justice in Chicago, which I use to expand our understanding of what "restorative justice" is, participates in debates in religious ethics and political philosophy. My effort to understand restorative justice through lenses of lived religion is a part of continuing endeavors to center everyday practice as a way of understanding religion. My challenge is carrying out these tasks in a way that is theoretically discerning enough to distinctively contribute to scholarly conversations, while not *so* fraught with theory as to become opaque to readers who make up another audience I address: those who approach restorative justice with interests in practice, implementation, and social transformation. These readers, I hope, will also find instructive insights from my engagement with practitioners across Chicago and from the analysis that follows.

This book emerged as the result of a long research journey. I developed and began teaching courses on restorative justice upon joining the faculty at an interdisciplinary institute devoted to matters of justice and peace. The topic naturally complemented my previous work on theories of justice in religious ethics, and in religion and conflict in public life. An exploratory paper entitled "Restorative Justice and the New Jim Crow" that I delivered to the ethics group at the American Academy of Religion in 2013 sparked interest from the audience. Shortly thereafter, Anthony Pinn, an editor for New York University Press's Religion and Social Transformation series, urged me to consider developing the paper into a book for the series.

As I started to work on this project, it quickly became clear that if I was to fully understand and engage restorative justice ethics and practices, I would need to move beyond a strictly academic context of case studies, ethical exposition, and philosophical argument. I would need to actually explore, observe, and open myself to understanding and learning from the ways that particular people and communities implement restorative justice philosophy and ethics, and sustain its practices in their everyday lives and local communities.

I embarked on this journey by undertaking community organizer training with the Community Renewal Society, a group focused (at that time) on organizing communities in support of restorative justice initiatives across Chicago. The CRS viewed these initiatives as vehicles for community-led and neighborhood-empowering approaches to public safety and violence reduction that could cut against the over-policing and retributive status quo administered by the Cook County criminal justice system. Community organizer training led me to a restorative justice peacemaking circle training program offered by the Community Justice for Youth Institute, guided by Ora Schub and convened at the Precious Blood Ministry of Reconciliation in Back of the Yards. Over the several days of the training I got to know, among many others, Ora, Father David Kelly, Sister Donna Liette, Pamela Purdie, Julie Anderson, Orlando Mayorga, and Jonathan Little—all pivotal figures in the chapters that follow. At the time, their willingness to welcome me and aid my investigations into their work led me to think that my project struck them as especially important. I came to realize that their welcoming and affirming support was, in fact, a sign that they were extending to me the same radical hospitality given to every person who sojourns at the center. Their generosity was far more a matter of simply living out their vocation than a signal of anything exceptional about my project.

The people I met at Precious Blood helped me access numerous activists and organizations across Chicago who work in a network of neighborhood grassroots organizations oriented by restorative justice commitments and practices—Emmanuel Andre, Ethan Ucker, Evan Okun, AnnMarie Brown, and the young people at Circles and Ciphers in Rogers Park; Sarah Staudt and Jeremy Winfield at Lawndale Christian Legal Center in North Lawndale; Matt DeMatteo at Urban Life Skills in Little Village; and Elena Quintana and Jayeti Newbold at the Institute on Public Safety and Social Justice at Adler University, to name a few. I undertook additional peacemaking circle trainings at Precious Blood, visited the organizations in the neighborhood hub network, regularly attended the monthly Circle for Circle Keepers meeting, and interviewed many of the people I encountered there. Precious Blood became the location I frequented most over the ensuing four and a half years. (My visits for fieldwork purposes, begun in the fall of 2015, were interrupted by the onset of the COVID-19 pandemic in 2020.[13])

Precious Blood revealed itself to be, in effect, a "hub of hubs"—a central node of a collaborative network of restorative justice neighborhood-based, community-led initiatives. The partners in this network began collaborating in 2012. Over a decade later, as I was finishing this book, this network was still continuing to expand and collaborate. Precious Blood, a pivotal element in this citywide restorative justice network, hosts monthly four-day peacemaking circle trainings run by the Community Justice for Youth Institute, and countless other circle meetings and restorative justice events facilitated by partner organizations across Chicago. It also convenes the monthly Circle for Circle Keepers, where restorative justice practitioners, especially those who regularly lead—or "keep"—peacemaking circles across the city, "sit in circle" together to learn from and support one another, and to further cultivate their restorative justice capabilities.

I approached this study as an exercise in "critical participatory action research."[14] Critical participatory action research is not traditional "ethnography," where outsiders journey to an unfamiliar context to engage in participant-observation, nor is it reporting from an "insider" participant perspective. It is, at its heart, an intrinsically ethical enterprise. It blurs a dichotomous insider/outsider opposition in research and recognizes the inevitability of bringing one's normative commitments to one's analysis. The assertion that scholarship ought (somehow) to be "nonnormative" is, itself, a normative claim and value commitment that have impelled many to pursue the chimera of "value-free scholarship."[15] I do not engage in ethnography in the chapters that follow. In some chapters I provide what ethnographers call "thick" description, using my observations to help illuminate and engage in ethical analysis of the self-conceptions, practices, and impact of these particular restorative justice practices and contexts.

Critical participatory action research prompts researchers to be as explicit and critically reflective as possible about their overarching purposes and motivating commitments (rather than, say, pretending that they have none). However, it does not name those motivations and commitments in order to attempt to "set them aside" to achieve an allegedly pure objectivity, or even neutrality. Instead, this mode of research recognizes how such commitments inform who the researcher is. To claim that one has cleansed or altogether separated oneself from one's commitments, interests, biases, and value orientations invites those elements of one's perspective to have unrecognized or un-self-critical sway.[16]

Critical participatory action research also intentionally explores and takes seriously the content and significance of the values, commitments, and purposes of the group(s) the researcher is engaging. It orients the research plan toward opening spaces where these people and groups can speak, and the researcher can listen and be challenged.[17] This allows people to account for what they understand themselves to be doing (one aspect of the expansive conception of what Clifford Geertz referred to as "thick description"), but also express their perspective on why and how the work they are doing is vital for social transformation.[18]

Critical participatory action research is anchored in and oriented by the relationships implied by "participatory action." This means that researchers are neither "extracting data" (ethnographic or otherwise) for abstract, scholarly purposes (as "outsiders") nor merely presenting "another country heard from" as ethnographers.[19] Of course, neither are they full-fledged participants (so-called insiders) straightforwardly committed to and participating in the practices occurring in that context. This approach means, rather, that researchers strive to cultivate relationships with those they engage with so as to understand them better and learn from them, but also with the hope that their own work might support actual sociopolitical change. This participatory dimension leads researchers to elicit and then focus on understanding the questions, needs, critical insights, demands, and stories of those they engage. It asks how these challenge and shape researchers' questions and purposes as the research journey unfolds. These purposes might aim to impact policy, foreground misrepresented or underrepresented initiatives and communities, support organizing and activist efforts, and/or illuminate critical insights that practitioners may want to take into consideration. Most basically, in the words of Michelle Fine, such "participatory" research aims to "trouble the common sense about unjust arrangements that seem so natural or deserved; to destabilize what we think of as 'normal'; and to reveal where resistance gathers and where radical possibilities might flourish."[20]

As a result, critical participatory action research creates relationships that become multidirectional—both institutionally and personally. So, for example, venturing into the South and West Side neighborhoods of Chicago time and again over five years during the fieldwork for this project led me to invite the practitioners and young people active in the hubs I encountered to come and speak to my classes, lead workshops, present their work at Notre Dame–sponsored conferences, and deliver lectures for students and faculty all across my university and for members of the South Bend community. They described their work and taught me, my students, and my fellow faculty members about the transformational potential of restorative justice, and about their efforts to implement sustainable restorative justice initiatives in the city of Chicago. The relationships that emerged further led me to accompany students from my classes, and from other Notre Dame programs, to Back of the Yards to interact with, listen to, and learn from the restorative justice practitioners and local community members. These relationships in turn facilitated placing our students in community-based learning opportunities and internships at Precious Blood, in collaboration with (and funded by) Notre Dame's Center for Social Concerns. These relationships continue into the present, well beyond the point at which I stopped frequenting Precious Blood and the other Chicago hubs for the purposes of participant observation and interviews.

Personally, these relationships led me into numerous situations—often while sitting in circle—that compelled me to reckon with the forms of increasing self-awareness and self-criticism intrinsic to the processes that Paulo Freire calls critical praxis. They required, in other words, that I examine and re-examine the sensibilities and understandings that I, as White, male, and economically advantaged, in particular, must strive to cultivate in order to seek solidary instruction from and critical participatory engagement with these practitioners, activists, and communities. This is especially the case when the "participatory action" on my part takes the form of research, teaching, ethical reflection, and writing.[21] Such personally directed "teaching moments" were necessary for me to learn how to illuminate and challenge the impact that White supremacist structures and cultural processes endemic to the US prison-industrial complex have on neighborhoods and local communities—including my own.

The "critical" dimension of critical participatory action research means that engaging in a relationship-oriented methodological approach is not mere reporting. This approach does not naively presume that the people in question always comprehensively articulate what they are up to or exhaustively grasp the full extent of the implications (or presuppositions) of their work. Who, after all, can do this? Rather, this approach calls researchers to engage in theoretically informed exposition and ethical reflection for the purposes of intervening in the contexts and practices they describe and redescribe. It might use theoretical tools or specialized vocabulary in order to more carefully illuminate and explain aspects of the work, insights that practitioners and advocates might benefit from or want to consider. However, even here the researcher-practitioner relationship is not unidirectional. I found that most of the people and groups that I observed, and whose work I follow now, already engaged in complex forms of analysis, self-criticism, and reflection on their practices. Indeed, this is a pivotal component of practicing restorative justice as a critical praxis. So even where theoretically equipped researchers might be most incisive, and have insights to offer, they must remain open to instruction through dialogue with practitioners.[22]

Critical participatory action research is intently object-directed—it is answerable to how things are with the subject matter it studies— but not "value-free."[23] It is based on a commitment to respond in certain ways to what researchers encounter and observe. As a scholar and teacher trained in religion, ethics, and politics, and working in peace and justice studies, I approach such work oriented by the integrative norm of "justpeace." That is, I aim to understand as charitably as possible and to critically enrich efforts to cultivate justice in ways that simultaneously reduce violence in all its forms.[24] In doing so, I try to avoid the temptation to graft an account of restorative justice onto preexisting controversies among interloping professional academics. These might include interminable arguments over whether something is "religious" or "secular," or the trashing of all invocations of the "spiritual" as either insufficiently traditional or irrevocably co-opted by secularity, among others. While these arguments have their place (and I address some of them directly in the two final chapters), getting sidetracked by them throughout would be harmful to understanding the kind of restorative justice I am concerned with in this book.

As you can see from this brief description, using this approach, the researcher is an observer, explorer, and critic, but a student as well, striving to remain teachable. In this project, I am motivated and guided by the hope that walking alongside practitioners of restorative justice—or perhaps more accurately, following at a distance—might provide critical yet charitable observation, understanding, redescription, and ethical illumination. I want to highlight how restorative justice can change scholarly discourses and classroom goals, but I also aim to give an account of restorative justice that helps those striving to implement it to enrich and expand their own conception and practice.

Conclusion: The Greatest Temptation

In the chapters that follow we will encounter restorative justice as a range of ethical practices of self-formation and community formation. In these, local neighborhood people and community-led initiatives cultivate relationships that help them transform conflict, heal and build up communities struggling with persistent violence, and practice a justice that centers accountability. They also aim to repair harms and heal people and their neighbors. Yet they do not have a strictly oppositional relationship to the justice system. They maintain, rather, a kind of strategic and selective critical praxis. This praxis certainly resists, but it also builds relationships within this system in order to transform it, piece by piece. It requires, in other words, working with willing collaborators who represent various facets of the justice system. There are better and worse ways to go about this. Doing so necessitates a persistently vigilant shifting and catching of balance, relationally and institutionally. The risks of being co-opted by the system are dangerously real. How to critically engage this system, and the people who maintain it, *without* being co-opted is the subject of a continuously unfolding argument among the restorative justice practitioners in the places we will visit together. It is also a central question I try to ask and answer in this book.

The greatest temptation for restorative justice is not that it might devolve into a milquetoast spirituality and navel-gazing self-help therapy that, in effect, preserves the violence intrinsic to the contemporary US retributive justice system. (Such temptations are real, of course, and it is necessary to resist them.) Instead, the greatest temptation is that restorative justice will neglect—or never claim—responsibility for the nature and character of the distinctive form of *justice* that is its namesake. This is a kind of justice that has the potential to heal through truth telling, practices of accountability, and repair of harm, but that, in order to do so, must simultaneously and relentlessly train its attention on the systemic and structural causes and conditions of *injustice*. To hold accountable through repair and healing, it must deploy itself as a form of critical praxis that challenges, resists, and strives to transform those causes and conditions.

The trap for restorative justice in the United States, in short, is that it will fail to lay claim to and exert its full capacity to analytically and practically cut to the roots of systemic injustice and structural violence, and provide transformational, dignifying alternatives in their place. To charitably yet critically demonstrate, explain, and amplify these capacities is the central purpose of this book.

1

South Africa to South Side

What Is Restorative Justice?

Amy Biehl arrived in Cape Town, South Africa, as a twenty-six-year-old Fulbright scholar in 1993. Strict racial segregation had been ironclad law there for fifty years. As an organizer for racial justice, Amy helped coordinate the first "all race" elections that would mark the end of South African apartheid. One afternoon, while she was driving several Black co-workers and friends to the local town of Gugulethu, a crowd emerging from a political rally surrounded her car. Calls for violent resistance to the cruelties of apartheid had provoked the rallygoers that day. Despite pleas from her friends that "she is one of us," a group of men dragged Amy from her car and stoned and stabbed her to death on the road. Four young men—Eazi Nofemla, Ntobeko Peni, Vusumzi Ntamo, and Mongesi Manquina—were convicted of Amy's murder and each sentenced to eighteen years in prison.

With the official termination of apartheid in 1995, President Nelson Mandela launched South Africa's Truth and Reconciliation Commission (TRC). The TRC's strict application process meant that applicants had to verify that the harms they had committed were politically motivated. If applicants were granted entrance, taking responsibility and public truth telling would result in pardon for the offense and immunity from further prosecution, otherwise known as amnesty. The four young men's applications were supported by Amy's parents, Linda and Peter Biehl. It was, the Biehls said, what Amy would have wanted.

The logic and objectives of the TRC were straightforward. The hearings aimed to do something that the normal, adversarial justice system did not permit: to induce thorough, open fact-finding, promoting public transparency and truth telling in the hope that healing would follow. Where possible, they facilitated reconciliation between those who had suffered and those who had caused the harm. Criminal prosecution was an option for those who would not acknowledge and fully disclose the harms that they had caused. In Amy's case, each man testified publicly about what he had done, why and how he did it, and the context surrounding that day. The Biehls met with the men's parents in their homes. They sought to understand the history of apartheid and the oppression—both personal and societal—that had precipitated their daughter's murder.

The TRC process in this case was indeed transparent and public. In fact, it was broadcast nationally on television and radio. The men sat on a dais together, each telling his story. A commission representative of those affected by their actions examined them. The community, Amy's family, and commission investigators all provided questions. The purpose of making the encounter public was to transform a personalized intervention into a practice of public accountability and, if possible, a shared practice of lament and healing. The public nature of South Africa's TRC promoted collective participation by allowing members of the public to observe and share vicariously in the process. Ultimately, all four men were granted reprieve from their prison sentences. Two met with Amy's parents following the hearings. They later accepted employment in the foundation launched by the Biehls to promote racial justice and reconciliation, the cause to which their daughter had devoted her life.

Many agree that South Africa's TRC was effective in promoting post-apartheid reconciliation to help victims heal and in holding wrongdoers responsible for their actions and reintegrating them into society. But the TRC's ability to actually deliver reparations to the parties who were harmed has been more ambiguous. And its ability to address and alter the forms of structural and cultural violence that were inscribed in South African society over the half century of apartheid has been faint, at best. The TRC could not address the savage socioeconomic inequalities that cut along racial lines, the ensuing forms of disempowerment, and the de facto forms of racialized geographic segregation and humiliation that were held over from apartheid.[1] This raises a question for the restorative justice ethic at the heart of South Africa's attempt to transition from the violence of apartheid. Is it possible for restorative justice to address and alter the injustices inscribed within justice systems, and to transform the structures and cultures of violence that hold those injustices in place?

Transitional Justice

It seems clear to many people in retrospect that the South African TRC too quickly emphasized interpersonal healing and relationship building. It stressed these goals over the painful, grinding, and sometimes alienating processes by which deeply rooted systems of racialized inequality, economic marginalization, and humiliation must be addressed directly. It focused on the personal healing process at the expense of dismantling systemic racism.

But it is also clear that this focused objective of the South African TRC was intentional. While it can be oriented by the values and practices of restorative justice, a truth and reconciliation commission is not, itself, restorative justice. These commissions, implemented at moments of great national change, are intentionally transitional measures that can deploy restorative justice values and practices in the wake of violence, prolonged injustice, human rights violations, and even mass atrocity.[2] In such a mode, restorative justice is "transitional" in that it is employed for a specific purpose and during a designated period of time. TRCs can reflect the values and commitments of restorative justice, in part, by aiming to heal harms through relationally focused repair.[3] They can do this through practices of mutual recognition, reciprocal respect, and public accountability, via truth telling, responsibility taking, apology, and restitution. These practices are tailored to the needs of the victims, survivors, communities affected, and even the wrongdoers.

South Africa's TRC occurred during such a period of transition and embodied restorative justice values.[4] Transition was necessary after the cessation of mass violence, sustained racial injustice, and human rights abuses that characterized the National Party's apartheid regime (1948–1994). It was also necessary in light of the longer histories of European conquest and settler colonialism out of which apartheid was born. The commission conducted nationally visible investigations. It reconstructed what actually occurred and facilitated public acknowledgment of politically motivated violence and killing.

Where there had been silence, the TRC enabled victims to name—and make dramatically present to others—the wrongs they suffered. Where there had been a void of information, it gathered and shared facts. Where there had been denial, it mandated public truth telling. It facilitated contrition and apology. Victims and families who had been suppressed and pushed to the margins were brought into the light and asked to share their stories. Where there had been persistent resentment and desire for retribution, the TRC facilitated public practices and interpersonal engagement that might aid survivors in coping cathartically with rage. It allowed repressed anger to be handled in constructive ways rather than emerging violently and unpredictably, as happened in the murder of Amy Biehl.[5] The commission hoped to open possibilities for repair, perhaps forgiveness, between victims and those who had harmed them. Its architects aimed to promote healing and shared, societal recovery.

Politically, the TRC was trying to avoid a situation in which the newly installed government simply vanquished its opponents, in effect exacting revenge through legal retribution. Legal prosecution of those who harmed others during apartheid would have been an undertaking so massive—and so certain to meet with refusal to cooperate and denial of responsibility by wrongdoers—that it would have further polarized and retraumatized a still wounded and deeply divided society. The new South African leadership sought, instead, to facilitate a peaceful and healing transfer of power. The purpose of the TRC was to bring South African society to a recovery point from which it might cultivate and gradually normalize more equitable forms of justice, civil rights, democratic practices, and even civic friendship between former enemies who were now trying to imagine a future common life.

From Transitional to Restorative Justice

Prison abolitionist, activist, and scholar Angela Davis holds up the case of Amy Biehl as an example of a restorative justice approach that might provide an alternative to what Davis calls the prison-industrial complex in the United States.[6] This description, a play on the more common "military-industrial complex," points to the fact that the problem of US mass incarceration is both deeply embedded in the structures and culture of the United States and driven toward permanent institutional expansion.

US mass incarceration is not simply a phenomenon of out-of-control physical growth. It is more than the sum of jails, prisons, and detention centers in the United States (over 6,296 as of 2022) plus the eleven-fold increase since the early 1970s of the masses of people they incarcerate, monitor, and incapacitate.[7] This population went from 200,000 in 1973 to 1.9 million as of 2022—5.7 million if we include those "in the system" on probation and parole.[8] This result is also entwined with the growth desires of the industries that underwrite and profit from mass incarceration. The phrase "industrial complex" gestures to the business interests, corporations, lobbyists, policy makers, lawmakers, law enforcement departments, and prosecutors who participate in (and often profit from) sustaining these conditions. It entails the political platforms, ideologies, and slogans that orient and inform lawmakers' supporters or constituencies (like "tough on crime," "zero tolerance," "three strikes," and "war on drugs"). It also gestures to the many cultural perceptions involving race, ethnicity, gender, and class that feed into and perpetuate the alleged unavoidability of mass incarceration (so-called "missing Black fathers," "welfare queens," "bad hombres," and "super-predators," in addition to countless forms of unconscious bias). The phrase further points to the impact of mass incarceration on local communities across the country. Prisons, for example, sometimes serve as economic engines of rural towns. The "prison-industrial complex," understood like this, is profoundly motivated toward its own preservation and growth in a way that causes deep and lasting tears through the fabric of neighborhoods and communities all across US society. What hope might there be for the restorative justice practices and values at the heart of the South African TRC to offer alternatives to these US institutions, practices, and ideologies?

The differences between post-apartheid South Africa and US mass incarceration are vast. The idea that a person could take lessons from one and apply them to the other depends on any such lessons being adapted in highly context-specific ways. These adaptations would need to be sensitive to the histories of explicit and structural violence that may be related to others around the world but that are also unique to US contexts. They would have to address, for example, the ways that structural violence typically veils itself behind racialized forms of cultural violence.[9] These include the pretext of seemingly "commonsense" perceptions and justifications, such as that certain groups of people are inclined to "commit more crime" because "it's their culture," and rationalizations such as "they do this to themselves," "they deserve it," or "they are their own worst enemies." Moreover, since the South African TRC occurred during a moment of transition, we would have to think about how its lessons might apply to a US context that is not in transition in the same way and that needs sustainable, not transitional, initiatives. Any effort to implement such a model would have to focus on the complex root systems of racialized injustice and structural violence from the start, and not incidentally or as an afterthought. It would have to lead to structural change and facilitate cultural transformation. Is this possible?

Restorative Justice

"Restorative justice" is a term that names both an ethical framework that has elaborated a particular understanding of personhood and justice, and a range of community-based and victim/survivor-centered justice, healing, and peacebuilding practices. In the United States, it occurs most frequently as small-scale "diversionary" practices and initiatives. These "divert" wrongdoers from a standard course through the criminal justice system. They funnel them into alternative justice practices and programs. These may offer third-party or court-sponsored options in which a person convicted of crime can decrease their punishment by agreeing to participate in a restorative process. Such restorative justice paths are born out of the conviction that harsh punishment solves no problems—that, indeed, it makes those problems worse and usually creates additional problems that were not there before. Instead, at their best, these diversionary measures aim to repair all harms that have been caused by destructive conflict and violence, including those suffered by wrongdoers.[10]

Studies of restorative justice initiatives in the United States report a consistent reduction in so-called repeat offending (recidivism) when compared with standard retributive justice approaches—by as much as 44 percent.[11] Those who have caused harm also report increased perceptions of fair treatment and increasingly empathetic views about the impact their wrongdoing had upon others. Survivors of harm also report improved perceptions of fairness, greater satisfaction with the justice process, and improved attitudes toward the offender. They are more willing to forgo punitive feelings toward the person who harmed them and more likely to feel that the outcome was just.[12] All these results, too, demonstrate the contrast with traditional approaches.

Yet, when deployed primarily for diverting alleged offenders out of the standard (and, typically, most destructively punitive) paths through the criminal justice system, restorative justice initiatives fail to address the ways that the US justice system itself has come to be predicated on structural and cultural forms of violence inflicted on the people and communities enmeshed in it. Such violence occurs in an array of forms, including high inequality, exclusion, and humiliation. The system of mass incarceration criminalizes and profiles people of color and poor people of all colors long before it incarcerates them.[13] Racially uneven application of zero-tolerance discipline codes in schools and war on drugs policies drive hyper-incarceration from a remarkably young age.[14] Broken windows policing practices, named for their intensive focus on pulling people into the criminal justice system for minor offenses such as graffiti, loitering, open container violations, running a stop sign, or biking on the sidewalk, are driven by the long-disproven concept that these are a harbinger of more serious crimes.[15] Instead, employing overt and implicit biases, they manifest in the overuse of police force in poor and urban minority communities. The system shames and stigmatizes the people it entangles, keeping them locked out of decent jobs, housing, livable wages, and meaningful opportunities even after they have "paid their debt to society."[16] It splinters social bonds and relationships in local communities over generations.[17]

When compared to standard retributive and punitive approaches, diversionary restorative justice practices can—and do—make a positive difference in the lives of many people ensnared in the system. Nonetheless, these efforts also risk making a draconian justice system look and feel "kinder and gentler," while leaving that system hardly less racialized, unequal, exclusionary, and liable to stigmatize people and fragment neighborhoods. Is it possible for restorative justice ethics and practices to respond effectively—and transformatively—to such structural and cultural forms of violence that hold systemic injustices in place? As we saw in the case of the South African TRC above, this is no simple task.

2

Resurrection in Back of the Yards

The Past Inhabiting the Present

Jonathan Little grew up in Back of the Yards, a neighborhood at the heart of Chicago's South Side. He lives and works there today. At seventeen he started selling drugs, mostly to buy food for his younger brothers and sisters. When he got arrested, Cook County funneled him into its adult jail population. After a week there, he made up his mind that it was a place he could never go back to.

"Growing up in the neighborhood, it was a struggle. It was a struggle," Jonathan recounts.

> Every day you would wake up in the morning and have nothing to eat. You had to get up and go make something happen. I always say, I don't applaud robbing people, I don't applaud selling drugs, I don't applaud [anything] negative. [But], when you wake up in the morning and your sister is saying, "Mama, I'm hungry," you've got to do what you've got to do. My thing was that I sold drugs back in the day. It was a breaking point because you have to look over your shoulder at every moment. That is no way to live. You are worried about the police, being locked up, and worried about other people either trying to rob you or take what you've got. It was a struggle. Just seeing my younger sisters and brothers go through the same struggle that I went through is kind of what brought me into this work.[1]

As a first-time offender, Jonathan qualified for a job placement program. He found work at a Catholic community center in his neighborhood called the Precious Blood Ministry of Reconciliation, which models the more holistic account of restorative justice I offer in this book.

Precious Blood sits between Throop and Elizabeth Streets in Back of the Yards, a block north of Sherman Park. It occupies the top floor of an old Catholic school building that once served the colossal St. John of God parish. A vacant field now stretches out where the church once stood. The history of the site—its growth, struggles, entanglement with larger currents of racism and "urban renewal," and present life as a hub of restorative justice work—tracks with that of the neighborhood writ large.

A Polish congregation founded in 1907, St. John of God grew as large as 2,400 families. At one point it was one of nine Catholic churches within a radius of a few blocks.[2] In their heyday, these parishes served the influx of immigrants who were arriving mainly from Eastern Europe, although sometimes still from Ireland and Germany. These mostly Czech, Polish, Lithuanian, and Slovak immigrants converged on the neighborhood seeking work in Chicago's Union Stock Yards a few blocks north. The invention of the refrigerated rail car in 1878 gave Chicago's meatpacking industry national reach, as slaughterhouse owners could now ship their perishable meats to the coasts. Business boomed. Countless railroad lines already converged in Chicago, and the stockyards on the South Side stood at the heart of them. The Union Stock Yards quickly sprawled to become the largest of their kind in the country.

Though officially they lived in "New City," residents came to refer to their blocks of dilapidated worker tenements, permeated by the slaughter-yard stench, as the "back" of the Stock Yards. The name stuck—"Back of the Yards."[3] The year before St. John of God was founded, the journalist Upton Sinclair portrayed the neighborhood in his novel *The Jungle*, a book Jack London called "the *Uncle Tom's Cabin* of wage slavery."[4] Sinclair's gut-wrenching accounts of the squalor of impoverished immigrant life, the cruelties of child labor, and bare survival in the meatpacking district compelled a young reader named Dorothy Day to push her baby brother's pram along the South Side streets of Chicago, rather than along the genteel Lake Michigan shore. Walking through Back of the Yards first wakened Day to a vocation to live and work alongside the people that the New Testament calls "the least of these." These early experiences shaped her into the writer, radical activist, and founder of the Catholic Worker movement who is now a candidate for sainthood.[5]

In 1939 the legendary activist Saul Alinsky led Back of the Yards residents in forming a neighborhood council. Their successful campaigns to transform neighborhood blight, to procure living wages, secure humane housing, and reduce youth violence all laid the foundation for a model of community organizing that would spread throughout the country. Leaders trained in Alinsky's approach implemented his methods across the United States in the Industrial Areas Foundation.[6] Community organizing transformed the neighborhood through the 1940s and 1950s.[7]

During the postwar period, federal policies led to a series of massive "urban renewal" projects that often had exactly the opposite effect, prioritizing easy automobile transportation from new suburbs to downtown and thereby destroying housing in city neighborhoods. In the late 1950s, urbanist and organizer Jane Jacobs successfully led neighborhood campaigns that saved New York City's Greenwich Village and Washington Square Park from Robert Moses's efforts to plow an expressway through those communities. Jacobs modeled her campaigns on the organizing in Chicago's Back of the Yards. She held the neighborhood up as an exemplar of community self-empowerment and successful "unslumming" in *The Death and Life of Great American Cities*, her masterwork on the ways that urban neighborhoods can flourish or dilapidate.[8]

With the rise of the interstate highway system and trucking industry in the 1950s, meatpacking companies decentralized, shifting their processing to local and regional facilities. Chicago's Union Stock Yards gradually receded until they finally closed in 1971. The jobs vanished, and Back of the Yards gradually morphed into the cluster of impoverished, predominantly African American and Mexican American ghettos that visitors find today. This is the commonly told story of the neighborhood's decline, at least. The reality, however, is very different. While the stockyard closure contributed to neighborhood hardship, Back of the Yards did not just transform because these specific jobs went away. Racist policies and systemic discrimination played a more substantial role in this transformation.

Racism and the Death of a Neighborhood

Historically, Chicago has been one of the most racially segregated cities in the United States.[9] This is no accident. Present-day enclaves of generational poverty and racial segregation in a physical setting of intermittent vacant lots and boarded-up houses are the result of racist historical practices of so-called redlining, blockbusting, and contract home sales by real estate speculators. Such practices were facilitated by White residents who fought like hell to keep their communities all White.[10]

Between 1917 and 1970, several waves of Black Americans fleeing the cruelties of the Jim Crow South and seeking higher and (they hoped) more equitable industrial wages converged on Chicago. As a result of the Great Migration, the city's population of African Americans swelled from 2 to 33 percent, spurring the Chicago Real Estate Board to innovate tactics to maintain racially homogeneous neighborhoods. Cities all across the United States took its efforts as a model.

Earlier European immigrants to Back of the Yards—newly minted Irish Americans and German Americans, then Polish, Slovak, and Lithuanian Americans—had themselves fled poverty, conflict, and often persecution. In the United States they confronted interethnic animosity, suspicion, bigotry, and criminalization in the face of Anglo-Protestant nativism.[11] "Anyone who carries a hyphen about with him carries a dagger that he is ready to plunge into the vitals of this Republic whenever he gets ready," president Woodrow Wilson warned in 1919.[12] Yet, in Chicago and around the United States, the rigid boundaries of identities imported from old Europe gradually softened and blurred, assimilating these different ethnic identities into Whiteness.

This was not an accident; rather, across the nineteenth and early twentieth centuries new immigrants realized that, in the United States, they would need to be recognized as "White" in order to claim legal and social rights as landowning, voting, working citizens and to avoid the kind of repression directed at those identified as Black or, in some parts of the country, "Mexican" or Asian. There was no faster track to integration for disparate European ethno-national groups than what James Baldwin later described as "the moral choice to become white."[13] African Americans, meanwhile, remained excluded from the possibility of being seen as equal to Whites. Assimilation and exclusion, as this recounting suggests, are never merely abstract moral choices. They are embedded within historical and context-specific circumstances. They occur by way of material and social mechanisms and processes. They become codified in cultural developments and perceptions. Such is the case for "the moral choice to become white," to seek a dominant place in society rather than making common cause with those on the underside.

The emerging field of social work and the concurrent settlement house crusade across South and West Chicago—organized by a movement of college-educated, White women activists and suffragists—provided support, resources, and services for marginalized European immigrants. Perhaps most famously, Hull House, founded and operated by sociologist Jane Addams and Ellen Gates Starr in Chicago's Little Italy, a few neighborhoods north of Union Stockyards, received as many as two thousand guests per week.

Mary McDowell, who came to be known as the "Angel of the Stockyards," left Hull House in 1894 to help launch a University of Chicago settlement house initiative in Back of the Yards. It stood at Whiskey Point, a few blocks off Gross Avenue jutting closest to the stockyards. Saloons that lined the street there offered a free lunch to any worker who purchased enough beer and whiskey at the noon hour. The settlement houses instead offered literacy and language programs. They supported union organizing and advocacy for workers' rights and for sanitary housing and living conditions. They provided childcare and education. Such "laboratories of social service" aided marginalized and exploited groups in gradually transforming their embattled ethnic ghettos into thriving neighborhoods.[14] Addams won the Nobel Peace Prize in 1931 for her pioneering social work and research.

Access to such transformational initiatives fell largely along the color line. Jane Addams herself advocated for African Americans' civil rights and was a founding member of the NAACP. She fought for Hull House to embrace the entire Chicago community, though she never fully succeeded. Hull House and similar settlement houses served African Americans either on a segregated basis or not at all.[15] They feared generating controversy that could sabotage the gains they facilitated for other vulnerable populations.[16] Their "Americanization" work, both intentionally and not, also sought to dissolve ethnic specificity in favor of a single-common-denominator culture, a default Whiteness that mimicked middle-class food, housekeeping, and other standards.

At the same time, the Chicago School of Sociology at the University of Chicago produced study after study that gradually dispelled the pseudoscience of earlier social Darwinist analyses and interpretations of statistics that were either careless or merely bigoted. Many of those earlier studies had suggested that Irish, Italian, or Polish immigrants were inclined toward criminality. The Chicago School's studies stemmed the tide of perceptions that "foreign-born" immigrants were distinctively prone to violence and crime. These studies made their case, in part, by contrasting the cultures of European immigrant groups with the cultures of Black communities. The underemployment and elevated crime statistics of Irish communities, they argued, were skewed by a vastly disproportionate number of young males. Crime in Black communities, by contrast, supposedly reflected "racial inheritance, physical and mental inferiority, barbarian and slave ancestry and culture," as Charles R. Henderson wrote in one of the first academic textbooks on crime.[17]

Even Jane Addams's rejection of racial-determinist accounts of socioeconomic inequalities defaulted into a proto-variation of a so-called culturist explanation. A version of this argument would find its most influential manifestation in US senator Daniel Patrick Moynihan's infamous 1965 report *The Negro Family: The Case for National Action*. Moynihan alleged that Black delinquency and generational poverty were the result of a "tangle of pathology" that had come to characterize the "matriarchal, single-parent family structure" of African American subculture.[18] The language of statistical analysis in early twentieth-century studies baptized such research on apparently persistent Black crime, vice, and immorality with a sheen of scientific objectivity, and thus supposedly constituted proof of Black inferiority. If the cause was not intrinsically biological, as other manifestations of scientific racism would have it, then it was at least rooted in "their culture."[19]

The real estate practice of redlining kept the neighborhoods of New City racially homogeneous for the first part of the Great Migration in the 1920s and 1930s. Residents from supposedly high-risk areas—designated by literal red lines on realtors' city maps—were denied loans and homeowners' insurance, or could acquire housing only at prohibitive rates. Of course, "high-risk" usually meant a high proportion of Black residents. Homeowners in White neighborhoods therefore had strong financial as well as social incentives to form "neighborhood improvement associations" and enter "restrictive covenants" to resist encroachment from potential Black homeowners.

The teeming Black Belt on the South and Near West Side neighborhoods of Chicago began to spill over, however. Some Black people successfully fled the sewer-less conditions—and, thus, frequently sewage-flooded streets and unsanitary surroundings—that caused Black people to die at twice the rate of Whites from flu and tuberculosis.[20] Spotting an opportunity to maximize profits, real estate agents selectively began to "bust blocks" in White neighborhoods. Gradually and strategically, they let one or two Black residents move near or onto otherwise all-White blocks of row houses. After a single Black family arrived on a city block, the Federal Housing Administration would often deny mortgage insurance and home improvement loans to the entire block. Violence erupted as White homeowners sought to protect their investments. There were fifty-eight bombings (averaging one per month) of properties in Chicago purchased or rented by Black people in otherwise all-White neighborhoods between July 1917 and March 1921. Racial and ethnic tensions exploded in the summer of 1919 when a White mob stoned to death seventeen-year-old Eugene Williams, an African American youth who accidentally drifted across an unofficial "Whites-only" area marker while rafting at the Twenty-Ninth Street Beach.[21] The Chicago "race riots"—perpetrated by Whites against Blacks—lasted a week. Black Americans bore the brunt of casualties and deaths, with as many as two thousand of their homes destroyed.

White owners in the area quickly sought to sell and move. Housing prices plummeted.[22] This gutting of the housing market was intentional; real estate speculators were able to acquire the properties at rock-bottom prices. The brokers then sold houses directly to Black buyers "on contract for deed," since banks denied them mortgages because they were so-called high-risk borrowers. The result was, in effect, a high-rate rental scam. Investor-owners inflated monthly payments to well above the rates of the standard rental market. Charges and fees also fluctuated from month to month. The brokers retained ownership of the properties, but had none of the liabilities—or investments—that usually go along with being a landlord. Residents were responsible for upkeep and repairs, as stipulated by their contracts. And since they did not actually own their homes, they could not accrue equity until their entire balance was paid. A missed payment or inadequate upkeep meant eviction. Speculators sold these contracts, and new lienholders often flipped the properties by pressuring residents financially, either foreclosing on the home or evicting those living in them. Lorraine Hansberry famously dramatized the exploitative housing dynamics along Chicago's Black Belt in her play *A*

Raisin in the Sun (1959). Her own family's fight to move into a "restricted covenant," all-White Hyde Park neighborhood in 1937 inspired the story.

By the late 1950s, an estimated 85 percent of home sales to African Americans outside the redlined ghettos of the Black Belt and Near West Side were conducted "on contract."[23] The inability of such buyers to retain the value they had poured into their homes—sometimes over decades—meant that they could not pass them on as an inheritance to their children. Owning a home is one of the primary ways that people in the United States are able to save for retirement and/or make an investment in their future, in addition to passing down wealth. "Contract sales" are thus a form of theft, draining wealth from Black families to White speculators and helping create the generational poverty that persists throughout some areas of Chicago today.

Meanwhile, the construction of the Eisenhower and Dan Ryan Expressways between 1949 and 1961 carved up South and West Side neighborhoods, with as many as fourteen lanes of traffic in each direction in some places. The expressways dispersed the immigrant enclaves of Little Italy and Greektown, and fragmented others. Previously contiguous neighborhoods became today's parallel worlds, standing on opposite sides of canyons of traffic. Second- and third-generation immigrant entry into middle-class standing, along with access to GI Bill mortgages in the postwar period, facilitated "White flight" to the subdivisions of a Chicagoland suburbia that was just beginning to sprawl. The newspaper for Chicago's Oak Park neighborhood described this combination of White suburban exodus and urban highway building as the replacement of "appalling slums" with "orderly dwellings where orderly people are living in health and comfort." Areas immediately surrounding the new expressways were left behind for Black Americans; West Garfield Park, for example, went from 0.05 percent Black in 1950 to 97.98 percent Black by 1970.[24]

Martin Luther King Jr. arrived in 1966 to campaign against Chicago's housing market discrimination. King and his fellow activists argued that fair housing rights and humane living conditions were essential civil rights, as basic as the right to vote. "We are tired of being lynched physically in Mississippi, and we are tired of being lynched spiritually and economically in the north," he declared in his July 10, 1966, speech at Soldier Field. Lyndon Johnson signed the Fair Housing Act into law on April 11, 1968, a direct result of pressure from the movement, and prodded by King's assassination in Memphis seven days prior. The act established the Office of Fair Housing and Equal Opportunity.

King's Chicago Freedom Movement achieved vital improvements against racist housing laws and practices. Structurally, however, the damage to many of the affected neighborhoods had reached a point of no return. White exodus and real estate speculation had destroyed property values and thus the tax base in Back of the Yards, and the population cratered as well. At its height, in 1930, the area had eighty-seven thousand residents. Falloff of 5 to 15 percent across each successive decade left it with roughly forty-one thousand residents by 2015. The immigrant Catholic inhabitants had exited to Chicago's southwest suburbs. Seven of the neighborhood parishes closed, while two merged with churches elsewhere.

Inhabiting the Present

St. John of God shuttered in 1992, though the diocese let the church building stand for another twenty years without maintaining its upkeep.[25] Neighborhood youth transformed the nave and sanctuary into bowling lanes and a basketball court. The diocese finally demolished the crumbling structure in 2010.[26] It shipped off the dismembered remnants of the building's façade and two 135-foot bell towers to a new parish—St. Raphael the Archangel—on Chicago's high North Side. The majestic stained-glass windows followed northward to Loyola University's Rogers Park and Edgewater campus.

Sister Donna Liette of Precious Blood Ministry of Reconciliation worked with groups of neighborhood people to transform the vacant crater that the diocese left into a peace garden—a welcoming space, mowed, blooming, and usable. An area to the side of the lot is now equipped with a grill for cookouts and an asphalt basketball court. Sister Carolyn Hoying led the initial effort to turn a series of vacant lots along Fifty-First Street, on the north end of the old parish, into a community garden (now an urban farm) replete with multiple beehives. Neighbors from nearby blocks come together each spring to plan the garden together, and anyone willing to help out is welcome to plant and keep a raised garden bed. The harvest is shared with the neighborhood.

Led by a forty-year veteran of prison chaplaincy, Father David Kelly, these Brothers and Sisters of the Precious Blood moved to Back of the Yards in 2002. This religious order identifies its purposes and founding vision—its *charism*—as seeking justice and promoting reconciliation. They focus their attention on the needs of marginalized people, modeling themselves after the witness of Jesus in the Gospels. This charism fits the needs of the neighborhood. When they arrived, this corner of Back of the Yards sat on a fault line between rival gangs. The neighborhood also was home to a community with countless young people and families entangled in the Cook County criminal justice system. It still registers some of the highest rates of police violence in the city.

The Brothers and Sisters of the Precious Blood spent their first year in the neighborhood in temporary residence and discernment. They met and listened to people there, mainly to see what people needed, and to see whether they would invite them to stay. Invite them they did. Eventually, the brothers and sisters came to share the old St. John of God Catholic school building with Second Chance High School, which occupies the first floor. "Ultimately," Father Dave explains, "this is a place that seeks to create that physical space where people who are accused and people who are the harmed party can perhaps participate in each other's healing."[27]

The gangs in these neighborhoods have splintered and realigned into smaller sets in recent decades. But the neighborhood remains contested territory. A few trees and a building or two obscure Precious Blood's second-floor office windows from a direct view of the drug dealers on the corner of Fifty-First and Racine, in front of what was the Family Foods corner mart (before it too was vacated). Over a four-week period in January 2015, that intersection and back alley recorded five murders as rival drug crews fought for control of the corner. "I grew up in a lot of violence. A lot of violence in the neighborhood still happens today," Jonathan Little tells me.

> Actually, it kind of got worse because people are real quick to pick up a gun before they [fight]. Back in the day we would fight real quick. It was more about fighting, proving yourself as a man. Now it's changed. Youth have easy access to guns. It's as simple as going to ask somebody. If you get into a disagreement, you get into an argument, we fight; I go and

say, "Look man, I need a gun." They don't ask questions: where, when, what happened, nothing, they just give it to you. It is so easy to get a gun these days. That's why there is a lot of gun violence happening in our neighborhood.[28]

The violence that fragments the neighborhood is by no means limited to the young people in the community. Much of it originates with the police, and animosity cuts both ways. "We don't have respect for the police, they don't have respect for us," Jonathan explains.

> There are good officers out there; I am not saying they are all bad, but [there are] a lot of crooked cops. One of my friends was killed, shot in the head by people we grew up with. Within the next two days somebody was killed from they group. [One of my co-workers and I] were getting off of work and pulled down the block when the police pulled up on us. They were like, "You guys got 'em." We were like, "'We got 'em?'" We lost. "What are y'all talking about?" We had heard about the shootings, but we here at work. He was like, "You guys are getting better and better every day. . . . Y'all got him right in the head. Good job." Basically, they felt because our friend was killed and shot in the head that we retaliated and shot one of them. That wasn't the case. At the end of the day, how can I have respect for you when you talk to me like that? He was basically pinning that on me. Not only is they saying that to us, but we was cool with some of the boys from the other group. They came over and told us, "They said y'all did it." Now that is just causing more problems within these two groups. It is crazy how we can grow up together, but yet be so distant. At one point we were, like, the best of friends and now everybody is out for each other.[29]

Jonathan's story, which might have resulted in a downward spiral, instead moved in a transformative direction. He was captivated by the work he saw at Precious Blood, which included youth mentoring and after-school tutoring, and the different kinds of people he encountered there—young people, mothers, families—who were meeting for what they called "peace circles." "Basically, I knew nothing about restorative justice at all. . . . Just starting out, it was like, 'Wow. This is actually happening in my neighborhood and I never even knew about it.' I was interested in learning more. After my program ended, it was only a six-month program, I talked to Father Kelly about permanently working here. I got a part-time job at that point, and . . . have been here ever since."[30]

Jonathan stayed on at Precious Blood and worked his way into a position as lead mentor and case manager for young people at the center. Some are diverted from the Cook County courts by judges who view restorative justice as a way out of the system for first-time, low-level, and nonviolent offenders. Precious Blood has also been a fixture in the neighborhood long enough to get traffic from local youth harmed by, or themselves caught up in, violent conflict, who need a safe space to hang out. Some take part in the tutoring and mentoring meetings, or in skill development and job training offered in multimedia skills, car mechanics and repair, woodwork and carpentry, silkscreen t-shirt design and printing, culinary arts, and theatre and fine arts. Some of the young people need assistance navigating the criminal justice system. Others seek accompaniment in court as their cases wind through a labyrinth of lawyers, caseworkers, judges, probation officers, and parole officers. Sister Donna comments that many of the youth who approach her are not only seeking a safe place or practical assistance. Whether they recognize it or not, many are looking for help managing and recovering from the impact of violence and ensuing forms of trauma that they carry.

3

Pillars and Circles

"Accompaniment" is one of five "pillars" of Precious Blood's work.[1] In the realm of restorative justice, accompaniment means that "a caring, responsible adult will walk through obstacles, situations, or life's moments offering support, advice, advocacy, and education."[2] "Accompaniment is walking alongside," Father Kelly explains. "It's very much a biblical kind of thing of just accompanying someone on the journey. Being there on that journey. Not necessarily that I know where we're going, but I'm committed to you as a human being, and I'm going to be there for you."[3]

From the young people's perspective, "accompaniment" means, for example, that Sister Donna Liette is someone who will join them and advocate on their behalf at a court-related appointment. Young people often ask her to come with them and speak in what they call her "White voice" when their time comes to stand before a judge and answer questions, or meet with a caseworker or probation officer.[4] These youth are acutely aware of the racialized dimensions of the justice system, down to the very particulars of how they sound—how they are perceived—when they speak.[5] They know, and the adults who accompany them recognize, that in the justice system as elsewhere, "Whiteness" is not merely a skin color. It is also a background social norm, influencing how one is expected to sound, dress, walk, stand, and hold space, especially when questioned by a person in authority. Accompaniment names the central relational practice at the heart of the holistic restorative justice vision that Precious Blood aspires to embody.

But accompaniment also means walking alongside people as they try not only to navigate the outside world, but to deal with whatever they might be facing. At the Precious Blood center Jonathan Little leads a weekly group meeting called Saturday Sanction. Participation at Precious Blood is always voluntary. But some youth in that group get referred by judges who think it is a good place to fulfill their community service. Because of this, Saturday Sanction welcomes young men from several different neighborhoods from across the South Side. Some come from larger rival groups at odds over neighborhood territory, others from small sets from conflicting blocks who hang together for safety and to protect where they live. As a result, the young men in Saturday Sanction come from factions that may be steadily in sometimes violent conflict with each other. "What pulled me to the work [is that] I have been through it. I know the struggle. I know how they feel. I know where they come from, so I try to make them think a little bit outside of the box," Jonathan tells me.

> I grew up here and that's why I feel like the work is so powerful to them. They see someone that grew up in the same struggle as their own and I changed. . . . Even the drug dealers, they want to change. It just isn't as easy as changing [because] it is not going to happen overnight. It takes time and effort. . . . Without the Precious Blood center and the work that we do here, I think a lot of [our] youth would probably be locked up or dead right now.[6]

Jonathan's long experience in the neighborhood means that he can identify the continuities and dissimilarities between the kind of accompaniment he once needed himself and the kind he needs to offer Precious Blood's current group of youth. "At one point it was gang-related," Jonathan tells me. He goes on,

> When I was younger . . . it was always about gangs. I'm one of the Moes, you are one of GDs, and we don't like you.[7] That's what it was. Now, it's the same gang getting into it with the same gang. Everybody in this area is Black Stones, so the Black Stones all had to separate and they went into groups. [There is] a group that calls itself "EBK" and another group that calls itself "Just Us." You've got the other group that calls itself "Love None." All of these different groups are under different areas and they are into it with each other. It is not about gangs anymore. It is about territories.[8]

There is a complex history behind Jonathan's description of how the gang-fractured neighborhoods have evolved radically in recent decades. When the Chicago police succeeded in arresting the leaders of major gang organizations in Chicago in the 1990s and early 2000s, the gang hierarchies collapsed. The vacuum left behind quickly filled with splinter groups, often called cliques, sets, or crews. These are frequently leaderless and do not adhere to previously established codes or models of operation. Chaos erupts where major gang organizations once enforced order. Today many conflicts flare up and develop across social media. These flare-ups have been exacerbated by trafficked guns from gun shows and due to lax gun laws a few miles away in Indiana. As a result, rates of gun violence are now persistently high.[9] One former gang member from Little Village told me that an older White man in a business suit, stationed on a park bench in the neighborhood and reading newspapers, served as the order and purchase point for guns for him and his fellow gang members. "He could get you whatever you wanted: high-capacity mag[azine]s, whatever."[10]

In many neighborhoods, affiliation is no longer a matter of a person joining a group, or even being forced into membership. It is a designation assigned by default, by virtue of the block or blocks where one happens to live.[11] Segmented blocks and territories create spatial confinement. It is difficult for many young people to move freely across the New City neighborhoods, or the South and West Sides generally. There really is no choice in it. If you enter blocks where you are not recognized, you can expect to be confronted, sometimes violently.[12] You also are expected to confront unfamiliar faces when you encounter them in your own neighborhood. This fractured topography and general leaderlessness give people little recourse for remedying the situation. Their isolation only further spurs the need for connection that leads young people to turn to neighborhood cliques.

Radical Hospitality

Accompaniment—solidary "walking alongside," being in and maintaining relationship with others—is the beating heart of the holistic and transformational vision of restorative justice at Precious Blood. How does it initiate relationships across the South Side neighborhoods and across the city? If accompaniment is the first of the five pillars of the neighborhood restorative justice hub network, it leads directly to the second—"radical hospitality," which welcomes anyone, and promotes wider relationships between neighborhoods and groups across the city.

Precious Blood has been a fixture in Back of the Yards long enough to be known as a space that is open to anyone seeking safety and respect. This is what is entailed in radical hospitality. It "means that space is provided that welcomes youth in, that nourishes their spirits by being a place that is affirming and open to all willing to respect that space. . . . Within this space, youth can expect to be provided models for positive boundaries and positive relationships with others."[13] The only requirement for belonging to the space is a respect for the space and the people in it.

Though radical hospitality requires the offer of safe space, Precious Blood is not immune to violence and conflict. Staff have spoken to me of periodic fights during cookouts or basketball games at the center, especially when someone was not recognized and did not identify themselves, and who they were with, if they came from a different neighborhood. Even so, someone walking to the center and unknown in the neighborhood can invoke their affiliation with Precious Blood and perhaps move on unchallenged or unharmed. Jonathan explains,

> I've seen people from outside the neighborhood walking to get here. I've seen maybe one or two be like, "Who is that? Who are you?" But others from the center will be like, "No, bro, he's good. He's up at the center." It's like giving someone a pass. Whereas if he wasn't from Precious Blood maybe it would have been like, "Yeah, who is you? What you is?" Through here people think twice.[14]

Again, Jonathan cautions, this is not simply a reflection of "gang" conflicts as portrayed in movies and the twenty-four-hour news cycle. The motivation is rather a basic need for safety and mutual protection in an area where the risk of violence is a daily reality. "It's not even about gang banging," he reiterates.

> Nobody is worried about what gang this man is. It is about you not a familiar face and there is so much violence going on that I don't know if you walking up the street to run up on me and shoot me, I don't know what you're going to do. . . . I would rather know who [you are] than you

run up on me and shoot me, then I'm looking stupid because I just looked past you when I saw you walking up.[15]

Saturday Sanction works to counter the condition of being, in effect, confined to one's immediate block community. Mentors facilitate trips across the city of Chicago—beyond the boundaries of the neighborhoods and conflicted territories—to places that some might otherwise only hear of. The purpose is to build healthy relationships with these young people and enable their building such relationships with one another. It is also to widen the horizon of their experiences and help evade the constricted mobility and isolation that are effects of living in communities carved up and fragmented by violence. But after evening sessions, some people ask for help with a bus pass in order to get back home. A bus ride after dark might be the difference between getting home safely and getting jumped or even shot.

Circles

Nearly all of the programs at Precious Blood incorporate restorative justice peacemaking circles. Restorative justice values and practices can be traced to a variety of indigenous justice and peacemaking traditions from around the world (First Nations peoples in North America, Africa, and Australia, among others). At Precious Blood, participants in circles, as well as "circle keepers," gestured toward these uses among "their ancestors" when they spoke to me.[16]

In Jonathan's group, the young men belong to rival groups. They sit together in circle nonetheless. Peacemaking circles can be any size. The ideal number of participants varies with the purpose of a given circle—whatever size is best to build out a community of participants for the purpose at hand. The general wisdom is that the smaller sizes (ideally, eight to twelve people) are more likely to support the cultivation of relationships, especially for circles addressing conflict and healing.[17] Prior preparation for circles is important, especially for circles that bring together victim/survivors and persons who caused harm. In such cases, those organizing the circle meet with the participants separately in advance to introduce the circle practice. They identify other people (stakeholders) who will be important contributors and support people for each participant (parents, teachers, friends, community members), and invite them into the preparation process. If the harm occurred between a specific victim/survivor and a particular person who caused the harm, the circle keeper will convene separate preparation circles with each cluster of participants to help gauge each participant's expectations prior to gathering the full circle. This preparation process is a way for all the participants to clarify what they need, imagine how things might go, and prepare themselves to participate in ways most likely to serve their needs.

At Precious Blood, the chairs in each of the circle rooms are set around a centerpiece, which is a space in the middle usually marked out by a prayer rug or throw. Each rug is centered by a candle that is lit at the beginning of the circle session to set apart the time that is to unfold. A participant rings a bell, singing bowl, or tingsha to call the circle to awareness and mark the moments that follow as special, outside the normal course of life. A few "talking pieces" litter the center. Each piece bears some mark of its own story and significance, indicating that present circle members are joining in a practice that has been made possible by many people and events, in many places, that came before them.

The circle keeper—a person trained to prepare for, assist, and keep the circle—opens the session by marking the time, space, and theme, often with a meditation or poem. The circle keeper selects the talking piece from the center or may invite another participant to do so. Whoever this is may offer a brief account of the origin and importance of the piece. Only the person holding the talking piece at any given time can speak; everyone else listens. No one is *required* to speak; anyone can elect to pass the piece along at any point. But for each round in the circle, the talking piece passes until everyone has had opportunities to share, and then the circle finds consensus in silence. It is the talking piece that is the mediator in a circle. The circle keeper's primary contributions come ahead of time, in the preparation period.[18]

The introduction is usually followed by one or more trust-building exercises to help with names and familiarity. The aim is to promote a sense of ease, even playfulness, among the participants. The members of the circle then pass the talking piece left to "check in" for a round—that is, they report how they are feeling as they enter the circle time together. If a circle is meeting for the first time, or if a new participant joins, circle members then take one round to reflect together on the values that will guide their circle. Each offers a value that they want the circle to reflect, explaining why they consider it important. The shared values take the form of a written list, perhaps posted on the wall of the circle room or laid down as part of the centerpiece. One list I found read, "respect, confidentiality, understanding/open-minded, be present, self-care, listening, support."

A follow-up round builds out these expressed values to develop consensus on a set of guidelines for sharing in the circle. For example, the value of "confidentiality" typically becomes recast as "What's said in circle stays in circle." These rounds make explicit the norms and commitments the circle members agree to uphold, and that will bind them together over the course of the circle. Because the guidelines also take the form of a list posted around the perimeter, or added to the centerpiece, a circle that recurs from week to week (or over several days) will reconvene with the values and guidelines orienting the space in view.

Once the values that ground the circle are made explicit and the guidelines shepherding participation are clear, the rounds turn more deliberately to cultivating relationships. Sharing stories is the substance of relationship building. Circle rounds focus on how the circle members' stories may bear similarities or connect with each other. This kind of sharing is practiced in numerous ways. The "ribbon ceremony" is one example. Each member of the circle receives a differently colored, slender piece of ribbon. As the talking piece passes, each person talks about someone who has helped, mentored, and/or loved them. They then tie their ribbon to the end of the ribbon of the person who spoke previously. As the round unfolds, pieces of ribbon gradually connect at the ends to form a thread running along the perimeter of the circle. This creates a visible cue that the members of the circle are connecting in the present, in large part because of the people who have cared for them, loved them, and mentored them at some point in their lives. These preceding relationships intersect in the shared present of the circle through these recountings, and the circle will be a place where such relationships of care will be extended. Members then lay the completed circle of ribbon along the perimeter of the centerpiece as a visible reminder of how their stories connect.

Though the prioritization of interconnecting relationships is always essential, the specific purposes of peacemaking circles vary widely. Some possibilities include the following: to celebrate an occasion or accomplishment together, to welcome someone new to the community, to lay the groundwork for and sustain nurturing relationships, to mediate and transform conflict, to process harm, to facilitate healing, to engage in support and accountability for a person, and to cultivate consensus on a "repair of harm agreement" in the wake of destructive conflict. There are many others. But all of these goals depend on the relationships of mutual recognition and respect that begin within the circle. Pinpointing and illuminating places where relationships intersect are concrete ways that mutual recognition and respect begin to form—a far less aggressive, more constructive version of the same impulse that leads young people on the street to demand to know who a stranger is.

Toward the end of the session, the circle keeper will devote a round to asking circle members to respond to a prompt—perhaps to share something they are struggling with, their concerns, questions they have, or reflections or responses related to what has occurred in the circle. Participants may speak of harms they have experienced or have caused. Depending on the theme or purpose of the circle, they may share celebrations. If need be, they may decide to do a follow-up circle. They then "check out" and close. Much as they did while "checking in," in "checking out" each member of the circle shares their condition as they leave the circle: how they feel, something they learned or better understand, some hope they leave with, a concern or issue they will bring up in the next circle, and so forth. "Closing" often occurs as a ceremonial reading or poem that transitions members of circle from the "set apart" time and space of the circle back to the ordinary time and space of their lives.

Circles take time. Some circles unfold across multiple days. Some reconvene weekly or monthly. The process is slow and often unpredictable, and comes with no guarantee that the circle will succeed in meeting its explicitly stated goal. The most seasoned circle keepers and trainers persistently remind everyone involved to "trust the process." At its best, this methodical, ritual-like practice offers a safe space and intentional, methodical progression that embodies honest sharing and invites vulnerability, uninterrupted speaking, focused listening, and attuned response. Whatever the theme, purpose, or issue that serves as the focus for the circle, the intent is to elicit the voices and particular experiences of the members. It is through this process that recognition of each by the other, and, more importantly, mutual trust, can begin to take shape. Relationships gradually start to emerge.

To call the circle "safe" in no way suggests that it is immune from difficult, emotional, sometimes painful and conflictual exchanges and topics. Indeed, these are what circle processes specialize in slowly and carefully sifting. The reference to "safety" indicates, rather, that circle members commit to exercise charitable understanding and acceptance, holding back judgment of others' shared stories and contributions. This does not preclude practices of accountability, but defers them until later rounds of the circle. The circle is a delicate configuration that must be flexible enough so that explicit instances of accountability can emerge organically. In some, such as conflict and repair of harm circles, it moves to the heart of the process as the circle gradually unfolds.

Connections in circle materialize slowly through face-to-face encounter, openness, and truth sharing. Those who regularly sit in circle describe the process as democratic. This is because the relational power of the circle originates in the capacities of ordinary people to cultivate relationships, build community, transform conflict, and heal harms for themselves—whatever the purpose or issue at hand. They make this possible by gathering together in ways that enable them to enter deliberately into relationships of mutual recognition and respect.[19]

Allowing these relationships to emerge over time and through careful listening can enable the members of the circle to see each other differently. Preconceptions can be reframed and perhaps even altered. Adversarial orientations may soften. "You spend a lot of time building relationships with one another," Father Kelly explains. "After you have a relationship with those in the circle, *then* you deal with whatever the issue might be. But you don't get to the issue until you build relationships with one another—until you understand 'who we are' in this circle. So often, when you attend to the relationships, then the issue is so much less important, or so much easier to resolve."[20]

Jonathan gives an account of the impact he sees the circles have:

> Every Wednesday, every week we do a circle where we bring all of our youth together. It's a men's group, and we talk about our stresses and struggles of life. It won't necessarily always be that, because that would just be a sad circle all of the time. We talk about some good times too,

so we try to mix it up from time to time. Sometimes it is a little bit at the beginning where we start off with stresses and struggles, and then we try to end it with something good so that they leave feeling positive. . . . Circles are the biggest stress relievers for our youth, because that is the time where they put all of their pride aside. When you are on the streets you have to play the tough role, you have to be hard. You can't show weakness or you will be the person that is picked on or pushed to the side. Here we give them that chance to be vulnerable. Not only with themselves, because it is hard to do it within yourself, but in front of other people. I found that the best way for them to open up is for them to hear people that they know or other people in general open up. That makes them feel a little more comfortable, and knowing that they are not the only person in that scenario or going through that struggle makes it that much better.[21]

Through the relationships they build in circle, the young people learn how to accompany each other.

Conclusion: "That's What Can Happen in a Circle"

David was a teenaged boy growing up in Englewood, the neighborhood immediately to the south of Back of the Yards. When he arrived at Precious Blood he had already been arrested, charged, and convicted of breaking into a home along with three of his friends and stealing a computer. David had served as lookout for the others, but was the only one who got caught. The state's attorney contacted Precious Blood to see whether it would be willing to offer the option of a restorative justice "sentencing" process.[22]

The holistic approach to restorative justice practiced at Precious Blood does not conduct "sentencing circles." It does facilitate and practice repair of harm encounters. A repair of harm circle addresses the harms experienced by all the people impacted by destructive conflict, violence, and crime. The idea was to have the people who knew David and had relationships with him, the community in which he lived, and the people most directly affected by the harm participate in understanding, and then working together with him to decide how to respond to the harm—to put things right as much as possible—rather than have a judge sentence him to a particular punishment. As is typical at Precious Blood, Father Kelly was willing to facilitate the repair of harm circle so long as the state's attorney agreed to cede authority over the process. Specifically, they would have to let the "repair of harm agreement" that emerged from the process be final. The state representatives had to agree not to try to adjust or overrule the agreement if they found that it did not fit their expectations.

The request first came to the center by fax. Father Kelly went to visit the man whose house had been broken into. He then visited David, who was at home on electronic monitoring with his mother. In "pre-circle" conversations with each, Father Kelly described what the circle would be like, how the process would unfold, and what some of the questions and prompts would ask of the participants. He explained to David that the person whose house he had broken into would be present and would be able to speak directly to him and ask him questions. Father Kelly assured David that the circle process would be safe for him—he would not be verbally condemned or treated badly—but it could be a difficult conversation. David and his mother agreed to participate. Father Kelly then asked David to reflect on how he might respond to some of those potential questions. David was apologetic. He was eager to have the chance to tell the homeowner how sorry he was. This man, Mr. Jordan, a Chicago police officer, was also willing to participate in the repair of harm circle.

The circle convened several members from across the Englewood and Back of the Yards communities: a retired school principal, a coach, a couple of neighbors, grandmothers of young people in the neighborhood, a corner store operator from nearby, and some other young people so David would not be the only young person in the room. The circle unfolded over the course of the day. It started in the usual way—opening, icebreaker, discussion of the values that would ground the discussion, and then shared articulation of guidelines reflecting those shared values. Mr. Jordan was distant and reserved at first. He sat with his arms folded, as if to say, "What is this? What are we going to do here? When am I going to get to tell him what I think about what he did?"

As the storytelling rounds unfolded and people engaged one another, it became clear that David and Mr. Jordan shared a lot in common. Mr. Jordan had grown up in Englewood, not far from where David lived. Both were African American males living on the South Side. David talked about how he had been expelled from school and how hard that had been on him because that was where he had played basketball for the school team, which he loved. Mr. Jordan talked about growing up in the community, and how hard he had to work to become a police officer. During the ribbon ceremony, David spoke about how his mother was the main source of stability in his life. His father left home when he was young, and his mother meant everything to him. She was always there for him, even when he messed up, he said.

The rounds of relationship building served to form a community that could address the harm. Later in the day, when the time came, Father Kelly asked Mr. Jordan, "What was the harm? What happened?" Mr. Jordan answered, "You know, everybody says that the harm is the burglary, that they broke into my house." But, he said, "it's not really about the broken door, though, or the computer they took." He continued, "I have a five-year-old son. And I grew up in a time and a house where I didn't know my father. It was a little bit chaotic at times. And I vowed if I ever had children, I was going to provide a safe environment for them. My son, my children, would never lack for anything, as far as the love and protection of family. But after the burglary, my five-year-old son said, 'Daddy, I don't want to live here anymore,' that he didn't feel safe." Mr. Jordan looked at David and said, "You know I had to send my son to his grandma's, my mother's, for five or so days before we could help him come back into our home?" He said, "*That's* how you harmed me." Everybody was listening, and David in particular. That was the harm—the impact on the basic sense of safety and the security of Mr. Jordan's family in their home.

Father Kelly then asked David, "What happened?" David explained how he came to be with the group who broke into Mr. Jordan's house. He thought that he would be less involved if he volunteered to be "lookout." But he was caught and detained. And he kept saying how sorry he was.

Father Kelly then asked Mr. Jordan, "What do you need?" At first Mr. Jordan said he did not need anything—that he already had what he needed, namely, that David was sincerely apologetic. Mr. Jordan acknowledged that and said, "I don't need anything more than that." And then he stopped himself and said, "Wait a minute, I do need something." And he looked right at David and said, "David, I need you to go back to school." He continued, "And look at all these people that care about you.

You have a mother that has always been there for you." Mr. Jordan then proceeded to heap affirmation on David—"What an incredible person you are. You need to get back to school. You still have so many ways to have a positive future."

In the Chicago public school system, once a student is expelled, they cannot return to a Chicago public school. At the same time, however—as Father Kelly puts it—in Chicago, "it's not what you know, it's who you know." And the retired school principal who participated in the circle that day said, "I can help David get back into school, where he can play basketball, where he can be back in a community of sport." And so that was the "sentence"—that was how David would repair the harm. David had to go back to school, and he had to come back to Precious Blood and let everyone know how he was doing. He was required to periodically visit and reconnect with folks at Precious Blood as a community of support for him. The former high school principal was charged with helping David get readmitted to his high school. Father Kelly closed the circle. Everybody was getting ready to leave, and Mr. Jordan walked over to David and gave him his card. He said, "David, I'm not just a cop. I'm also a coach at a gym. Let's go hoop together." What resulted from that circle, ultimately, was that Mr. Jordan became a mentor to David. Father Kelly concludes this example of repairing harm:

> I've been in court thousands of times, and I've never seen anything like that happen there. But that's what can happen in a circle—when you tend not just to the incident, but to who we are as people. You build relationships first, a community, and then out of those relationships we can say, "Okay, what are we going to do to repair the harm done?" But so often in court, you never get to the harm. The person who was harmed really never gets to speak, unless they are asked to speak in order to get [harsher punishment] for somebody. And, for the person who caused the harm, there's really no attention given to, "How do I *repair* the harm?" A restorative process is all about "How do we repair?"

4

The Power of a Credible Messenger

"Hurt People Hurt People"

Chilly Mayorga—whose birth name is Orlando—never forgets to mention the name Francisco Hernon when he shares his story. He honors the name at every opportunity. It is the name of the young man who is the reason that Chilly is who he is today, he tells me—why he sought to work at Precious Blood with gang-involved young people on the South Side, and with men returning to their communities after incarceration.

Francisco Hernon was a young man whom Chilly killed when he was seventeen years old. He describes his younger self as an angry, scared child, whose home life growing up in Little Village was fractured by parental substance abuse and instability. He gravitated toward friends who were dealing with similar struggles—all looking for collective comfort. By thirteen, Chilly was drug-dealing, addicted, and gang-involved. He was incarcerated a couple of times as a juvenile. Eventually, he shot Francisco during a drug robbery. Because of a legal technicality, he was released from prison after serving twenty years of a forty-year sentence.

Chilly tells me he cried for weeks once the gravity of taking Francisco's life dawned on him. He knew then that he needed to change, he says. But it took a long time to grow beyond a self-absorbed focus on how his difficult childhood, and now prison, affected *him*, instead of exploring the impact his journey was having on the people around him. What finally broke him was a visit with his three-year-old brother. "I remember him telling me—he called me Nando, that's my nickname, Nando—he's like, 'Nando, you don't love me anymore? You don't wanna come home?' Up until that point, the understanding that he had was that I was away at college. And that was the reason that I was not coming home. But, it doesn't take much for a child to learn where a person is at, where he's going to visit a person."[1] Taking responsibility for how his choices affected his baby brother, his mother, and others in his family led him to wrestle with the effect that his actions must have had on Francisco's family. Months of depression and self-isolation followed.

Chilly was lucky. Several of the older cellmates he encountered mentored him, recommended books, taught him how to read carefully and critically, and discussed the reading with him. He recounts,

> I would like to think I came out a better person than I was when I went in. I believe that. I strongly believe that. But it only came because of the relationships that I allowed myself to have once I became incarcerated. I would have never thought I would be open to partaking in a meal with a Latin King. I would have never thought I would be best friends with a Vice Lord, right? But these are things that happened while I was in prison. And I want to clarify this—it does not take prison for these things to happen. I believe these spaces should be created out here in the communities we come from. And because these spaces aren't available, I believe that's why the communities we come from are the way they are.[2]

Ten years into his sentence, Chilly enrolled in a program called the Education Justice Project, run by the University of Illinois. He studied social justice issues and learned about the concept of agency. Most importantly, he learned about the power of relationships, mutual support, and mentorship for helping people develop both agency and critical consciousness. This was a concept of individual agency understood as nested within and enabled by mutually constructive, healthy relationships and community. To put these new concepts to use, he and others in the program helped develop and began to teach an English as a Second Language program for others living in the prison.

The point of the Education Justice Project, Chilly tells me, is for participants to become peacemakers in whatever community, whatever peer group they end up going home to. "It just means that maybe you could be that voice of reason, even though you may still be in the streets, that says, you know, that 'Maybe right now might not be the best time to do whatever it is that we're trying to do. . . . Yes, our friend just got shot, but maybe we should take that breathing moment.' And in that respect, that person . . . is being a peacemaker."[3]

"Healed People Heal People"

Chilly had been out of prison for a little more than a year when I met him. He figured he would be lucky to find work fixing refrigerators and air conditioners (jobs for which he has vocational training) or maybe lawn care. But a friend he shared in common with Father Kelly sent him to Precious Blood, where a long conversation turned out to be a job interview. He accepted Father Kelly's offer to mentor young people and serve as the center's reentry coordinator for people returning from incarceration.

Chilly is what restorative justice practitioners call a "credible messenger" to youth and young adults. This is someone who speaks out of firsthand experience. He survived the streets and a difficult family life as a young person, then survived two decades of incarceration. He has managed to return to his family and community to share the hard lessons he learned—and his own transformation—in hopes that the young people there can find different paths than those he walked.

> [I try to] provide those caring moments that I wish somebody would've provided for me. Like, I remember having to walk miles to get to the Boys Club when I was a shorty. Because I wanted to be in sports, and I wanted to, you know, play pool and play basketball, but I had to walk miles to get there. And I wish there would've been somebody able to take me there on a day-to-day basis. Because I didn't want to be on the street, right? I wanted to be somewhere doing something positive. But, that walking to that Boys Club got tiring. And I was like, "I'm not going to walk all that," and not only that, but I remember being at the Boys Club *hungry*, because I would be there all day. I would be there from the time I came out of school until the time it closed at 9:00 p.m.—*hungry*. And there would never be any food. So I think about the opportunities here, like, some of the boys are here all day, and sometimes they don't get anything to eat. Like, there's food out there [in the Precious Blood community room], but I take those opportunities to engage with them. "Hey, bro, you hungry? Let's go get something to eat," or "You need a ride home? Let's go, even though you live two blocks away, let's go. I'll give you a ride home because I know how dangerous it is to even walk home one block west from here," right? It's dangerous! So, I take those opportunities as a way to let them

know, "Look, man, I care." And as a result of those moments that I was able to provide some type of safety for them, that is what they respond to. "Hey, Chilly, you know the business!" I hear that a lot: "You know the business."[4]

An Ecology of Violence

As even this brief account has shown, neighbors in Back of the Yards struggle with multilayered causes and conditions of violence and harms. Acute, explicit violence perpetrated both between people in the community and by police on community members is often the occasion for convening circles. But this is only the surface level of the neighborhood's violence. Examining the longer history of the neighborhood brings into view the different forms of violence that manifest in these contexts and that community members must contend with daily.

Violent structures cause conditions that leave marks on the bodies and psyches of individuals and families. Historical legacies, physical landscapes, and structural forms of violence such as redlining, predatory real estate practices, "White flight" to suburbia, and the broken windows policing that followed in their wake set the stage for the direct forms of violence that we have also already met. Associations formed for mutual protection and entrepreneurship based on illicit economies are in many ways rational responses to the situations in which individuals find themselves. But together, they multiply the different forms of harm with which people in the community must contend in their daily life together. The key, Chilly tells me, is to reach out to young people with support and opportunities for relationships that are healthy and safe. Through those relationships you can help them deal constructively with their struggles, and how to manage impulsive responses they may experience to difficulties they encounter that result from those harms. This relational engagement is not merely interpersonal support. It also addresses the structural effects of the criminal justice system through relationship building. How so?

The criminal justice system operates by severing relationships. This is one of its *structural* features. It makes relationships as difficult as possible—if not formally impossible—to maintain. Within his first two to three years incarcerated, Chilly tells me, he had lost basically all the relationships he had with people outside. "Twenty years does a lot to destroy *everything*," he says. This made developing relationships with his cellmates all the more crucial to his well-being.

> One thing about jail and prison is that all those warring-type mentalities that we have out here end up going—for me, it went—to the wayside. Because the same people I was out here trying to cause harm to, were the ones taking the most time to educate me about being a better person. So all the people that I thought were my enemies ended up becoming my closest brothers, my closest friends, in jail. That again, kind of fed the other way of thinking, that again contributed to me being more conscious of my role in the community. Not as a perpetrator of wrongdoing, but how I can actually begin to be a person who can heal a community. Anywhere, right?

Chilly's release from prison was one of the most joyful moments of his life. It was also one of the most heartbreaking. Upon his release, the probationary terms set by the state required him to sever all ties—prohibited *all* communication—with the people who he had built such strong relationships with while incarcerated. As Chilly put it to me, relationships are all lost going in, and all lost coming out. Again, this is a *structural* feature of mass incarceration.

At one level, reentry is about helping people find housing and jobs. It is a struggle to counter all the ways that the structures and stigma of criminalization exclude and marginalize returning citizens. Most fundamentally, though, Chilly tells me, reentry must be about cultivating healthy, reliable relationships. These relationships must equip people who are returning with what they need to find stability in the face of the issues they struggle with. The same is true for the young people Chilly mentors who have not (yet) been swept up "into the system." Their struggles may be emotional, social, psychological, or more likely some combination of these. How do you help them make their way successfully through the challenges of transition into daily life? What Chilly describes here is accompaniment, as well as radical hospitality—which he finds most effectively done in circle.

> I sit with brothers that are sixteen to twenty-four. Sometimes a little younger. We sit down and have the same type of discussions that we as men at Danville Correctional Center had, [regarding] issues of adverse childhood experiences, issues of why that is, what makes us tick, and being able to outline for ourselves what it is that "safety" means for us—whether it's safety physically, socially, psychologically, emotionally, morally, all these different areas of safety. So that we learn to understand what it is that we need in order to feel safe, not only in this space but wherever we're at. And being able to talk about those emotions that come with trying to maintain emotional regulation, right? To be able to talk about issues of loss, like losing a loved one, losing a parent, losing our childhood, losing whatever it is that we lost in life, being able to verbalize that through storytelling. Which is why I love the circle philosophy—the circle process—because even before I learned what it was that restorative justice peace circles were, we were already doing that, not knowing that we were doing that.[5]

Cultivating and sustaining healthy, durable relationships with young people—and modeling for them how to do so—directly counters systemic structural violence. When young people are taught to understand and see how the system inflicts violence by severing relationships, they can respond by building up practices that both preempt and counter the isolating and fragmenting effects of that violence. When cultivated in the form of practices and initiatives that are intentionally sustained and built outward, relationship building becomes a type of transformation of the effects of structural violence.

Another aspect of the violence that cuts across many South Side neighborhoods is the way that the wealth and resources of their communities and their families have been, over time, plundered and siphoned off. Racially and socioeconomically driven exodus left the remaining residents exploited, their housing stock increasingly dilapidated. It left the tax base—on which the funding and resources for their schools and the general commonwealth of their community depend—drained. Catholic churches and numerous civic organizations that once catered to immigrant residents abandoned the area. Meanwhile, as we have seen, many poor and minority communities on the South and West Sides became targets for increasingly intensive policing over the later twentieth and early twenty-first centuries.

All of this set in motion a vicious cycle of marginalization, exploitation, poverty, and harm. Structural racism in its many forms promoted an ecology of violence, the environment that forms the air breathed by generations of community members in Back of the Yards. Circles cultivate participants' ability to recognize the presence and impact of such violence. This is the message that Chilly works to convey to the people transitioning from incarceration back to the neighborhood. "I read *The New Jim Crow*," he tells me—the question is how best to get the message across:

> Even for a brother that may not understand what Jim Crow even was, [I am] able to let them know, like, "Look, bro, there is a system set up, and you're a part of that system whether you like it or not. And the system is going to be fed simply because you are necessary for that system to work"—being able to provide knowledge about what that is in those places. Like, for me—thinking about seventeen-, sixteen-, fifteen-year-old me—I would not be able to understand a lot about what that is. But I do know that they respond to what it is that policing is. And letting them know, "Bro, there's a reason why there's constant police rotating around your block. You are worth dollars in the eyes of people that want to lock you up." And putting it in ways that I think they understand.[6]

Chilly is a "credible messenger" to young people because of his long history. This experience, along with his work as a mentor and reentry coordinator, has also made him a credible messenger to policy makers in the state of Illinois. In 2019 Chilly was hired as the reentry policy coordinator for the Justice Equity, and Opportunity Initiative in the office of Juliana Stratton, Illinois's lieutenant governor, and he enrolled in a doctoral program at the Crown Family School of Social Work, Policy, and Practice at the University of Chicago.

Conclusion: Agency in Restorative Perspective

The stories of Jonathan Little and Chilly Mayorga convey several key takeaways about resistance to the criminal justice system in Chicago. First, in contrast to seemingly "obvious" perceptions and news cycle representations, very few young people in these communities choose to "join a gang" or "volunteer" to be involved in violence. Nearly everyone would categorically exempt themselves if they saw a way to survive otherwise. The history and ecology of the neighborhoods in Back of the Yards create dynamics in which there is strikingly little room for individual "choice." "There is no [neutral status in the neighborhood violence] anymore," as one Chicago police officer stationed in an Englewood high school, in a neighborhood just south of Precious Blood, put it.

> It used to be if you played sports or you were academically better than the average kid, they didn't bother you. Now it's different. It doesn't matter. If you live here, you're part of them. You know, you live on that block, or you live in that area, you one of them. The way they get to school, they have to come to school with one of these factions, one of these gangs. They going to come to school with them. They don't have a choice. . . . I'm not saying it is OK to be in a gang. And I'm not saying I approve of it, I agree with it. If I could take them all, and say, "Hey, look here, ain't no gangs, you know?" I'd do that. But this ain't a fairy tale.[7]

These are some of the daily realities that young people confront in Back of the Yards.

At the same time, this is not to suggest that such situations are entirely predetermined and that individuals have no agency, as Jonathan's and Chilly's stories also demonstrate. It is to point out that the concept of abstract "individual choice"—of simply "choosing" one way or the other, and acting accordingly—is analytically deficient for understanding these circumstances. This is the case both in terms of the constraints those circumstances place on people and in terms of the possibilities for agency and change that they also offer. More importantly from the point of view of peacebuilding, the voluntaristic "individual chooser" is defective as a means by which to resist and transform these conditions. To conceptualize a life's events as merely a matter of personal choice and individual action is to blind oneself to the nature of situation and circumstance, and to set us up for failure in the search for an appropriate and effective response.

As we will see, structural harms and their manifold effects expose as an insidious lie the old Horatio Alger myth of the exceptional American individual, according to which any industrious, rationally choosing, and rugged individual can "pull herself up by her own bootstraps," regardless of historical and contextual specifics. Historically, it is simply false to think that any earlier generation of immigrant groups reinvented themselves in America and hoisted themselves up in this manner. In reality, every group relied on their neighbors' and predecessors' intervention, aid, commitment to the transformation of violence, and pursuit of a more just society. Most importantly, they also relied on social programs, resources, and support from city and state agencies. The racialized dimensions of this process also meant that, while some groups' prospects improved dramatically thanks to this kind of community support, others were left behind. Indeed, the prosperity of the groups that moved into the upper echelons of America's allegedly classless society was frequently predicated on the disadvantage—and, at times, outright exploitation—of people left behind (as in the case of Chicago's real estate market). Violence in the areas where the descendants of the left-behind live today is directly linked to the multiple forms of violence perpetrated there in the past.

"Choosing" is an abstract category that frequently enables outsiders to blame the people subject to these structures and circumstances for (allegedly) having brought their difficulties upon themselves or "becoming their own worst enemies." From this perspective they have always been able to "choose otherwise," and simply ought to make better choices. And presupposing neoliberalism's phantom human—the utility-maximizing, rationally "choosing self"—virtually guarantees a turn toward neoliberal institutions and systems in search for a cure. In the narrative told by these systems, the individual who makes the poor choice and engages in destructive behavior suffers, individually, the consequences of retributive punishment of those choices. In short, this is a self for which the US prison-industrial complex is tailor-made.

But restorative justice takes a different view of personhood. At the heart of restorative justice is the understanding that human beings are not detached from the time, space, and circumstances in which we live. Instead we are always situated in particular histories, structural positions vis-à-vis others in our societies, and constituted as ourselves by the relationships we share with others. I have told Jonathan's and Chilly's stories as they told them to me because I agree that this is a pivotal insight not only about personhood but about choice. A holistic vision of restorative justice develops a refined account of individual agency, like personhood, as historically situated, socially embodied, and relationally articulated. Restorative justice practices take seriously the depth of these causes and conditions of oppressive structures and cultures—the lasting harm and trauma they cause to persons and communities—and yet nonetheless cultivate capacities of persons and communities to understand, critique, resist, and transform those causes and conditions.

5

Restorative Justice and the New Jim Crow

The radical expansion of the criminal justice and mass incarceration systems in the United States is a relatively recent development. The effects of mass incarceration are not limited to the isolation and inhumane conditions of those locked away in jails and prisons. If we include all persons "in the system"—that is, including those on parole and probation—the US carceral population balloons to 5.7 million.[1] Even this, however, is not counting millions more who have a conviction and imprisonment history that makes it difficult to find work, obtain housing, and maintain stable relationships with other people. And as the stories from Back of the Yards have shown, the effects of mass incarceration also spill outward beyond prison walls into communities and families impacted by related policies.

Mass incarceration has taken root within a wider legalized system of race-coded social control. "Social control" is a primary aim of any legal or justice system, which tries to prevent people from committing certain acts and to encourage others. In the United States this system, while supposedly "colorblind," in reality is "race-coded": by defining a particular set of activities associated with racial minorities as criminal, and enforcing those laws with vigor in certain areas, it replicates many of the forms of marginalization, exclusion, and humiliation that characterized the long period in which the disenfranchisement and exclusion of Black citizens were the legal norm—a period of US history known colloquially as Jim Crow.[2] In fact, it is no longer possible to speak of resisting and countering the US prison-industrial complex without simultaneously addressing the racial caste system that interweaves this massive apparatus. Does restorative justice have anything to offer regarding these severe and deeply interrelated challenges?

This chapter opens by asking what unmasking this racial caste system may have to teach the restorative justice movement in the United States. It also considers, however, what such analyses might learn from restorative justice, as it already stands as a well-established counter-option to the retributive US criminal justice system. First, we will briefly explore how an array of "tough on crime" legislative and cultural developments that first emerged during the 1970s and were further pursued with the "war on drugs" of the 1980s formed a racialized system of mass incarceration now widely recognized, in Michelle Alexander's widely adopted formulation, as the "New Jim Crow." We will then move back and forth between the two frameworks of New Jim Crow and restorative justice to illuminate how each can benefit from the other's best insights. Both provide indispensable elements for opening possible paths beyond the prison-industrial complex in the United States. Both are necessary for countering broad cultural complicity in the criminalization and vastly disproportionate incarceration of African American and Latino/a youth and young adults, as well as poor people of all colors.

What Is the New Jim Crow?

The Jim Crow era instituted countless forms of legalized discrimination and segregation enabled by the (allegedly) "separate but equal" provisions established by the 1896 US Supreme Court ruling in *Plessy v. Ferguson*. This period is notorious for its "colored only" and "Whites only" drinking fountains, bathrooms, pools, beaches, bus seats, schools, movie theatres, lunch counters, churches, and so on. The Fifteenth and later the Nineteenth Amendments to the Constitution guaranteed the right to vote regardless of race or gender, but Jim Crow denied Black citizens voting rights anyway through a series of laws restricting voter registration, including literacy tests, so-called grandfather clauses ("you qualify to vote if your grandfather had the right to vote before the Civil War"), and poll taxes (monetary payments required for voter registration). So-called vagrancy laws and Black codes restricted Black citizens' freedom of movement and allowed police to detain them indefinitely for hard labor. State laws prohibited interracial mixing and interracial marriage. Numerous states outlawed interracial procreation or miscegenation, because (again, allegedly) it transgressed racial differences state lawmakers believed to be essential, and which they justified by appeals to a "higher" or "natural" law. In thousands of documented cases, interracial intimacy, sexual relations, or "flirting" (whether real or imagined) resulted in lynching, extralegal executions.[3] The period between 1877 and 1950 witnessed 4,384 lynchings, for these and other reasons. These instances of racial terror were a primary instrument used to enforce both Black and White compliance with Jim Crow laws and cultural norms.[4]

If the original Jim Crow was marked by explicitly racist laws, social practices, and justifications for both, the New Jim Crow of the mass incarceration era is marked by implicit, though arguably no less nefarious, forms of racial segregation and oppression.[5] The *New* Jim Crow of US mass incarceration and the prison-industrial complex is a system coded, in large part, by socioeconomic class: the types of crimes committed by poor and working-class people are far more likely to be punished by jail terms rather than fines, and poor and working-class people also are pursued at greater rates by police and have far less access to competent lawyers who can help them evade the justice system.[6] At the same time, the socioeconomic disparities of US imprisonment have always been interwoven with—and grossly outpaced by—racial and ethnic disproportionalities. Symptomatic of this is the vastly lopsided representation of African American and Hispanic people in the general US prison population. Indeed, Black Americans and Latino/as constitute over 60 percent of the current US prison population. African American men are almost six times as likely to be incarcerated as White men; Hispanic men are 2.3 times as likely. One in ten Black men in their thirties is in prison or jail on any given day, with the number of those "in the system" on probation or parole also disproportionate.[7] How can we account for these disparities?

One major issue with the criminal justice system is that what constitutes a "crime" has historically, in the United States, been deeply racialized. "War on drugs" legislation and law enforcement policies and practices have been the primary drivers of the New Jim Crow. As noted, these are recent policies and practices that emerged gradually through structural adjustments to the US criminal justice and mass incarceration systems over the past sixty years, beginning at almost exactly the same time that a new set of laws and court decisions struck down the old Jim Crow regime. These policies have primarily been pursued through "tough on crime" legislation. Examples include "zero tolerance" and "three strikes" laws for nonviolent drug offenses, mandatory minimum drug sentencing guidelines, so-called habitual offender statutes, and the racialization of drug war procedures and ideology, among others.

The US incarceration rate began to rise exponentially with the Nixon administration's declaration of a "war on drugs" in 1971, which deliberately targeted African American communities and anti-war activists.[8] It jumped again, above the steady expansion of the 1970s, with Ronald Reagan's relaunch of the "war on drugs" (1982), the ensuing Sentencing Reform Act (1984), the Anti-Drug Abuse Act (1986), and yet again with the 1994 Violent Crime Control and Law Enforcement Act, championed by Bill Clinton.[9] Each of these bills pushed for increasingly harsh and punitive responses to nonviolent drug-related offenses. These laws and policies, as enacted by a wide range of police, prosecutors, and judges, have had a savagely disproportionate impact on minorities in urban areas and impoverished socioeconomic groups. These bills therefore contributed to further cementing more long-standing structural violence against such communities and groups.

To take one well-known example, the Anti-Drug Abuse Act of 1986 established a sentencing disparity of a hundred to one between crack cocaine and powder cocaine. In other words, a sentence for crack was one hundred times more severe than a sentence for the same amount of powder cocaine. The controlled substance is identical in these two different forms. But crack was much more affordable and accessible in African American communities at the time. Powder cocaine, by contrast, was much more expensive, was considered a "glamour drug," and was used predominantly in White, wealthy communities. The Anti-Drug Abuse Act of 1986 instituted similarly disparate mandatory minimum sentences, such as a five-year minimum sentence for first-time possession of crack (five grams).[10] Congress revised the hundred-to-one sentencing disparity between crack and powder cocaine in the Fair Sentencing Act of 2010, but reduced it to eighteen to one rather than eliminating it altogether.

The war on drugs, however, goes well beyond the number of people incarcerated and impacts the far greater number of people permanently swept into the system more broadly.[11] For example, ascribing felony status to nonviolent drug-related offenses is another way the war on drugs policies came to mimic the forms of legalized exclusion and criminalization produced by Jim Crow laws. Sentencing and law enforcement reforms in the 1980s rendered idiosyncratic determinations, such as "intent to sell," as the bases for reclassifying misdemeanor nonviolent drug offenses as felonies. Though these policies vary somewhat on a state-by-state basis, people convicted of a felony (or, more likely, who enter a guilty plea in a plea bargain concerning a felony charge) typically have their voting rights revoked, a process known as "felon disenfranchisement." (Tellingly, felon disenfranchisement laws came into wide use after the Civil War as part of the old Jim Crow, used in conjunction with enforcement of laws against vagrancy and the like as a way to prevent Black men from voting; now, they are part of the New Jim Crow as well.) Felons lose access to public housing and are no longer eligible for food stamps. They are disqualified from federally funded health and welfare benefits. They lose eligibility for federal student loans, can have their driver's license revoked, and can be disqualified from attaining employment and professional licenses. They suffer informal employment and housing discrimination through background checks and employment applications that ask you to "check the box if you have ever been convicted of/pled guilty to a felony."[12]

The results resemble constraints that are constructed along "caste" rather than "class" lines. While class is at least theoretically subject to change, caste names a permanent condition. And typically, felon status is impossible to overcome. The stigma and forms of legal exclusion that ensue from having been convicted of or pled guilty to a felony, either in court or in a plea deal, are irreversible. There is no prospect of "upward mobility," as is presumed in the notion of "class." The combination of the inequitable application of this system to racial minorities and its permanent stamp is what analysts of the New Jim Crow call a "racial caste system" that pervades our justice system. It is not tenable to speak of resisting and countering US mass incarceration without simultaneously acknowledging and responding to the reality of this caste system.[13]

Central to "tough on crime" and "war on drugs" policies is the claim that a retributive model of punishment makes us more safe and secure. Allegedly, the more severe the punishment of the crime that the offender has been convicted of now, the less likely the offender will be to engage in criminal behavior in the future. This retributive concept of justice makes social control through incarceration appear to be a necessary, and even natural, process by which to measure and apply justice. The negative impact of such attempts at social control, however, falls disproportionately along racial lines. Once a set of actions is criminalized and effectively identified with particular groups and locations (for example, the policing and sentencing policies related to the so-called crack cocaine "epidemic" targeting predominantly Black communities), then the task is to administer what is allegedly a necessary law in what purports to be an impartial way. The apparent "virtuousness" of justice (in its retributive conception) motivates "tough on crime" ideology and policies. In this view, it is not only necessary to carry out such policies, it is also good to do so because they promote justice. However, this is a skewed vision of justice that also motivates preventive policing policies and practices targeting communities considered to be "high-risk" or to have a "high likelihood" of offending. Such policing policies emerged in the early 1980s and spread throughout the 1990s, in the so-called broken windows approach to policing.[14]

Broken Windows

Broken windows policing focuses on indications of so-called neighborhood dilapidation, small offenses, and "quality of life" infractions. The underlying belief that motivates this focus is that the occurrence of minor infractions indicates that more serious, violent crime will follow. The motivating idea is that the *appearance* of decay and disorder leads to *actual* disorder, and that seeming permissiveness toward small infractions, in effect, condones larger ones and increases the likelihood that they will follow. What then follows (allegedly) is increasingly expansive disorder (that is, criminality and violence).

This framework resulted in concentrated police focus on small infractions in predominantly inner-city communities—especially those deemed to exhibit so-called urban decay. War on drugs laws and policies offered a legal terrain perfectly matched for broken windows policing strategies. One example is the aggressive "stop-and-frisk" practices implemented by numerous police departments in the 1990s and 2000s. Police departments trained officers to stop, interrogate, and search citizens on the basis of "reasonable suspicion" (for example, movements they portrayed as "furtive" or "secretive"). Due to the racialized history that developed present-day demographics in US cities, the communities and groups most impacted by these policies and practices have been predominantly African American and Latino/a.[15]

Broken windows merged with the increasingly widespread computational-statistical tracking and analysis program Compstat, which instituted so-called data-driven policing practices. The result was an exponential increase in arrests for small, nonviolent infractions in communities where "indicators of disorder and decay" appeared. It also resulted in the overall downgrading and underreporting of actual crimes.[16] Federal and state programs such as the Byrne Justice Assistance Grant Program incentivized policing that could demonstrate high numbers of nonviolent drug-related arrests (including possession, use, and sales). Summonses and arrest rates were a central performance measure by which agencies awarded grants. Marijuana arrests increased 51 percent between 1995 and 2010. And though Black and White people use marijuana at identical rates, through 2010 Blacks were 3.73 times more likely than Whites to be arrested for marijuana possession across the United States.[17] Such approaches to policing and punishment are the primary means by which Black and Brown men, especially, are swept into the system of mass incarceration at rates massively disproportionate to their share of the general population. As we have seen, people enmeshed in the system then became legally ostracized and socially stigmatized. They become, in other words, members of a "system-involved" caste. As a result, mass incarceration has spread beyond the prison walls to segment and fragment their families and communities.

"The New Jim Crow" names this system in a way that helps us to see how the conception of justice as retribution has become, in effect, a deeply racialized means of social control. This mode of control, and the structurally institutionalized and culturally justified forms it takes, claims to serve the purposes of justice. Yet here the terms are insidiously modulated so that what appears to be ironclad logic ("don't do the crime if you can't do the time") actually justifies the stigmatization, repression, and direct management of specific segments of people and their communities. Insofar as restorative justice decenters/displaces retributive punishment as defining what achieving justice looks like, it challenges and seeks to replace one of the central tools of social control by which the prison-industrial complex implements the New Jim Crow. By seeking to repair harm, heal, and (at their best) decriminalize and empower individuals and communities, rather than administer punishment, restorative justice practices offer a different path to a different conception of justice.

Understanding Restorative Justice

Restorative justice approaches in the United States have long identified and critically assessed the insidious self-subversion of a justice system in which retributive punishment is the primary focus. More importantly, they have developed counter-practices and alternative programs to this system. As they began to take shape in the early 1970s in the United States, restorative justice programs worked locally and in grassroots communities to challenge the predominant conception of justice as payback, according to which an offender receives his or her due in the currency of incapacitation, isolation, pain, and humiliation.

Restorative justice responds to many of the underlying beliefs that underpin and hold in place the New Jim Crow. First, it introduces a counter-ethic and a range of concrete counter-practices as alternatives to retributive justice. It recognizes that a strictly punitive conception of justice ultimately contributes to the very state of affairs that it purports to combat: it leads to more crime rather than less.[18] In the current retributive conception, the primary entities that justice serves to vindicate are the state and, in principle, the rule of law. The needs of the survivors of harm and the complex circumstances and needs of wrongdoers—along with the way that these complex relations and circumstances affect the community—are relevant, if at all, insofar as they happen to pertain to the defense of the state and maintaining the integrity of its laws. In short, the contemporary justice system, with its retributive orientation, focuses on a specific set of questions:

(1) What laws have been broken?
(2) Who did it?
(3) What do they deserve?
(4) How do we punish them?

The alternative proposed by restorative justice programs in the United States replaces the questions above with the following:

(1) Who has been hurt?
(2) What do they need?
(3) Whose obligations and responsibilities are these?

(4) Who has a stake in this situation?
(5) What are the processes that can involve the stakeholders in repairing the harm and transforming the causes?[19]

Restorative justice introduces a counter-vision that emphasizes relationships emerging from, and in the context of, community leadership and participation. In fact, restorative justice is often referred to as "community-based" justice. As this descriptor suggests, restorative justice is predicated on "the power and capacity of ordinary people to identify and resolve their own problems."[20] Such power inheres in the community's processes of mutual recognition and reciprocal accountability. This "power" is intrinsic to all community relations, even if it might remain latent and unused. The power intrinsic to community relations might also be poorly—or destructively—used. Nonetheless, restorative justice practices are predicated on recognition of this power as a shared community resource. They facilitate uses of that power in ways that put right and heal harms, process trauma, and meet the needs of victims of destructive conflict and violence in all its forms. These community practices also aim to meet the needs of wrongdoers, understanding that they too are entangled in systems of structural violence. The harm that people cause is frequently precipitated because they have suffered (or suffer) harms and have ensuing needs and residual trauma that remain unaddressed. Restorative practices identify and respond reparatively to harm—and illuminate and address all its causes and conditions—rather than punish.[21]

How do restorative justice practices respond to the "needs" of the wrongdoer? They do so in ways quite similar to how they respond to the needs of the harmed party and the community. They invite wrongdoers to participate in practices that cultivate their agency and empower them, along with the other stakeholders. This includes inviting wrongdoers to protect the rights of survivors of harm, strive to meet their needs, and promote healing and repairing of the harms they have suffered. It also includes inviting their participation in justice practices such as encounter groups or victim-offender mediation, among others. Restorative justice practices invite wrongdoers to accept responsibility through truth telling, rather than confronting them with indictment and accusation, which incentivize denial or diminishment of responsibility. It also aids wrongdoers in cultivating empathy for the people harmed by their actions. It does so by inviting them to make, and facilitates their making, amends, through apology, expressions of remorse, changed behavior, and material or symbolic restitution, among other possible forms.[22] In each case, the "stakeholders" cease being passive recipients of the state criminal-legal justice system. They become active participants in practices of justice by facilitating empathy, interdependence, accountability, and tailored repair.[23]

Restorative justice programs, as currently practiced, take a range of approaches. Some present restorative justice programs as alternatives that stakeholders may opt for once they have entered the retributive criminal justice system. This model is referred to as the "augmentation model" because it works with the system. Parties may opt for restorative alternatives at the start, or these may be made available at various points along the way (by, for example, prosecutors or judges). If stakeholders choose not to participate in restorative practices, their case is handled by the standard criminal justice procedure—that is, by the courts.[24]

The "safety net model" instead proposes restorative justice, as practiced by established community initiatives and figures, as the default approach to responding to wrongdoing in a given community. The criminal justice system then serves as a secondary alternative (a so-called safety net) when restorative practices or engagement is refused. Similar to this model is the "parallel model," in which restorative and criminal systems operate independently of each other in a given context, and the stakeholders decide which process to opt for.[25]

Another model—a "unitary model"—presents restorative justice as the sole response to conflict, harm, and wrongdoing, having displaced the strictly retributive system. In this vision, restorative justice is "unitary," in that "all crimes, victims, and offenders are to be addressed in a restorative manner."[26]

These models do not exhaust the options. They are, rather, a range of descriptions of how restorative justice practices and initiatives can—or must (some argue)—interact with and/or oppose the contemporary retributive criminal justice system. Restorative justice thinkers and practitioners debate at length which model—or how integrating the different models—might succeed (or not) in structurally transforming the contemporary system, as well as the causes and conditions of the New Jim

Crow. As we will see in the chapters that follow, even the strongest proponents of restorative justice must inevitably interact with the criminal justice system. If they are to be strategically oppositional and constructive (rather than reactive and/or terminally deconstructive), they must navigate real situations that are partial and heterogeneous, rather than formed along a simple dualism between the system and its opposite.

Conclusion: Can Restorative Justice Transform Systemic Injustice?

In what ways might restorative justice address the contemporary dynamics of the US justice system, which are co-constituted by newer forms of a much older racial caste system? The prescriptive portion of Michelle Alexander's *The New Jim Crow* begins with a plea for humanizing people and communities stigmatized by the current criminal justice system. The point is not simply to *identify* the deep structures of exclusion and humiliation that are inscribed legally in the criminal justice system, although identification is necessary and a good start. Nor is it only to see how these violent structures are propped up and rendered supposedly necessary through what are, in fact, contingent processes of cultural violence. Their "naturalness" is constructed, built up in our minds by "commonsense" sloganeering about "getting tough on crime" and declaring a "war on drugs." These concepts purport to promote safety, keep the peace, and administer justice in contemporary society. In fact, they accomplish the opposite. They also camouflage and perpetuate cultural violence by using coded language that makes dehumanizing policies seem normal, necessary, or at least not wrong.

If restorative justice is to effectively address systemic injustice and structural and cultural forms of violence, then it will have to address and then fundamentally change those forms of violence and injustice. In short, restorative justice will have to transform not only the effects of incarceration, but the causes and conditions that produce it. But this is precisely what some people say restorative justice *cannot* do.

6

Restorative Justice *Is* "Transformative Justice"

How Restorative Justice Transforms Structural and Cultural Violence

Some argue that restorative justice cannot address more than the repair of interpersonal relationships and harms.[1] For example, they might consider the story of David and Mr. Jordan a very positive response to a particular instance of harm.[2] It repaired damaged relationships and cultivated new, more stable, positive relationships. It removed the state from playing a role in deciding whom to punish and how. It also rejected the concept that punishment was a worthwhile purpose to begin with. Instead, it centered the situation on reducing and repairing harms through a process that directly involved the people who were in relationships with all the individuals—and with the community—impacted by the harm. These are all good things, such critics may suggest, but they serve a niche purpose only. They provide some valuable alternatives that can divert people away from a standard path through a destructive, punitive system of mass incarceration.

However, none of these alternative responses do anything to actually name the injustices internal to the criminal justice system itself, nor to challenge and change them. They do not address the structurally racist and classist dimensions of the punitive orientation of the school system that first expelled David, and then made it impossible for him to ever return to school (a hallmark of the "school-to-prison pipeline"). They do not name and challenge the generational poverty, lack of access to basic goods like quality health care and education, and all forms of structural racism that these marginalized communities must confront. Restorative justice, the argument runs, does nothing to challenge and change the prison-industrial complex itself. As a result, truly transforming systemic injustice and structural violence requires inventing an altogether different form of justice—what some have come to call "transformative justice."[3]

As developed by those who think that the (allegedly) "strictly interpersonal" purposes of restorative justice necessitates a separate conception of "transformative justice," there can exist many points of overlap and complementarity between the two. One key difference is that many advocates for transformative justice describe it as intrinsically "anti-state."[4] As one transformative justice advocate explains, "Transformative justice responses and interventions 1) do not rely on the state (e.g. police, prisons, the criminal legal system, I.C.E., foster care system[,] though some TJ responses do rely on or incorporate social services like counseling); 2) do not reinforce or perpetuate violence such as oppressive norms or vigilantism; and most importantly, 3) actively cultivate the things we know prevent violence such as healing, accountability, resilience, and safety for all involved."[5] Numbers two and three directly overlap with the purposes of restorative justice. And advocates of transformative justice sometimes describe it and restorative justice as two interactive phases of a complementary process, perhaps even as interchangeable, depending on how they are implemented.[6]

Even so, many such critics argue that restorative justice is essentially compromised by its recognition of and alleged deference to the state and government authorities. Transformative justice thus distinguishes the anti-state, anti-institutional orientation of the card-carrying "prison abolitionist" side of a "reform versus abolition" dichotomy. Sometimes it does this by delimiting (definitionally) the purpose of restorative justice to "repairing relationships" in the first place, or reducing it to a means of returning to the way things were prior to the harm.[7] Some versions reject restorative justice insofar as it does not identify the state as a distinct entity and oppose it (thus naively leaving its own practices suffused with state power and, however tacitly, a state-centric orientation).[8] Transformative justice then functions to mainly cut against instances of restorative justice that do limit themselves to interpersonal repair or that become a tool of the state, and to guard against the implementation of restorative justice without an eye to transformation of perspectives, structures, and people. It is true that it is possible for instances of restorative justice to fall into these traps. Of course, it is also possible to correct such (mis)applications of restorative justice using resources and insights that are central to restorative justice itself.

In contrast to those who portray it as strictly "interpersonal" and concerned to reconstruct prior conditions, and then call for an altogether different model of transformative justice, this chapter makes the case that intervening in and countering structural and cultural violence and systemic injustices are *intrinsic* to restorative justice when it is holistically understood and practiced. For those well-versed in restorative justice literature, this claim is no surprise. Indeed, the most influential writings on the history, character, and practices of restorative justice make the case that transformative purposes and effects are, in fact, integral to it.[9]

Restorative justice is a contested concept. However, when we view it as an encompassing framework (or a "way of life," as some practitioners describe it), it is possible to identify three recurring elements that thread throughout its various formulations. These are, in effect, nonnegotiable: (1) encounter (various stakeholders meeting and/or otherwise engaging one another), (2) forms of accountability that aim to repair harms, meet needs, and promote healing, and (3) transformation of the causes and conditions that precipitate and perpetuate harms by changing "perspectives, structures, and people."[10] If we understand restorative justice as an "encompassing framework," we would not describe as fully "restorative" any initiative that lacked any one of these dimensions.[11]

The "interpersonal" aspects of restorative justice (encounter and repair) must therefore also attend to the transformation of the causes and conditions of the harms. Whatever form that might take, the key insight here is that illumination of, resistance to, and efforts to transform systemic injustice do not occur after, separately from, or as an adjunct to cultivating and sustaining relationships that are healthy and just. Rather, they occur *in and through* the cultivation and maintenance of such relationships. This opens up possibilities for restorative justice to present practicable ways to challenge and transform structural violence occurring in retributive systems. How is this possible?

In order to highlight the ways that restorative justice practices can and often do address structural and cultural violence and systemic racism, it is helpful to re-describe them in terms of *critical praxis*. Recall, the term *critical praxis* refers to both practice and an ensuing critical reflection (often theoretically informed) that feeds back into and refines further practice in the wake of new experiences and applications. Critical praxis develops an understanding of any given set of circumstances that is multidimensional and incisive. Its purpose is twofold: to analytically challenge, but also to practically transform, the causes and conditions of injustice and violence. Critical praxis integrates theory and practice.

Restorative justice as a form of critical praxis occurs in several ways. We see it, for example, in the ability to facilitate people's recognition of the sources, nature, and character of the injustices they experience in their lives and communities. It appears in their self-empowerment through resisting structural and cultural conditions that have persistently ensnared, silenced, and disempowered them. It is evident in their participation in constructing just and sustainable alternatives, in their continuing critical reflection upon those alternatives, and in their further adjustment in the light of new challenges and experiences. This is what critical praxis entails. When implemented in these ways, restorative justice practices provide means by which people can develop capacities to engineer their own liberation.

Perspectives: Restorative Justice as Critical Praxis

My observational journeys into restorative justice communities across Chicago indicate that, at its best, restorative justice deployed as critical praxis opens a range of practices of resistance and transformation for those communities. These include practices by which ordinary people come to understand and make explicit the forms of structural violence and systemic injustices that affect their lives and their communities. These practices, further, enable the formation of critical consciousness and methods for relational struggle through which they can resist forms of structural violence, work to change them, and transform the conditions under which they live.

By cutting against the dehumanizing dynamics of various forms of oppression, critical praxis has the capacity to "humanize" everyone involved. In other words, participating in the practices by which humans pursue justice and strive to liberate themselves from oppression—from forms of *de*-humanization—opens possibilities for every participant in the endeavor to build and strengthen those elements of personhood that most distinctively illuminate their humanity and dignity. Through liberatory struggles, they achieve, expand upon, innovate with—perhaps set new examples of—the potentialities implicit in what it is to be human. They cultivate the capacities for more expansive forms of freedom and develop more encompassing forms of justice.[12]

Such humanization is especially rich among those who develop critical consciousness for purposes of resisting the forms of oppression that they confront and must change. But it also opens possibilities for those who are, in effect, dehumanized by the forms of domination they perpetrate upon others, or from which they passively benefit. Critical praxis does not merely take back power, but also illuminates, challenges, and seeks to reorganize the structures and distribution of power by which "violence" and "crime" are identified in the first place. It cultivates practices that enable resistance and transformation of those causes and conditions. It also alters the culture and reshapes the awareness and dispositions of all the people affected by injustice. This opens up possibilities for those who benefit from oppressive structures (intentionally or not) and who suffer the dehumanizing effects of that role. They can learn how to participate in the humanizing processes of critical-empathetic awareness raising and understanding, self-examination, and self-transformation. These processes reorient oppressors (or beneficiaries of oppressive structures) to change by educating themselves and seeking solidarity with the oppressed for purposes of transforming the causes and conditions of injustice and oppression. In learning how to become the kinds of people who can recognize, empathize with, accompany, be led by, and support others' work of self-liberation, beneficiaries of oppression learn how to liberate themselves.[13] How does this clarify the distinctive account of justice at the heart of restorative justice?

Structures: Transforming Structural Violence through Relational Justice

The conception of justice at the heart of restorative justice derives from an account of "relational personhood." This centers the cultivation of relationships that dignify and enable individuals' agency and self-reliance, while simultaneously healing and nurturing the bonds that enfold particular persons and other members of the community. It aims to repair the ruptured portions of broader relational webs caused by harm, destructive conflict, and various forms of violence. This means that restorative justice is intrinsically participatory. It begins with the active participation—and amplifies the voices and experiences—of the people who live in the community and who directly suffer from the forms of violence that are present there.

Human relationships, as we have seen, never occur in a vacuum. They are situated within particular social locations. Those social locations have histories that are reflected in their socioeconomic, political, and cultural dynamics. These dynamics in turn inform and inflect the relationships established in these places. Those relationships are implicated in the inequalities, privileges, advantages, and access to resources—among other differentials—that give any cultural ecosystem its own particular contours. To name this a little differently, because of the historically situated political, socioeconomic, and cultural forces that shape these contexts, the relationships formed within them are necessarily shot through with dynamics of power. If it is to address the justness of relations in a given context, restorative justice thus cannot limit itself to attending to distinct interpersonal relationships, or even to broader relational webs. Rather, it must simultaneously attend to the structural and cultural dimensions of the contexts with which these relationships are interwoven.

Insofar as it promotes a genuinely holistic and just relationality, restorative justice must illuminate and work to counter structural and cultural violence *in and through* cultivating interpersonal, communal, and societal relational forms that promote human flourishing. It must also resist forms of relationality that fail to promote such flourishing. In other words, at its best, restorative justice will attend to the structural causes and conditions of harm, as well as cultural conditions that may appear to justify (or camouflage) that harm. Restorative justice practices and initiatives can and will proactively promote just structures and cultures, even as they cultivate just relationships among persons and communities. How might this occur?

Restorative justice recognizes that the retributive conception of justice in the United States ultimately promotes the very state of affairs that it purports to combat—that is, it increases, rather than reduces, crime and maleficence.[14] Retributive punishment isolates and incapacitates persons. In doing so, it further damages the very relational forms that must be cultivated—where necessary, repaired and/or altered—to achieve the just relationality that promotes the flourishing of persons, communities, and societies more broadly. The US retributive system ignores the concrete needs of survivors of harm, the humanity of offenders, the destructive impacts of crime on communities, and the structural causes and conditions that precipitate and perpetuate the criminalization of people and groups. Restorative justice contests the cultural and conceptual presuppositions that make the punitive features of the New Jim Crow seem or feel "right," or at least "not wrong." It does so by challenging and, in practice, displacing retributive punishment practices as the necessary form or "true" meaning of justice.

To actually be restorative, restorative justice cannot simply seek to counter the savage disproportionality of retributive punishment that fuels mass incarceration by instituting greater proportionality in punishment—lowering sentences for crack cocaine to meet those of powder, for example. Nor can it respond to wrongdoing with merely "kinder, gentler" forms of correction. Rather, the historical and sociopolitical account of the New Jim Crow clarifies that it must recognize mass incarceration in the United States as a racialized caste system that is intrinsically self-defeating, as witnessed by its astronomical rates of recidivism and the trauma it heaps on the people it incarcerates and the communities it stigmatizes. This requires not just responding differently to crime, but calling into question what gets classified and categorized as crime in the first place, and why. It requires interrogating which people or groups come to be profiled for these violations, how those patterns and profiling trends came to be, and what holds them in place. It requires thinking in terms of *decriminalization* of certain types of situations or actions as a means of decarceration. It must illuminate the historical racism that drives US mass incarceration and promote anti-racist policies and practices instead.

People: Transforming Relationships

You will recall that restorative justice intrinsically works to dislodge the victim, offender, and community from being oriented by, and locked into, a state-centric, retributive-punishment conception of justice. This approach can challenge and facilitate practical alternatives to the structural formation of the contemporary US criminal justice system in several ways.

First, restorative justice practices can facilitate various forms of "taking back power" from a state-centric system that renders participants passive and persistently disempowers them. It can do this, in part, by empowering all parties to see themselves as direct participants, with agency and voice, rather than as passive subjects of the system. For example, members of peacemaking circles that respond to harm and wrongdoing will often generate binding "repair of harm" agreements from the emergent consensus of the restorative justice practice, rather than permit solutions to be imposed from outside by a prosecutor and/ or judge. Such justice is restorative because the circle's practices of relationship building cultivate an inclusive "nondominated consensus."

Nondominated consensus emerges when all participants act in good faith and take part in an equitable space for dialogue. Everyone has an opportunity to be heard and to listen to others. Each is able to give voice to their views, is accountable to the others, and is attended to and respected throughout the process.[15] This practice of justice wrests power back from a system that allows prosecutors, judges, administrators, and/or other representatives of the system to operate largely without accountability to persons accused of wrongdoing. These actors within the system are even typically unaccountable to the victim and community impacted by the harm. This is a form of cultural violence that Johan Galtung has identified as *marginalization*. It keeps those subjugated "on the outside," disconnected from decision-making processes that directly affect them, and without even information about how such decision processes are made and implemented.[16]

Restorative justice practices, by contrast, contribute to genuine relational justice because they afford active agency to all participants in the substantive practice of justice (understood, in such cases, in terms of relational repair of harms). They enact mutual accountability by encouraging participants to speak truthfully, engage in attuned listening, participate in tailored response, use consensus-based decision making, and develop action plans for purposes of repairing harms and meeting needs. The justice of restorative justice is enacted, most fundamentally, by illuminating and amplifying the ways that each participant is a somebody, not a nobody.[17] Each member in a circle commands respect by finding, formulating, and conveying their stories, articulating their experience and their judgments in their own voice. Doing this takes power back from the state's top-down implementation of laws that target and categorize communities of color in the United States.

Galtung names two other forms of structural violence beyond marginalization that are active in communities like Back of the Yards. The US war on drugs, as we have seen, culturally manifests in ways that stigmatize people and communities of color. The neighborhoods in which many live are portrayed as ganglands and ghettoes.[18] Broadly shared perceptions of the people who are allegedly most likely to engage in crime, and the spaces most likely to be criminalized, are manifestations of the cultural violence that has long stigmatized these groups of people and the places where they live.[19] These perceptions are promoted, or sometimes passively accepted and naively unquestioned, by people who benefit from these groups' stigmatization. At the same time, they also risk being internalized by many members of the stigmatized group. This reflects a twofold dynamic of cultural violence that Galtung calls *fragmentation* and *penetration*.

Fragmentation refers to how structural violence internally divides marginalized groups and incapacitates their pursuit of solidary resistance by keeping them separated from and divided against one another.[20] It is one way that the New Jim Crow differs most profoundly from the original Jim Crow. Racialized stigma during the earlier Jim Crow era (legalized inequalities and terrorism of Black communities) actually generated community solidarity and motivated collective resistance by the oppressed group. As Alexander puts it, "Racial stigma during Jim Crow contained the seeds of revolt." The stigma of "criminality," by contrast, has encouraged members of the same racial group to see and create internal divisions; it has "destroyed networks of mutual support" that once existed among Black Americans of all classes, and "creat[ed] repressive silence about the new caste system among many of the people most affected by it."[21] Fragmentation suppresses possibilities for the very forms of collective action necessary to challenge and dismantle the mass incarceration system. Indeed, the system even induces some people to appeal for further and harsher "tough on crime" policies in their own communities. Thus, the very social and communal bonds upon which community organizing (and any broader social movement) depends are stigmatized in ways that result in silencing and repression—and even an insidious inversion—of the mutual support and relational agency through which a bottom-up response for constructive change could coalesce.

Penetration is another form of cultural violence, and one that especially targets people of color in a society infused by White supremacist structural and cultural features. In this dynamic, the perceptions of value, meaning, beauty, and self-esteem that characterize the regime of oppression come to be "implanted within" the oppressed.[22] A frequent result is that oppressed people come to desire, value, consider beautiful, or aspire to images and practices absorbed from (or oriented by) the regime of oppression and its culture. This can be an especially powerful form of racialized cultural violence. Martin Luther King Jr. identified this as a temptation that African Americans needed to overcome in order to successfully pursue true justice and their own liberation. King described it as "cultural homicide." It occurs in many forms of psychological and spiritual captivity to the valuations of a society saturated by White supremacist values, resulting in self-abnegation and a pervasive sense of "nobodiness."[23] Penetration also names the means by which the prison-industrial complex implants its expectations, values, and influences within the souls, and across the bodies, of those it disciplines and administers, as well as those it benefits.[24]

Indeed, penetration afflicts the beneficiaries of the White supremacist dynamics of the New Jim Crow as well. As King diagnosed it, the valuations of a White supremacist society create a false sense of "normalcy" and/or "privilege" in White people. It is a false normalcy and illusory esteem because it is predicated on social formations that subjugate African Americans (and non-Whites, more generally). It is destructive relationality, and thus cannot be the basis for true relational justice. Recall that European immigrant groups' quest to be classified as "White" was a *moral choice*, not merely a factual statement about skin color, and moral choices have moral consequences. The White supremacist structures and cultures that dehumanize people of color, thus, also distort the personhood of White people. This is a central implication of the Nguni concept at the heart of South African conception of restorative justice Ubuntu (see chapter 9), and its ethical implication that "whatever dehumanizes you, dehumanizes me." While its destructiveness for White and

Black people is never simply equivalent, nonetheless, White supremacy penetrates the hearts, minds, and souls of White people in ways that dehumanize them and diminish their ability to flourish.

What might be the antidote to such insidious forms of violence? Michelle Alexander recommends something as straightforward as affirming shared humanity:

> Rather than shaming and condemning an already deeply stigmatized group, we, collectively, can embrace them—not necessarily their behavior, but them—their humanness. As the saying goes, "You gotta hate the crime, but love the criminal." This is not a mere platitude; it is a prescription for liberation. If we had actually learned how to show love, care, compassion, and concern across racial lines during the Civil Rights Movement—rather than go colorblind—mass incarceration would not exist today.[25]

These lines conclude one of the most searing and sustained analyses of structural and cultural violence on record. Is this really what Alexander would propose as a prescription for change? To "hate the crime, but love the criminal"? To demonstrate love, care, and compassion, especially across racial lines?[26]

Of course, compassion, care, and concern are essential for any structural and cultural transformation that will do more than preserve and camouflage the White supremacist system in a new form. Compassion, care, and concern form the heart of restorative justice. Yet realistic, constructive analysis requires that we inquire concretely into the social and cultural mechanisms—the forms of practice and action—by which such changes can be cultivated in particular contexts (and broader US society itself) that suffer from deep histories of violence and marginalization. What does restorative justice have to say to this?

The relational ethic and the spiritual ethos of restorative justice can make multiple interventions, but we will examine two. As a practice of restorative justice, the slow trust building that happens through listening, truth telling, and relationship building in peacemaking circles can illuminate, interrogate, and combat dynamics of penetration. As such, restorative justice can function as a form of critical praxis.[27] When it is intentionally undertaken, it can create a situation where, as James Baldwin put it, "we, with love, shall force our [White] brothers to see themselves as they are, to cease fleeing from reality and begin to change it."[28] The relational nature of the justice that forms the heart of restorative practices combats the cultural violence of penetration in its multiple directions, if this justice is genuinely made present in the world.[29]

Second, restorative justice has the capacity to counter the stigmatization or humiliation through which *fragmentation* occurs for all stakeholders affected by wrongdoing, and criminalized wrongdoing especially. These are social acids that denude the prospects for solidary action and organizing. For example, restorative justice practices can challenge the imposition of the "criminal" label by the state and broader societal perceptions by affording space to, and centering the voices of, the individuals and community members caught up in harm, wrongdoing, destructive conflict, and violence in all its forms. Community-led peacemaking circle initiatives can problematize and challenge the top-down labeling and categories imposed by the criminal justice system. At the same time, peacemaking circles can facilitate the cultivation of local relationships oriented by trust building and truth telling. Together, these practices can counter the community-fragmenting acids of stigmatization through criminalization. At its best, restorative justice resists fragmentation through practices that *create* the genuine care, compassion, concern, and love that Alexander cites. As a form of bottom-up community building, sustained over time and scaled outward, this can combat the larger-scale violence of fragmentation.

Conclusion: Transforming Structural and Cultural Violence

Penetration, stigmatization, fragmentation, and marginalization[30]—these dynamics drive the lived conditions of communities that are criminalized within the US prison-industrial complex. These conditions are characterized by the absence of shared concern, interpersonal compassion, care, and social hope. Here the spiritual character of restorative justice becomes especially pertinent in contexts beset by forms of structural and cultural violence.

When implemented in a way consistent with the normative implications of its relational dynamics, practices and initiatives of restorative justice will not merely divert people from or moderate disproportional punishment. They will not even merely heal and repair particular harms. Rather, they will cultivate and build human relationships that reflect holistic relational justice, and thus manifest compassion, care, hope, meaning, and empowerment that can lead to both resistance to subjugation and constructive action for positive change. In this, restorative justice concepts and practices can illuminate and directly counter structural and cultural forms of violence that impact consciousness formation, the effects of which tend to write themselves upon the mind, heart, and human spirit.

Just as a restorative justice practice can cultivate nondominated consensus that is binding and final for "repair of harm" agreements, so it can also determine that a particular action should not be categorized as "criminal" in the first place, and respond accordingly. Local neighborhood and community initiatives can—and have—scaled outward to form collaborative networks of restorative justice initiatives that provide parallel, alternate, or critically cooperative arrangements with contemporary systems of justice.

As an ethical framework, an account of justice, and a set of peacebuilding practices that can facilitate the cultivation of community-wide, citywide, or society-wide networks of initiatives, restorative justice can construct a "durable, interracial, bottom-up coalition for social and economic justice" to combat as well as illuminate the New Jim Crow.[31] It can also guard against such a caste system being, in effect, preserved or re-instantiated through what appear to be vital reforms and corrections to that system.[32] Thus, restorative justice presents theory and practice that can intervene in and counter structural and cultural violence. To determine the extent to which it successfully does this requires concretely examining the places where it is implemented. This is the task we return to in the following chapters.

7

Restorative Justice with a Hammer?

Beyond a "Damage-Centric" Account of Trauma and Care

If the only tool you have is a hammer, it is tempting to treat everything as if it were a nail.
—Abraham Maslow, *The Psychology of Science* (1966)

Days in Back of the Yards

Chicago has sustained some of the highest and most persistent rates of gun-related violence and homicide in the United States for many years.[1] One day I spent in Back of the Yards followed a weekend that tallied the city's highest number of shootings for that year—seventy-four between Friday afternoon and Monday morning, twelve of which were fatal.[2] Everyone in the neighborhood, from small children to elders, lives amid a persistent threat of violence. Pamela Purdie, a circle keeper and trainer at Precious Blood, spoke candidly about this to me. Four days prior to our meeting, three young men who were regulars at Precious Blood and employed in the woodshop there were hit in a drive-by shooting. They were sitting in a car across from the center, just down from the intersection of Fifty-First and Racine, waiting for a center director to come open the woodshop and street-side art gallery (both fashioned from a vacant house Precious Blood had appropriated and refurbished). A jeep pulled up alongside them and sprayed their car with bullets.

"Thank God it wasn't fatal," Pamela tells me. "DeShawn is in surgery today. Paul got hit in the hand. Willy jumped out the window but didn't [get hit]. The damage is the trauma. . . . The damage is the trauma." The ecology of restorative justice long cultivated at Precious Blood enabled the community to respond instantaneously, and in intentionally restorative ways.

> By being a restorative justice community . . . we put out an announcement [that] at one o'clock we need to meet as staff and family, young men, to talk about how we have been affected by that—the day that it happened. It happened at ten thirty in the morning. We met at one. And it was incredible because Willy was sitting right here—he's the one that jumped out the window. He was able to join the circle, talk about what that looked like, what it feels like. Police got involved because there was another young man in the circle that had just been picked up by the police the night before, questioned him all night and then made him walk home—that's trauma. . . . So we were dealing with that, and in dealing with what . . . it feel[s] like to be a young Black man in Chicago, to be shot at by young Black men that look like you, probably grew up in an impoverished neighborhood like you. What is that *like*? How does that make you *feel*? These things can't happen and you *not* check-in. They can't.³

If the harms go unnamed and undealt with, Pamela explains, they almost assuredly result in some kind of retaliation by the victims, usually within a day or two. Everyone affected—especially the young people—internalizes the harms and carries the trauma, often in ways they do not recognize. The harm also metastasizes. Its effects can migrate subtly from one location and circumstance in a person's life to a different, seemingly unrelated circumstance and moment. "Hurt people hurt people" is a common refrain among the staff at Precious Blood. In the restorative contexts I frequented across Chicago, I found that this truism is followed with another time-tested truth: "Healed people heal people."

Pamela emphasizes the fact that the community convened a peacemaking circle on short notice to name and begin articulating and sifting the harms and needs experienced in this particular shooting, and made worse by the police involvement. Responsive circles of this kind are often convened on short notice in order to intervene in the typical cycle of action and reaction that follows immediate conflict and harm. Such circles aim to anticipate and disrupt the predictable responses (typically, direct retaliation and escalation). Yet an immediate or short-notice restorative response can be effective only if it occurs within an intentional and practiced restorative environment. It requires the preemptive cultivation of restorative justice training and a sustained practice of everyone involved in the community—relationships of trust that can only be built over time, but can then be activated productively in a crisis. This is one of the reasons that Precious Blood integrates peacemaking circles and strives to cultivate a restorative vision and way of life in every aspect of the life of the community.

To be effective and sustainable, then, restorative practices must be embedded within an encompassing restorative environment. This is a pivotal insight. It requires a *qualified* embrace of emphasis on trauma, as I argue below. The environment must be restorative all the way down, with attention to trauma embedded in and infused by trauma-informed approaches—rather than vice versa. While trauma awareness and trauma-informed approaches are indispensable for a holistic and healing effectiveness of restorative justice practices—most especially in contexts fraught with structural and cultural violence—restorative justice is not therapy. Indeed, recognizing that restorative justice can (and must) be trauma-informed without reducing it to trauma therapy helps illuminate how it embodies a form of relational justice that is not merely interpersonal, but that can address—and potentially transform—structural and cultural forms of violence.

A Qualified Approach to Trauma

Dr. Elena Quintana directs Adler University's Institute on Public Safety and Social Justice in downtown Chicago. The institute provides support for the various groups and initiatives at Precious Blood, as well as the other restorative justice community hubs across Chicago. Her research focuses on adverse childhood experiences, childhood trauma, neurobiology, and epigenetics. She studies the ways that persistent traumatic experiences—and the stress hormones with which they persistently flood the brain—leave lasting impacts on neural cognitive development and behavior.

Bodies respond to generational trauma by changing and evolving. The impact of trauma does not dictate anyone's destiny, but a person can accumulate an increasingly daunting set of obstacles that have to be dealt with and overcome for that person to flourish.[4] How, then, to promote the kinds of healing of the person and wider community that are necessary in contexts persistently beset by multiple forms of violence? In Back of the Yards and elsewhere, healing must address not only the individual, but the community and social environment as well. The key to addressing trauma nonreductionistically and restoratively is to keep relationship—and thus the practices of relationship building—central.

"What you will see," Dr. Quintana explains, "is that when you look at the very hard sciences, and you're looking at CAT scans . . . [you find that] people are healed by positive human connection. If we are really clear about that, then it is important to think about ways of listening to each other, learning from each other, and then healing each other." Dr. Quintana invokes this as an answer to my question of whether peacemaking circles provide an "evidence-based" way of constructively responding to personal and collective trauma, and to the challenges of living in contexts in which the threat of harm persists. Generally speaking, trauma is a "disconnective disorder."[5] "People heal in community, and restorative justice is a very important part of that. Restorative justice in all of its forms is about positive human connection, and human connection with accountability to one another," she explains. "I see it as a very effective and evidence-based way of healing people and of breeding not just trust and interdependence, but also public safety through those means."[6]

Prolonged experiences of trauma and repeated exposure to extreme threats generate a wide array of symptoms, including nightmares and sleep deprivation, daymares, substance abuse, low academic performance or outright avoidance, depression, anxiety, impulsiveness, episodic free-floating anger and rage, and hypervigilance against anticipated threats and aggressions, among others.[7] Statistically, having suffered trauma increases the likelihood of behaviors that place people at risk of being in violent situations.[8] At the same time, acting from a place of trauma is liable to make people prone to further marginalization by service systems that have little patience for the very behaviors that manifest the traumas from which people need help recovering. To address the symptomatic behavior by punishing it—or responding aversively, without comprehending and attending to the underlying causes and conditions as an intrinsic part of the justice process—only increases the likelihood that the behavior will recur. Most likely, it will go downhill, prompting even harsher responses. The result is a vicious cycle that any viable relationship building will have to anticipate and respond to.[9]

The trauma to which circle processes aim to speak does not only stem from direct violence. It emerges just as much from institutionalized and systemic violence (including structural and cultural violence). Typically, these different types of violence interweave. Reducing one form may result in (or be predicated upon) an increase or expansion of another. Willy, the young man who survived the drive-by shooting physically unscathed by jumping from the car window and crawling under the far side, was still at the scene and in shock when the police arrived. Rather than engaging him as a victim in the incident, the police treated him as a suspect. They handcuffed him and placed him in the back of their squad car. They questioned him for several hours, and when they found no reason to detain him, laughed at him and the circumstances.

Pamela recognizes Willy's treatment as part of the practices of racialized policing in a neighborhood that reflects the deep historical legacies and present realities of racialized ghettoization in Chicago. Much of the trauma that Black, Brown, and poor youth and young adults across Chicago experience results from interactions with police and, further, from anticipated interactions with police.

> Since I've been working here, I live in Oak Park. I live in a neighborhood with White people. So where there is White people, there is protection and there is no having the stuff they allow to happen, that happens in Black and Brown neighborhoods. You understand? So coming here was traumatizing for me. But I've come to want to be here, can't wait to come to work 'cause I'm making a difference. But it makes me so angry when I see stuff that I know I would *never* see in Oak Park. Never. And that's why I have to be here. I *have* to come here, and I have to *impose* circles. I have to. The [young people at the center] call me the "circle police" [*laughs*].[10]

Pamela focuses on the importance of "checking in" following the drive-by shooting. This seemingly trivial component—the entry point into the peace circle—is, itself, no simple formality. Registering to the other members of the circle where you are in the moment, how you feel, what you are dealing with, and how you are doing is a means of initiating connections and establishing honest sharing. It opens up possibilities for articulating and processing pain.

Pain cannot be addressed and healed without first being named, Pamela explains. Of course, it is never as easy as simply "naming" pain and harms. In fact, what makes trauma so insidious is that it damages the very capacities to "name" what one feels or is experiencing in the first place.[11] Here again, the alleged unobstructed introspection of the voluntarist self, critiqued earlier, is analytically insufficient. Such a self is, purportedly, capable of "peering into" its inner environs to inspect its thoughts, feelings, and motivations. Circles, though, take a more capacious account of personhood, seeing it as relational. In doing so, they reveal themselves not to simply be psychotherapeutic "talk therapy" by more ritualized means. On its own, "trauma" language—despite its increasing prevalence in restorative justice contexts—does not fully utilize the kinds of healing, community building, and peacebuilding that restorative justice practices can afford. The latter are not focused on the individual in isolation from their community, but on the dynamic between the two that is required for both to heal and flourish.

The Indispensability but Insufficiency of the Trauma Lens in Restorative Justice

Trauma language was not prominent in restorative justice discussions until fairly recently.[12] In recent years, there have been efforts to holistically integrate trauma healing discourse into restorative justice's focus on the "harms, needs, and obligations" that follow from destructive conflict, violence, and crime.[13] Still, the engagement between the two fields is relatively recent and not fully refined.[14] This combination is a precarious one. The sudden pervasiveness of trauma language risks semantically absorbing more long-standing restorative justice language of harms and needs, accountability, obligations, repair, and healing. Conducted uncritically, and with insufficient care, appropriation of trauma discourses risks (however inadvertently) creating a "damage-centric" understanding of restorative justice that undermines its normative relational aspect, which importantly emphasizes the wider network affected by particular harms.[15]

By focusing solely on how persons are traumatized by harm, such an approach can also unintentionally drift into a deterministic account of the impact of trauma and its effects on people and communities. The temptation to view survivors as defined only by their experience of violence risks defining people's future possibilities according to the harms they have suffered, the developmental impact of those harms, and the residual psycho-emotional and physiological impacts of them (for example, the perpetual risk of re-traumatization).[16] At its worst, fixating on trauma can cause people to "get stuck in a victim identity."[17]

Damage-centric accounts focus on identifying, assessing, managing, and where possible "fixing" the damage that people suffer. Deploying "trauma" as the exclusive category for this process risks medicalizing the ways these harms are understood, and thus narrowing the responses considered viable. "Trauma" language can also shade into a language of expertise. It risks leaving harms, needs, accountability, obligations, and healing ultimately beholden to experts in trauma treatment. Anyone not officially credentialed in the necessary ways would need to qualify their work as not formal or "clinical" trauma treatment. This might limit the community's ability to respond to harms, and thus diminish its agency in circumstances most directly affecting it.

I argue that restorative justice can be justice, and not merely therapy by another name, so long as its relational moral and spiritual dynamics remain the normative orientation that trauma discourse supplements and supports. For restorative justice to address structural violence and systemic injustice, it will have to resist the temptations to over-medicalize and place undue emphasis on measurability and cure. Such approaches risk stripping away restorative justice's distinctive relational understandings of personhood and community, and obscuring the ethical dynamics of its practices, especially when they claim to provide comprehensive explanations and solutions to the effects of violence they confront.

At the same time, integrating trauma discourse into restorative justice contexts has been demonstrated to be effective in a wide range of specific contexts.[18] The uses and limits of this discourse can be helpfully illuminated when we attend to the moral and spiritual features of restorative justice practices. The central question is, Can restorative justice practices and understandings avoid a rigid either/or—either using a medicalized and clinician-driven model of trauma and treatment (or its temptations), or else deploying the term "trauma" so casually that it becomes a catch-all category for whatever harms happen to emerge? I think that it can.

The key is not to become "anti-trauma." It is, rather, to integrate the insights and resources of trauma discourse in ways that are critical and situationally specific. At the same time, we should recognize that restorative justice is more than assessment and treatment of trauma, and that it cannot be absorbed without remainder into trauma discourse. It is in thickly describing and explicating precisely the moral and spiritual dynamics of restorative justice practices that the critical integration of trauma discourse and restorative justice becomes possible.

Harvard University's Center for the Developing Child has demonstrated a single most frequent factor that enables children and young people to persist, recover, and adapt in healthy ways, despite having experienced trauma. It is at least one stable, dependable, trusting relationship with a caring adult in their lives. Such relationships—even one—actually protect against the future impact that experiences of trauma can have on people in their formative years.[19] In short, relationship is a key to resiliency and well-being.

For restorative justice practitioners, a central purpose of peacemaking circles is to cultivate such healthy, positive, reliable relationships. They do so by using circles to cultivate mutual recognition and reciprocal respect, nurturing trust and care, and facilitating accountability for and, when necessary, repairing harms. While these practices accentuate individuality and develop self-reliance, they also open up paths for constructively flourishing together in community. This term names a sense of "us" and "who we are together," mutually interdependent, that does not diminish individuality, but is more than the sum of the collection of discrete individuals.

At Precious Blood, only rarely have I found circles described in those terms by less trained participants. Instead, young men speak to me of circles as the best way of "getting stuff off your chest" or "relieving stress." This language highlights a grave risk of peacemaking circles—namely, that they become places of cathartic release, but not transformational practice. But this language can also be misleading.

There is always a danger that the circle can devolve into trivial therapeutic introspection. But the form that I observed circles take at Precious Blood is hardly "self-help navel-gazing." When young people there speak of circles "relieving stress," they are often speaking more colloquially to the ways that circles aid in processing harm from experiences of direct violence. The circles provide space where they can give voice to, and perhaps release, the tension that comes from living with recurring threats of violence. In places characterized by real and persistent threats, conflict, insecurity, and aggression, the safe space and truth sharing of the circle are not "wallow[ing] in some New Age nirvana," as some critics claim. Such critics dismiss circles for (allegedly) exemplifying a "diffuse spirituality" of self-help dressed up in cultural appropriation of indigenous peoples' peacemaking practices (for example, through "talking sticks and peace circles"—which they allege are "caricatures of indigenous folkways").[20]

In reality, when we carefully pay attention, listen, and open ourselves to learn from what people are actually saying and doing—their practices in these particular contexts—it becomes evident that peace circles are vital to the creation of durable relationships and a restorative community. For example, a component of the circle that may sound trivial—"checking in," in the example that opened this chapter—can be a key moment in maintaining the mental, emotional, and spiritual well-being of the community, and the particular persons who share in that context.

John had been coming to Precious Blood for seven years when I spoke to him. He initially came as a teenager because it was a place he could get a summer job in the neighborhood. He connected with Jonathan's Saturday Sanction group and started participating in one of the weekly peace circles. I asked him to describe the impact he saw from sitting in circle each week. "Basically it is always about, 'How are you doing?' 'How did you come to the circle and how are you feeling?' Basically getting everything off of your chest that you want to talk about," he recounted to me. "When you come into circle, everybody is going to listen, and when it's your turn to talk you can say anything that is on your mind. That made me feel like if I have something bottled up, I can just come to the circle. At least someone will listen to me, for the time being."[21] However, he states, it is the mutual sharing of experiences, more than an individual's release of stress, that is more important in a context where there might be few other opportunities to find out what you have in common with others. "Sending the talking piece around and listening to people's stories, you find out that people are going through the same thing that you even wouldn't know or were scared or ashamed to say. That was kind of good that you can get stuff off of your chest. You don't have to be scared to say if you've got something on your mind or that's bothering you." John's description captures the ways that circle practices aim to create a safe space for possibilities of vulnerability in connection with one another. This is the central condition for relationship building to begin.

Of course, restorative justice is not a *formal* technique for dealing with trauma—not, at least, in terms of the "traumatology" studied by psychologists. Precious Blood makes no pretense of providing trauma recovery services. This is a pivotal caveat for generating a necessary balance, and innovative tension, between resources and approaches to addressing the harms caused by multiple and recurring forms of violence, on the one hand, and the manifold purposes and multiple dimensions of restorative justice, on the other.

"Trauma" concepts and terminology are both valuable and necessary instruments for understanding and responding to the harms and experiences that many young people carry with them to Precious Blood. At the same time, although trauma language now recurs in the informal vernacular at Precious Blood, that language is used in ways that are distinctively inflected by the values of restorative justice. Insights and approaches derived from a trauma lens are interwoven with, and oriented by, the moral and spiritual dynamics of restorative justice.

Precious Blood employs an approach to restorative justice that strives to take the nature, character, and reality of trauma seriously. While staff members are not formally trained or credentialed to diagnose and treat trauma, they strive to be "trauma-informed" in whatever they do. For this, they collaborate with organizations that specialize in trauma treatment and training. This approach makes room for therapeutic concerns without reducing restorative justice to trauma response. Support organizations, such as Adler University in Chicago,[22] provide education and support to staff and community members. Relationship and accompaniment can be a means by which trauma-associated experiences and struggles can be understood and addressed in ways that promote accountability, healing, and resilience, and shared in ways that transform conflict. More broadly, understanding trauma can aid in constructively rebuilding and further cultivating the relational fabric of the community. One central conviction of restorative justice is that positive human connection can work as an antidote to harm, destructive forms of conflict, and the effects of trauma that ensue.

Relationality is the basic orientation by which Precious Blood avoids approaches that are reductionist or that would permit a dichotomous frame to hold sway (trauma *versus* health; "damage" *versus* "normalcy"). This relational orientation enables restorative justice practitioners and participants to develop, over time, a multidimensional understanding of how individual people experience and process harm, how they heal, how their agency might be supported and amplified, and how people come together to cultivate and enrich sustainable community bonds. Destructive conflict and violence in all its forms, including crime, are construed, most basically, as violations of relationships—interpersonal, communal, and across broader webs.

Conversely, the work of repair and the building up of relationships is referred to at Precious Blood as "co-creating community." This framing attunes itself to the effects of multiple forms of violence in terms of trauma and sustainable responses to trauma. But it also expands on such an understanding. It frames the relational dimensions of human flourishing and healing as multiple—simultaneously spiritual, emotional, social, and implicitly (where not explicitly) political and socioeconomic. This approach frames the understandings and practices of relationality as ethical practices that are at the heart of restorative justice, and that make such co-creating a matter of justice. Human and community liberation and flourishing are its ground and goal. Precious Blood takes a distinctively holistic approach to restorative justice by anchoring all that it does in this concept of relationship and practices of relationality. When it comes to implementing restorative justice ethics in the forms of initiatives and institutions, this is a root condition that is easy to get wrong.

"We Don't Do 'Programs'": Holistic, Elicitive, and Community-Led

Restorative justice is not merely a process employed for addressing specific harms or conflicts. By this I mean that it is not merely peace circles and conflict transformation processes (conferencing in the form of circles, victim-offender mediation, impact panels, and so forth). Broadly construed, it is a holistic vision for relationship and the forms of mutual recognition and respect, reciprocal accountability, and healing that are both the elements of healthy relationships and the fruits of such relationships. It is justice that takes the form of fair, equitable, healthy relationships of mutual regard and support. It takes the form of relational practices that further promote such relationships. These features point to the additional pillars on which Precious Blood founds itself as a restorative justice community—*building relationships with youth and families* and *relentless engagement with stakeholders and systems.*

"We don't do programs," Father David Kelly says emphatically. He clarifies that they neither "provide services" nor pretend to offer something that they cannot, such as trauma therapy. Building relationships with youth and families is the central focus of the center. As a result, the form restorative relationality takes—through practices, shared projects, and institutional mechanisms—is determined organically and situationally. It is elicited through relationships with the people who live in the neighborhood and participate in the life of the center.

> What I say oftentimes is, we're relational first and programmatic second. The first thing we do with a family or young person is build relationships with them. . . . "How are you?"—get to know each other, a relationship. Then to discover in that relationship, "Oh, you need counseling" or "Oh, you need to get in school" or "Oh, you need to get a job," and then we embark on that journey to help them. If it is "in house" [at the center], then great. But if it's not, we help them receive or access the resources that we discovered, that they told us they need. [Unlike] a lot of places, we don't have programs and say "Okay, fit in one of those programs." We have relationships and ask, "How do we build programs around that?"[23]

Father Kelly's exposition illuminates how the five "restorative pillars" (accompaniment, radical hospitality, building relationships, relentless engagement, and learning community) do not quite capture the dynamism and interwovenness of the central concepts and practices that provide the groundwork for the restorative enterprise unfolding in Back of the Yards. The "pillars" are perhaps better analogized as interwoven threads that form a single rope. The sisters, brothers, and staff at Precious Blood understand building relationships with youth and families in terms of the practices of accompaniment. The accompaniment character of the relational engagement requires, in turn, journeying together to "relentlessly engag[e] stakeholders and systems." They persistently seek support from, and connect people in the community to, resources that they are not equipped to provide.

"The programs that we do have would have never happened if it was me designing some program," Father Kelly continues.

We do a ton of arts, because what we learned in those relationships is that our young people are victims of trauma. Our families are being terrorized, in a lot of ways, because of that violence and horror of that violence. [Also, we learned] that trauma often does not embed in the part of the brain that is verbal. I can't *tell* you how I'm doing. I might be able to rap about it, I might be able to doodle it with some sort of [artwork]. We began to do some arts—not therapy, because we are not therapists—but it is therapeutic. In a lot of the arts we try to give voice to what we're feeling, and that voice can then be expressed and accepted, if you will, or received. So that's why we do a ton of arts. Again, it came from that relationship. We have an educational program here, not because we want to be an educational system, but rather, we know that our local schools are not giving our young people what they need to have a future, like college or whatever the case.[24]

Building relationships with youth and families interweaves seamlessly with the pillar that calls for the "relentless engagement of stakeholders and systems." This is the ability to effectively connect youth and young adults to the resources they need in order to flourish. But even when staff members are connecting people to resources outside the center, it is important to note, "relationship" remains the DNA of the holistic vision of restorative justice at Precious Blood. It forms the foundation on which the respective needs and resources can be obtained. It is the primary orientation by which folks at Precious Blood work alongside, and with, people throughout the neighborhood and broader community of Chicago. As we will see, it is this intentional and holistic conception of relationship that most essentially makes Precious Blood an enterprise in restorative justice. Relationship is the primary category within which the meaning of "trauma" must be situated.

The fifth and final restorative justice pillar at Precious Blood is a *commitment to cultivate collaborative relationships with other restorative justice initiatives* across Chicago. This requires sustaining teaching and learning relationships with other organizations. For example, as noted above, in order to become adequately trauma-informed, Precious Blood has entered into relationship with Adler University's Institute on Public Safety and Social Justice in downtown Chicago. The institute provides support for the various groups and initiatives at Precious Blood, as well as the other restorative justice community hubs across Chicago. It places graduate students in psychology at the center as interns to support Precious Blood staff, and to consult with youth at the center in need of help, especially with traumatic conflict, harm, and direct violence.

Precious Blood's collaboration with the institute brings into focus how these restorative justice initiatives aim to transform the justice system, alter the culture of punishment that surrounds it, and transform the impact of incarceration on communities that are necessary for that system to exist. Their collaboration brings specific forms of institutionally articulated systemic injustice into view. "[Threats to] public safety [are] mostly about people acting out of their own trauma," Dr. Quintana explains. At the same time, "[It's] also about institutionalized violence against groups of people who act out of their own trauma."[25] This insight reminds us that acute forms of violence, and the effects of harm that ensue, interweave with institutional norms to create systemic injustices. These then become inscribed in the ways that institutions respond to people who have suffered and who act out of the forms of trauma they have experienced. The result is a vicious and very difficult to break cycle of different forms of violence that compromise public safety.

"The young people that we work with are systematically kicked out of many traditional systems," Dr. Quintana explains. "It becomes difficult for them to do things like get a medical card, go to school, get into sports programs in school, get a job, get a tattoo removed. If you or I showed up some place to get services, a service provider would be more likely to want to help us because we are pleasant to deal with. Whereas, young people who might not have all of their documentation together, who might be confused, who might be angry, who might be defensive, and who might be [late are] a pain in the ass to serve. This relentless engagement of resources and systems is really about accompaniment."[26]

Dr. Quintana's description of the restorative justice pillars, and how the pillars interlock with each other, brings our analysis full circle. This is the basis on which Chicago's restorative justice hub network grounds its work. Even the trauma specialists' conception of trauma dovetails with the more basic conception of relationship and relational personhood at the heart of restorative justice, anchoring it in relational practices of radical hospitality and accompaniment. This is central to how both trauma and accompaniment are conceptualized and distinctively repositioned by restorative justice in these contexts.

8

What Does "Spiritual" Get You That "Trauma" Does Not?

Accompaniment as Spiritual and Critical Praxis

I have claimed that restorative justice can be a theory and practice of justice because it promotes modes of association that are moral and spiritual. What does this mean? What does it look like in practice? What do "spiritual" practices and relational dynamics provide that surpasses the limits of "trauma" analysis? Answers to these questions begin with the proper understanding of "accompaniment" in these contexts.

Accompaniment is "the commitment we have to the young person," Father Kelly explains. "It is also the understanding that we don't have answers."

> The young people, or their family, a lot of these know what they need. They just don't have access to it. Or they don't have the strength or someone to walk along with them. So accompaniment is walking alongside a young person or family member to help them access the resources that are needed. If it's about school, we go with them to the school. It's not a referral. We sit in the front office. We wait to be called in. We go in with them. And we come home with them. If we are successful, we celebrate. If we are not successful, we do it again the next day.[1]

Accompaniment, so understood, is not *doing for* another, nor is it a relationship that is unidirectional, even implicitly. Its express intent is to aid in the cultivation of another's agency and flourishing. What that looks like varies on a case-by-case basis. What results, however, is a relationship of mutuality, one where the person supporting another in cultivating their own capacities and potential is reciprocally enriched through relationship with that person. The hope is for the person accompanied to participate (through their presence and participation) in the "co-creation of community."

Here we see how accompaniment interweaves with a range of ethical concepts and practices that are co-constitutive of it. At this point, the tapestry of restorative norms and practices begins to come into full view. To place neighborhood people at the heart of the enterprise of co-creating community is to begin from their knowledge, talents, aspirations, needs, and resources. This insight forms the heart of what it means to "co-create community," and it flows from a holistic vision of restorative justice.

"Nothing Stops a Bullet Like a Job"

What does it look like in practice? And how does it address some of the pressing needs members of the community articulate? Safety, housing, job skills, and jobs are important for neighbors in Back of the Yards. This is especially the case for young people returning from incarceration or who are "system-involved." For them, finding a lease and employment are extremely difficult. The staff at Precious Blood walk alongside to support them in meeting those needs in ways that simultaneously build capacities to go on meeting those needs without support from the center.

Consider an example: In relationship with people in the neighborhood—and in response to the needs that so many expressed—Precious Blood has developed job-training initiatives. Staff members put together a carpentry apprenticeship program, enabling young people in the community to equip themselves with skills in carpentry and construction. They calibrated this initiative to work in tandem with a housing rehab project they undertook on neighboring blocks in order to provide jobs for the young people that directly aid in improving the conditions of the neighborhood itself. This also serves the marginalized community of returning citizens.

The center fundraised enough to purchase a few of the dilapidated vacant houses nearby. Youth at the center who sought job skills and a paycheck apprenticed with volunteer local union carpenters to rehab them. The finished properties became rental residences earmarked for people returning from incarceration. Apartments fashioned from a row house rehabbed in 2019 were reserved for returning citizens who had served a minimum of twenty years. These are people welcomed into the community who otherwise would have tremendous difficulty acquiring even basic rental housing because of the stigma associated with incarceration.[2]

In this case, job skills training and meaningful employment opportunities coincided with creating quality housing for people enmeshed in the structural violence of mass incarceration within the immediate community. These are concrete ways that all the parties involved co-create and sustain community together. Moreover, they do so in ways that illuminate and critically address the structural violence there (housing and job discrimination against formerly incarcerated people). This is a praxis of accompaniment. It is as integral to a holistic vision of restorative justice as any peacemaking circle. It names and also actively resists and transforms structural violence, bit by bit.

But there is more here than first meets the eye. This approach also illuminates the ways that spiritual or "lived religious" dynamics and explicitly theological commitments and motivations can overlap within a holistic vision of restorative justice. Father Kelly is fond of quoting another priest involved in similar enterprises, Father Greg Boyle of Los Angeles's Homeboy Industries: "Nothing stops a bullet like a job."[3] Contrary to how it might sound at first, this phrase is not an instrumental invocation of "a job" as means of occupying "idle hands" that would likely "get into trouble" (such as becoming involved with a gang) without one. Rather, the statement calls out to the Catholic social teaching that labor is an intrinsically dignifying enterprise—provided, of course, that the opportunities for work that are available are ennobling and dignified, and not demeaning, monotonously mind- and soul-numbing, abusive to the body, and economically exploitative. In Father Kelly's mouth, "Nothing stops a bullet like a job" is a tacitly theological claim. He understands this kind of labor as human participation in God's continuing creative action—both corresponding to and expanding human dignity.[4]

At the same time, embedded in a holistically conceptualized approach to cultivating restorative justice community, that same assertion about jobs can also function as a claim of "everyday religion," or a non-tradition-specific spiritual sensibility that many practitioners who explicitly disavow any connection with religion nonetheless associate with restorative justice. The theologically particular Catholic social teaching claim about work's creative, ennobling potential can be understood to simultaneously overlap with a broader understanding of labor as a practice that facilitates the dignifying, creative processes of "meaning making." These occur through capacity building and self-empowerment, self-respect and respect for others, and service in the context of cultivating a compassionate, interdependent community. The overall objective is to amplify the individual's and the community's agency and self-reliance. In the most literally workaday of ways, then, dignified and dignifying work cultivates purpose and a sense of significance.

The key point here is that, from theological and nontheological vantage points alike, the "job that stops a bullet" is anything but merely a source of income and means of occupying idleness to "keep someone out of trouble." Rather, the "spiritual" and/or "theological" dynamics of this holistic approach to restorative justice are lived out, in that the job training programs at Precious Blood are intentionally skill-based and craft-based. They purposefully contribute to the co-creation of community by cultivating the agency and self-reliance of the individual, but also by demonstrating their potential to create community for and with others who will live in the housing they rehab and build.

In the carpentry program I described above, youth and young adults learn to plan projects, read blueprints, select and use tools, measure and cut wood, and assemble parts to complete a task and/or create a finished product. Likewise, those who train in the woodshop and silkscreen printing shops develop the skill to use all of the equipment and manufacture the items that they then market and sell. They also assist in the artistic design, advertising, and sales segments of the enterprise. That is, they participate in the various facets of operating a small business. The fact that they do this in collaboration with their neighbors and friends in the community—other youth and mentors participating in the life at Precious Blood—and then also sit in peacemaking circles together with many of the same people, expands the restorative justice dimensions of the enterprise, enriching its significance and impact. The urban farm initiative works similarly. It integrates agricultural know-how and skill development with service to the neighborhood.

The job and skill training initiatives at Precious Blood are not an appendage to the restorative justice orientation of the community, a way to raise some funds and keep kids off the streets. They are, instead, part and parcel of co-creating community in ways that dignify, empower, meet needs, and help repair harms identified by the people involved. In Back of the Yards, these practices are intrinsic to a restorative justice that promotes human flourishing and dignity in a relational, not individualistic, understanding of what those mean. They exemplify what it means to describe a vision of restorative justice as holistic. Precious Blood and its partners are not merely regularly inserting peace circles (or other forms of restorative conferencing) into the daily life of the community. Rather, peace circles provide a methodical means of intentional relationship building that gradually both discloses needs and goals and establishes the context that enables these to be met. This restorative vision of relationships is anchored in a vision of flourishing elicited by the needs of community members and the harms that they struggle to overcome. It all begins with accompaniment.

Of course, there can be no accompaniment without embodied practices of radical hospitality already up and running. Radical hospitality is precisely what standard social services lack, as Dr. Quintana describes. Such hospitality requires commitment, resilience, and persistence in one's response to people who may be prone to act out of their pain after experiencing both visible and structural harms, often for their whole lives. At the heart of radical hospitality are practices of sustained commitment (fortitude) and radical patience. There can be no meaningful relationship—however embryonic—without trust. Cultivating trust with people who have experienced abandonment can be an especially slow and arduous process.

"Kids aren't always where I want them to be," Father Kelly explains.

> A lot of times they say, "Father K, thanks but no thanks. I want to do what I am doing." Well, I have to be in a relationship with that kid; I have to engage that kid. Not to berate him or nag him to change, but rather to say, "I know you're out there doing your thing," whether that's drugs or whatever the case may be, "but I care about you and want a relationship with you." I don't say it in those kinds of words, but that's my attitude, and my engagement says that, hopefully. So that when that kid decides he's going to change, that relationship is already there. He can say, "Damn, I got busted last night, I got to get my act together. Can you help me get into school? Can you help me do this?" We're there. So relentless engagement because they can act like knuckleheads. It's not easy. It's kind of a temptation to slam doors shut.[5]

Radical forms of hospitality, patience, and perseverance are all necessary precursors to—and simultaneously constituent features of—accompaniment. They make possible a relentless commitment to "walk alongside" with an attuned openness to the experience, resourcefulness, and wisdom that the people one is accompanying already possess. This is the spiritual relationality of accompaniment.

The impact of deep and lasting harm in the lives of particular individuals ramifies outward through families and into community. Whether as the result of something one has undergone, or actions one has undertaken, or some combination of these, experiences of harm make it challenging to enter into, much less sustain, relationships of mutual vulnerability and trust.[6] Practices of hospitality that are radical in patience and resilience are conditions for the possibility of accompaniment and the restorative relationality that might follow. Dr. Quintana helpfully describes the ways the restorative justice pillars interlock:

> Commitment to offer welcoming and hospitality—*radical hospitality*—[means] really meeting people where they are even when it's difficult—*especially* when it's difficult. We go to people who are in traumatic situations, that are carrying weapons on a regular basis [because they don't feel safe]. We go to them again, and again, and again. And we realize that they don't feel protected, they don't feel that they can trust, and they have probably been betrayed, and are probably hurting a lot of people. And we still go to them—again, and again, and again. That's radical hospitality. We have a space so that you can be welcomed in, and we will accompany you to hear your goals and your plans, to not judge where you are at the moment, but to keep walking forward and building relationships with young people. *Relentless engagement of systems and stakeholders* means that since we work with young people that other people have often already refused to serve, *our* relationships with schools, service providers, governmental agencies [are] really key in terms of being able to get them in the door and say, "Hey, I know you kicked this person out, but if you don't take them back, they won't be able to get to the next step."[7]

Circles as Spiritual Praxis

From my own observations, when restorative justice community members who disavow being "religious" do use the word "spiritual," they tend to use it in two senses.[8] The first coheres with the sense of "spiritual" as understood in relation to a community in which the members share an orienting sense of interrelating with one another and a resulting sense of interdependence. In the second sense, the word "spiritual" signifies a compassion and care for others that lead one to move beyond a self-centered focus to a shared sense of "who we are together." Both can infuse various dimensions of the circle practices, in addition to whatever else a given circle may be devoted to (for example, addressing and repairing some harm, welcoming new people to the community, celebrating an accomplishment, simply cultivating relationships by getting to know one another, deepening those relationships over time, sharing one's difficulties, and so forth). Whether construed religiously or not, the intrinsically relational features of such a holistic vision of restorative justice reflect such moral and spiritual dynamics. It is in relationship, and through a critical praxis of co-creating community, that human beings can facilitate each other's flourishing—and, where necessary, assist in each other's healing—in the face of meaninglessness and the threat of nihilism. The multiple purposes interweave and work together.

For example, the aim of processing traumatic experiences "in circle" is their expression in the voices of particular people. This occurs slowly, as relationships of mutual respect and trust begin to emerge through the circle process. Circles address some problem or issue only as a small piece of enabling each circle member to apprehend, sift through, interpret, and express their situation and role in the broader context. Doing so facilitates their finding and developing their own particular and concrete point of view and expressing that in their own voice. It also enables them to reject or at least resist the view of reality suggested to them by the justice system or broader society and the temptation to internalize how that reality sees them, as a "gangbanger," "drug dealer," "shooter," "delinquent," or "criminal," among other stereotypes. Though sometimes grindingly slow because it requires extensive trust building, out of this concrete particularity comes the possibility of developing, together with the members of the circle, a range of practical responses. So, through practices that cultivate relationality, circles can simultaneously enable, ennoble, and amplify individuality. How does this relate these moral and spiritual dynamics to insights from trauma discourse? The short answer is that the moral and spiritual dynamics of restorative justice practices are crucial for addressing the harms and needs (and ensuing obligations) that frequently get named in terms of trauma discourse. How so?

Consider an example. Neurologically speaking, prolonged experiences of harm and trauma prod the amygdala, the part of the brain responsible for activating the "fight or flight" reaction in response to immediate or anticipated threats. In the wake of trauma, the amygdala remains activated and on "high alert." This is especially so when the person revisits situations related to the traumatic experience. This can make even seemingly straightforward social situations and conversational exchanges unpredictable, and potentially inspire "quick-tempered" responses.

Every facet of relationship building in the peacemaking circle contributes to a stability that, in effect, counteracts these. The order of the process is clear and predictable. The physical formation and tactile features of the circle gather, help focus, and sustain attention. For example, items contributed from participants are assembled to form the centerpiece, the talking piece is always passed in a predictable way, and each participant can see and be seen by the other members of the circle. The progression of the circle is intentionally unhurried and uncomplicated. The values and guidelines emerge from several consensus-building rounds and are kept in view. Such a set-apart time, designated space, and ritual-like practice generate a sense of steadiness. It is a methodical and predictable practice that creates a sense of "being safe" because participants know what to expect during the circle. The circle process at its best is also a form of critical praxis and pedagogy. It is critical reflection on lived experience that is aimed at effecting some further change or transformation in the person and the world around them. It is not hyper-personal, self-help, or psychologizing analysis, though it aims to cultivate meaning, a sense of purpose, and self-value.

Another example helps to illustrate how this takes a form of "spiritual praxis." One staff person I spoke to was stationed at Precious Blood from the Institute for Nonviolence of Chicago. He keeps a circle for men in the neighborhood designated "high-risk." These are young men he describes as likely to be shooters and decision makers in gangs. His circle transforms the cultures of conflict and violence among these men by aiding them in developing self-awareness and self-value. "We strive to cultivate self-value," he explains, "because trauma devalues you." "Safety" for these young men is "a guy [partner] and a gun," he tells me. "When you bring up emotion with these young men, the initial response is typically 'I ain't no . . .' insert female expletive," he remarks. "In their minds, it's women that feel emotion, not men. You try to get them to think in terms of their 'future' and they smirk, 'cause there is none." The circle facilitates intentional, methodical relationship building that can lead to change because it develops the men's awareness that they have been traumatized, and then makes space for them to cultivate self-esteem and self-worth.[9]

In effect, this staff person describes a variation of the "nihilism" that Cornel West and Michelle Alexander identify as the heart of the effects of mass incarceration that must be challenged and overcome. West describes this as the pervasive and persistent experience of "the loss of hope and absence of meaning." Such nihilism generates various self-, other-, and community-debasing forms of attempting to deal with the onslaught of meaninglessness. He diagnoses such nihilism as coinciding with "a numbing detachment from others and a self-destructive disposition toward the world"—"a disease of the soul."[10] This must be "tamed by love and care," because "any disease of the soul must be conquered by a turning of one's soul" and "through affirmation of one's worth—an affirmation fueled by the concern of others."[11] It is equally fueled by the quest for reclamation of community-sustaining forms of justice. At their best, peacemaking circles provide the context, time, and methodical relationship building practices where the self-love, mutual recognition, reciprocal respect, accountability, compassion, and care for others necessary to dissolve such nihilism are cultivated.

The peacemaking circle is strategically elicitive. Because the circle is intrinsically interrelational and multi-perspectival—through the sharing of each person's stories, experiences, personal histories—it involves the circle members in a process of critical spiritual and ethical discovery. Some report realizing that they are not alone in what they have experienced or are struggling with. They report that their experience is part of a wider pattern of conflict, difficulty, or harm that is also suffered by others. They might reframe or reinterpret those experiences. They hear and process potential responses or courses of action—potential forms of resistance.

The circle aids in uncovering, illuminating, and then making the person critically aware of institutional, cultural, and historical forms of violence. It then points toward ways of responding constructively at the level of the local community. The circle can enable the cultivation of *communal* critical consciousness, aiding circle members, together and individually, in making a critically reflective turn in their understanding of their own situation and that of their communities. As this happens, they come to understand justice as more than a response to harm and crime, growing to have a broader conception of justice as a form of flourishing and well-being. They also grow into deeper practices of it themselves.

The move to the structural level requires a reconceptualization of what structural transformation is and how to go about accomplishing it. Again, rather than imagining structural transformation *in contrast to* cultivating healthy and durable communal bonds in the form of interpersonal and communal relationships, we need to see structural transformation as enacted *through* relationship and trust building, not before, alongside, or after it. Integral to this understanding is the effort to change the culture by creating a safe environment where people can trust enough to be vulnerable with one another: to tell their stories, share their experiences of harm and their needs, and thereby transform their relationships. The practices must be engaged in regularly for the values and understandings to take hold and seep in. This is a persistent, ethical practice of mutual recognition and respect, compassion, care, reciprocated aid, accountability, and healing. Once these relationships are formed, the people in the group are better able to see the way structural violence has shaped their experience and thereby also to begin imagining collective ways of overcoming it.

Resurrection: Restorative Justice as a Mode of Moral and Spiritual Association

We are now in a position to reconsider Michelle Alexander's prescription of an ethic of genuine care, compassion, and concern for every human being as the central way to subvert the individual and community-debasing impact of the New Jim Crow. As noted earlier, her solution to addressing the New Jim Crow and its role in the prison-industrial complex seemed to be highly idealistic, perhaps even wishful, thinking. Yet, in Back of the Yards, compassionate and care-driven forms of engagement constitute the substance of the practices by which community members together confront, counteract, heal, and work to transform the causes and conditions of multiple forms of violence. These are practices of care and compassion that require interrogating the structural conditions under which the actions in question came to be designated as crime—and the persons in question as "criminal" or "delinquent"—in the first place. It is the methodical and deliberate cultivation of relationships and communal bonds that promote person-specific and collective agency, which then provide the foundation on which structural transformation becomes possible.

Transformation occurs in several specific forms: community-led practices of conflict transformation; justice and repair of harm; naming, challenging, and resisting criminalization, and then contesting and altering what constitutes "delinquency" in the first place; cultivating and restoring healthy, nurturing, and durable relationships among people within and across neighborhoods; resilience and healing from trauma and post-traumatic stress; employment and education through mentoring, tutoring/educational programs, skill, and job programs; and more broadly, promotion of flourishing through the co-creation of community.

Positioning the vocation and work of Precious Blood in relation to Alexander's diagnosis gives her prescription a weighty tangibility, as well as a sober realism, without which some readers might overlook or dismiss all that is really at stake in her proposal. It also points us to the heart of community, care, and compassion that grounded the earliest movement for prison abolition, where the concern was for a sustainable, grassroots approach to the relational transformation of communities. Alexander argues, however, that following the civil rights era, activists became divorced from the people and local community contexts on whose behalf they work. Some took an exclusive focus on legal remedies and others hesitated to work on behalf of people who had been labeled "criminals," with the exception of death penalty cases.[12]

The approach to restorative justice practice at Precious Blood corrects this problem because it emerges organically from the people in the neighborhood. Neighborhood people are active participants in the processes by which conflict, harm, or crime is addressed. They participate in challenging and redefining what the prison-industrial complex has defined as "delinquency" and "criminality." And they have an incentive to do so, as they and their loved ones have been the victims of these processes of criminalization. This kind of critical praxis is no longer advocacy on behalf of people involved in violence. This approach instead brings forms of generational trauma and deep legacies of structural and cultural violence to levels of conscious awareness through the collaborative, deliberative processes of peacemaking circles. These and other practices seek to heal in the wake of present and recent harms. They seek to collectively reconfigure—from the bottom up—the processes and institutions by which such harms are addressed in the future. In this context, the transformation of violence takes the form of illuminating, naming, and disrupting a system designed to create crime and a perpetual class of people labeled criminals—in fundamentally racialized ways—rather than to eliminate crime or reduce the number of criminals.

Alexander's prescriptive words then become both grounds for hope and a prescription for both responsive and preemptive action. How do we see care and compassion restoratively conceptualized and routinized at Precious Blood? We find it in the intentional self-conception of restorative justice as a community-based and community-led set of practices that promote moral and spiritual forms of association and relationship. Restorative justice is what it is only in virtue of its enmeshment in a web of ethical concepts and practices: radical hospitality and the arduous cultivation of patience that such hospitality requires. The refusal of a service-providing or program-driven account of accompaniment is key. All of this is in-spirited—animated and sustained—through practices of conceptualizing and sustaining hope. This hope is many-faceted: hope for the possibilities of healing particular lives and communities; hope for the possibilities of transformation of the causes, conditions, and circumstances of violence and trauma; and hope that resiliently persists. However one grounds such hope, it is the substance of restorative justice as a moral and spiritual approach to life together and cultivating individual flourishing and self-reliance, and it takes the form of concrete, ethical practices.

As one might expect, Father Kelly considers this ethical impetus to be drawn from a central feature of the Christian story, although one that receives little attention. "My work is in between Good Friday—which is a death—and Easter [which is a resurrection]," he explains. "Too often, Christians want to move from Good Friday to Easter, and we forget about Holy Saturday, which is the real place of the work of the church. Because most of us—most people—are living in the shadows of the crucifixion, wanting that new life, that resurrection, that freedom, that liberation. But we're not there yet. And we work in this Holy Saturday moment."[13] Father Kelly refers to a point in time where a real sense of hopelessness can exist, and where hope must be actively cultivated and sustained through practices of common life together.

One need not share Father Kelly's theological grounds for hope to subscribe to, and practice, restorative justice, a point that he himself is quick to acknowledge. Some people, he points out, do not see restorative justice practices as religious at all. He describes it as a philosophy that reflects spiritual dynamics of, as he says, "standing in a breach, standing in the muddled mess and trying to give witness to the possibilities of hope, and healing, while working to repair."[14] He attributes the capacities of circles, and restorative justice more broadly, to embrace people with different or no religious commitments and backgrounds as an effect of what he describes as the spiritual aspects of this philosophy. Whether construed religiously or not, the intrinsic relationality of such a holistic vision of restorative justice reflects dynamics that can be helpfully described as spiritual. It is in relationship, and through a critical praxis of co-creating community, that human beings can help heal one another and facilitate each other's flourishing. This sense of "spiritual" situates the work at Precious Blood as "in between"—in between harm and suffering, on the one hand, and recovery, renewal, persistence, and cultivation of a sustainable, just, and peaceable community, on the other. It's a process of recovery that strives toward, and holds out hope for, some point of "things made new."

At Precious Blood, it is in this notion of "between-ness" where people find the grounds for and orientation toward hope. This orientation provides resiliency in the face of the daily realities of violence. One might believe that this notion is grounded in the story of Jesus, which is then reenacted in daily or weekly mass, as it is for the sisters and brothers of Precious Blood. One might, on the other hand, see it as the time and space in between loss and need, and processes of resistance and recovery that people have the wherewithal to pursue when they intentionally bring their individuality and relational capacities into concert with one another. Such forms of solidary, collective agency do not lose the flourishing and individuality of particular persons in acting together upon the world in order to change it. They amplify those.

This all reflects a social and historical pattern that recurred in the Back of the Yards more than once over the course of the twentieth century, as waves of residents fought variously for workers' rights, suffrage, fair housing, and neighborhood restoration over many decades. It was and is the capacity of people to act, organize, critically reflect, build community in ways that name and challenge violence in all its forms, and cultivate movements for sustainable change that effected, and continues to effect, transformation. Earlier we saw examples in Back of the Yards of "secular" activists (Upton Sinclair), radically religious activists (Dorothy Day, Mary McDowell, and Martin Luther King Jr.), and those who are some combination of these (the pragmatic humanism of Jane Addams or the agnostic Judaism of Saul Alinsky). Restorative justice is another example of an emergent transformational movement in the space between crucifixion and resurrection, or, for the nontheistically minded, oppression and liberation.

It still remains to ask exactly how these restorative practices cut to the roots of systemic injustices and structural violence. How do they actually displace the New Jim Crow and its role as driver of the US prison-industrial complex? To think about the roles that such restorative justice will play in transformation at the neighborhood level requires changing how one thinks about both the structures of power that operate in those places, and the nature of violence. One must begin by grappling with the deep relational histories and manifold varieties of violence that interlace those contexts and contribute to the causes and conditions of harm experienced there. This has come to be known as "historical trauma," in some cases. As we saw above, in Back of the Yards this requires unmasking the legacies of racism and White supremacy with specific attention to the ways that these deep histories inhabit and perpetuate present-day realities. This must be done even though present realities may appear to be divorced and distant from those relational histories and contexts. To fail to connect present conditions to the legacies and deeper causes of the current conditions is to invite misdiagnosis and misunderstanding of the types of response and repair that are necessary.

The variations of restorative justice unfolding in Back of the Yards emerge from the local grassroots. They are elicited by the experiences and needs of the people living in the neighborhood. Restorative justice invites their participation in developing and coming to guide initiatives that address their situation. I do not mean to suggest a romanticized and isolating vision of local organizations acting in isolation, refusing to seek out resources available at the level of the city, county, and state. These initiatives literally cannot afford the vision of "subsidiarity"—a view that independent, charitable organizations can generate the capacity to work on their own, at the most local levels possible. Without partnering with government resources, they would not be able to come close to addressing the breadth and depth of the needs of the community. Most of these organizations recognize the indispensability of working collaboratively yet critically with, and seeking support from, resources and services in the city and county governments (judges, social workers, police, and so forth). That realization falls within the purview of "radical engagement of resources."

Nonetheless, a different approach is taken toward how to interact with these government agencies. As we will see, the people at Precious Blood and their partner initiatives strive to maintain a critical posture and vigilant skepticism toward any top-down approach to community engagement. Outright reliance on government service providers risks ceding their agency, and thus compromising the intentionally restorative character of the values that guide their practices. Such reliance would also risk having their efforts co-opted by the justice system. "The criminal justice system is broken and cannot be fixed," Father Kelly says. "But it is possible for people [currently working] in that system to enter into deep relationships with communities that are restorative." Moreover, it is possible for those people to do so in a way that contributes constructively—and even transformatively—to that restorative purpose and identity.[15] The challenge comes in striking and sustaining a necessary critical tension between working with influential institutions and developing on-the-ground practices along with the organizational initiatives that sustain them. At Precious Blood, staff constantly strive to remain vigilant against becoming "system-led," or subtly co-opted, without defaulting into a simple "system-averse" posture.

At this point it is important to anticipate and respond to a central objection to positioning restorative justice as a form of "justice." Where does this relational conception of justice come from? And how does it constitute *justice*? How is it not better described as a form of therapy, charity, or humanitarian assistance? These questions take us to the heart of the philosophical and ethical dimensions of restorative justice. In the chapter that follows, we will explore the philosophical and ethical dynamics of restorative justice, and articulate a theory and practice of justice that flow from it.

9

But Is It *Really* "Justice"?

The Power and Impact of Restorative Justice Ethics

Restorative justice practices aim to repair harms and respond to the effects of trauma by cultivating healthy and durable relationships, facilitating repair of harm, and building (or rebuilding) sustainable communal bonds. Why, then, claim that these practices constitute a form of *justice*? Why not refer to them as forms of restorative therapy, healing, or community building instead? Or simply as an alternative to the dehumanizing bureaucracy and proceduralism of the US retributive "justice" system?

At one level, to speak of restorative justice rather than "restorative alternatives" simply reflects the use of these practices to respond to the effects of harm and destructive conflict. Restorative justice practices are equipped to address violence and its aftermath in a nonretributive way. In this mundane sense, restorative practices pertain to justice because they fall within the scope of, and provide an alternative response to, the typical paths that "victims" and "offenders" go through in the criminal justice system.

Some argue that to portray restorative justice as a form of justice is a mistake. Doing so creates an obstacle that keeps restorative practices and initiatives quietly participating in forms of unaccountable power and impunity (domination) that are dressed up in "justice" language. Justice language is ultimately beholden to the contemporary criminal "justice" system (which, they argue, is wholly mis-associated with "justice" to begin with). Any connection with "justice" in this way, these authors assert, makes restorative justice "doomed to fail."[1]

Contrary to such claims, there is a more fundamental—and more transformational—sense in which restorative practices are properly thought of as justice. Specifically, restorative justice practices arise out of a restorative understanding of what justice is. As with all conceptions of justice in the abstract, this account takes the form of a theory. A theory lays out conceptual groundwork, normative presuppositions and implications, features, and consequent practices in ideal form. Of course, this requires that we press outward to explore possibilities and examples of implementation to see how our theory bears out in practice. But detailing a theory of restorative justice demonstrates why and how this framework and the practices that embody it properly constitute an account of justice.

A theory of *justice*, broadly understood, is an account of what each person is due.[2] It provides a justification for how persons ought—and ought not—to be treated. It explains why and how people ought to recognize each other as persons and citizens, demonstrate respect for each other, and hold each other accountable for the claims and actions each undertakes. In a constitutional democracy such as the United States, accounts of justice articulate what each is owed in terms of equal protection under laws, equal rights, and equitable opportunities and access to resources.

At this theoretical level, identifying restorative justice as a form of justice requires us to recall the conception of personhood that restorative justice practices presuppose. We then have to clarify what persons are due based on that conception, and how restorative practices make it possible to uphold the rights and fulfill the obligations entailed in that account of justice.

Restorative justice, as we have seen, identifies human persons as intrinsically relational creatures. This implies that relationality is basic to an account of what all human persons *deserve* in virtue of being persons. Restorative justice, then, understands justice, or what each person is due, using this relational understanding of personhood. Other accounts of justice, by contrast, might identify persons as essentially isolated individuals. It is this account of relational personhood that makes restorative justice justice rather than therapy, healing, or community building per se—though restorative justice interacts with each of them.

At the heart of a restorative theory of justice is the claim that all persons require for their well-being, and thus are due, relationships that meet basic needs and promote well-being.[3] If such relationships are to be just, they require just socioeconomic, political, legal, environmental, and cultural contexts to support and sustain them. They require protection from arbitrary (mis)treatment by the institutions that govern the contexts in which they exist. In short, to be genuinely just, restorative justice must interweave symbiotically with social contexts characterized by just structures and institutions. Such a theory of justice also must be built up from an ethical groundwork.

The Ethical Bases of Restorative Justice

Restorative justice ethics and practices derive from many different points of origin—from indigenous and aboriginal justice practices in various contexts around the globe, as well as from religious traditions.[4] For example, the restorative justice norms and practices of South Africa's Truth and Reconciliation Commission (TRC) derived from indigenous African understandings of personhood, community, and justice. South African conceptions of restorative justice presupposed a conception of "relational personhood." In local terms, this was known as Ubuntu—a word from the Nguni South African languages that translates roughly into "I am because we are." South African Anglican archbishop and TRC chair Desmond Tutu glossed the meaning of Ubuntu in this way: "My humanity is caught up, is inextricably bound up, in yours, for we can only be human together."[5]

Much in this spirit, restorative justice understands individual personhood as intrinsically and irreducibly—though not exhaustively—relational. In this understanding, individual persons are distinctive, unique, and have individual agency. At the same time, they become persons in and through their relationships with other persons. This is reflected in, for example, the inescapable relationships of complete dependence and constant care that we all experience as infants and throughout childhood, and often return to in old age or illness. We see it reflected as well in the intrinsically shared character of cultures and languages.[6] We find evidence of this intrinsic need for relationships in the physiological and psychological necessities of social interaction and human connection for basic mental and emotional health and individual well-being all throughout the human life cycle.[7]

Humans always have been in relationships. The operative question, then, is not *whether* humans will be in relationship; the question, rather, is whether that intrinsic relationality will be recognized and acknowledged within their communities. Will those relationships be healthy? Will they meet these basic needs? Will they be oriented by and participate in the common good that is shared by the members of the community or society? Will those relationships be *just*? In other words, will they reflect and promote equity, reciprocal accountability, fair treatment, and mutual aid? Will they facilitate human thriving, individual and collective? Or will the intrinsic and indispensable relationality of human personhood be denied, ignored, passively neglected, exploited, and/or used for destructive ends—and, therefore, obstruct or degrade human flourishing?

Restorative justice, of course, aims at promoting human flourishing. As we might expect by now, this goal is grounded in a relational vision of what it means to "flourish." From the vantage point of restorative justice, the intrinsic interrelationality of human personhood has normative implications regarding how humans ought to be treated in order to promote their well-being.

Human relationality is "intrinsically normative." This means that the relational dimensions of personhood entail a distinct value orientation with implications for how persons ought to interact with and treat each other. To be a person is to be a "norm-using" creature—the kind of creature that both acts on the basis of reasons and makes judgments of how others do so. We make such judgments, for example, when holding another accountable for their claims (what they say), their commitments (what they believe), and their actions (what they do).

The normative implications of relational personhood originate in the mutual recognition that this other is "like me." Each is an agent who holds others accountable, and to whom the other ought to be accountable for how they relate to and interact with that person. Because persons are norm-using creatures, they ought not to be treated arbitrarily, like an object or a thing to be manipulated. We are not accountable to "things" in the ways we hold other people accountable for how they interact with and treat us, and vice versa. To use phrasing common in modern theology and ethics, each person ought to be treated as a "Thou" in an I-Thou relationship of mutual recognition, reciprocal respect, and accountability, as opposed to an "It" or an object in an I-It relationship.[8]

Unaccountability allows one person or group of persons to exert power over some other or others without having to answer for, or be held accountable for, what they do. In this, they dominate those others. They thus violate the normative character and moral implications of relational personhood—namely, that persons are the kind of creatures that hold each other accountable to norms, and thus, ought to treat each other in ways that recognize and respect each's norm-using character.

Dominating others is not only a factual error or a mistake in knowledge, a so-called epistemic mistake, that incorrectly treats a person as a thing. It is, at the same time, a moral error. In other words, interacting with persons in ways that are unaccountable is something one ought not do. For in treating others in ways that are unaccountable to them, I either actively engage in or make myself available to engage in behavior that dominates them. This ignores or denies their ability to hold me accountable for how I treat them, and therefore disrespects their humanity as norm-using creatures. It thus disregards their dignity as persons, treating them as though they were things instead. At the same time, in disrespecting and degrading the humanity and dignity of others, the dominator simultaneously disrespects and disregards their very own humanity and dignity. That is, the one who dominates others also comes to be dominated by the domination they impose upon others. (We will see why this is the case in greater detail in the section that follows.)

In principle, then, the normative character and implications of relational personhood ought to prohibit circumstances in which one is (or some are) in a position to be unaccountable to others. Indeed, as a creature caught up in relationships of mutual accountability, the other is intrinsically deserving of recognition, respect, and care.

It is important to add at this point that relational personhood does not *reduce* the individual to their relationships or roles in community, leaving no room for the individual self. Just the opposite, in fact. The interrelatedness of "each other together" illuminates the uniqueness and irreplaceability of the individuals in the relationship. The partners in relationship are never identical. Each person is unique and concretely particular *in virtue* of always and already being caught up in distinctive relationships. In fact, it is through the relational practices of mutual recognition and reciprocal accountability that the individuality of each is understood, enriched, and amplified.

This is so because the mutuality and reciprocity that lead to relationship mean that people cannot submerge their concrete particularity and irreplaceability. So, if interrelationality creates a situation of passive dependency, or promotes mere imitation of another's uniqueness, the situation becomes less than genuine interrelationality. In this situation, one person would become a mimic or would-be mirror reflection of the other. He would now be something less than a fully agential partner and distinctive contributor to the reciprocal give-and-take of the mutually accountable relationship. He could not, then, actualize his potential to cultivate, innovate with, and expand his distinctive and particular humanity. This is why the basic relationship, the necessity of the other to one's own identity, does not destroy individuality but ultimately illuminates and calls people further into the cultivation of their own distinctiveness and irreplaceability, though always in and through, rather than apart from, the realities of being in relationships with others.

"'I Am' Because 'We Are'": The Ethics of Ubuntu

The relational dynamics of personhood suggest a range of ethical implications for the ways people ought to relate to one another—that is, they suggest an account of justice. Mutual recognition means that others are relational partners with whom our own well-being is interlaced. Intrinsic interconnectedness or relational personhood means, as Archbishop Tutu explained, that whatever dehumanizes you, dehumanizes me.[9] I may not consciously recognize the ways that the dehumanization of others negatively impacts me, or I may view such dehumanizing as having a negligible impact on me. But it does have an impact.

Assume, for example, that someone is a beneficiary of a social system in which her well-being, self-understanding or self-esteem, prosperity, and/or privilege is, at whatever remove, predicated upon the exclusion, marginalization, domination, or humiliation of some other members of her society. She may not recognize that the hardship of others is a condition of her fortunate status. If confronted with this state of affairs, she may be inclined to deny that her good fortune depends on their misfortune. She may search for justifications of the naturalness of her advantaged position, or perhaps claim that she has earned it completely of her own accord, and thus deserves it. However, her very failure to recognize—or her effort to deny or justify—her benefiting from this social system is, itself, a luxury afforded by her privileged status and condition. This obliviousness (whether through unawareness or denial) is symptomatic of the destructive impact that such systems have even on those who are passive beneficiaries of such systems. In short, under such conditions, people suffer from a form of moral and relational ignorance that makes them more limited "selves" than they could otherwise be. It might make someone less aware of people around him and conditions in which they live, less inclined to practice or less capable of practicing empathy toward others, less able to understand and act reflectively or beyond the immediacy of his own situation and self-focused concerns, less liable to seek out, challenge, and alter conditions that benefit him in virtue of harming others, and thus, less able to render to people the kind of treatment that they are due (and so on).

It was precisely in this way that Martin Luther King Jr. diagnosed even the most passive forms of racism in the United States as causing a kind of spiritual and personal sickness in those who benefit from them. Segregationist laws and culture, King argued, "distort the soul and damage the personality" of *all* the people affected by them. Peoples directly harmed, marginalized, and oppressed by such laws and cultures, whether under the old or the new Jim Crow, were and are the most obvious recipients of such damage. They encounter daily the experiences and effects of a system that aims to dehumanize them. In the United States, minority peoples are subject to sources of authority that are not reciprocally accountable to them. Subjugated peoples are always at risk of absorbing and internalizing the experience of inferiority and humiliation inflicted on them. As a result, King warned, segregationist structures and cultures can produce an abiding sense of "nobodiness." These effects upon the souls of Black folks, he said, must be relentlessly rooted out as lies.[10] We might recognize this diagnosis as that also made in Back of the Yards today.

At the same time, King noted that people in his own day who benefited from segregationist structures and cultures suffered from a sickness of soul that could be even more insidious if it was not recognized and actively struggled against. Segregationist arrangements conveyed to White Americans the false and soul-contorting self-perception that they were superior, or at least "okay" when compared to their Black and Brown fellow citizens. Such claims of superiority were often made explicitly (as with avowed White supremacists). But they could remain tacit as well, manifesting in subtle ways beneath the level of self-awareness and self-reflection. For many beneficiaries of White supremacist culture, their range of social and political advantages remained un-reflected upon. But the effects of this violence were—and are today—nonetheless written upon the souls, hearts, and bodies of those who benefit from domination. The entire situation misshapes their psyche, disposition, and soul.

This is the logic of Ubuntu. It is an embodied, relational logic that is conveyed in the claim that "whatever dehumanizes you, dehumanizes me." At the heart of restorative justice is this account of relational personhood and the claim that flows from it, that what each person is due includes, though perhaps is not limited to, mutual recognition, reciprocal accountability, and inclusive nondomination.

How do peacemaking circles embody and enact these elements of restorative justice? In the chapter that follows, we will see that they are not New Age dialogue sessions with a little burning sage added. They are, rather, concrete ethical practices of mutual recognition, reciprocal accountability, giving and asking for reasons. They are also an inclusive, nondominating form of taking back power that uses this retrieved power to cultivate and amplify personal and collective agency. Circles are practices of relational justice at their very core.

10

Peacemaking Circles as Ethical Practice

Recall that peacemaking circles open by calling participants to be fully present and mindful through, for example, candle lighting, bell ringing, and/or an opening reflection. This is often followed by a brief icebreaker or introductory activity to cultivate familiarity and ease. Typically, participants then engage in a collective exercise where each member of the circle contributes one or more values that they think the circle process must reflect. The circle members then collectively compose guidelines for living out these values in the circle process. The values and guidelines that emerge make explicit the norms of relationality that the circle embodies. They articulate the ethical elements of what mutual recognition, reciprocal accountability, trust, and justice will look like. How so? And how does this process guard against forms of unaccountability, arbitrary treatment, and thus, domination?

While it may sometimes appear to be a mere formality, articulating values and guidelines is actually essential for a peacemaking circle to be what it intends to be and do what it intends to do. Making explicit the values on which the circle will be based and cultivating a consensus on a set of guidelines is how each circle uniquely sets its own terms for the practices of sharing and accountability that will unfold there. It is true that each circle participates in a long tradition of peacemaking circles and that therefore many values and guidelines reoccur. At the same time, the practice is flexible and dynamic; every specific instance exhibits its own particularities. This makes innovation possible. Each circle at once, then, replicates certain features of a general form and innovates within the overall framework of reciprocal recognition and mutual respect.

In making explicit these shared values and deriving guidelines from them, each member of the circle recognizes each of the others as people to whom they are accountable regarding what they will say and how they will listen. Each member has a say in the norms according to which everyone will listen and respond. If we are considering the circle as an ethical practice, these are processes by which circle members commit to see every other person as one to whom they are accountable and then make explicit their mutual recognition. This mutual recognition, and these committed attitudes, generate a reciprocal and collective accountability.

Power

The circle is a practice that embodies the power-laden-ness of the commitments on which the circle is based. The explicitly stated values and guidelines that characterize and guide participation derive from making explicit the dynamics of the relationships that institute each particular circle. Having circle members formulate values and guidelines for themselves, rather than importing them from outside or leaving them unarticulated, means that the circle takes responsibility for the power that is implicit in the relationality in which the circle lives, moves, and has its being. This is not power presumed, introduced, or imposed from elsewhere. The circle takes responsibility for itself.

To say that recognition and accountability never occur in a power vacuum is to acknowledge that social, economic, and political constraints are always in place (even if in the background) in any given practical context of mutual recognition and accountability, including circles. Structural and cultural violence may generate misrecognition and various other forms of domination. Young people in the communities described in this book are sometimes tempted to misrecognize themselves, for example, using terms like "gangbanger" or "dealer" to suggest that these are somehow a fixed and unchangeable part of "who they are" in virtue of what they have done. In contexts ridden with structural and cultural violence, such misrecognition can become baked into systems and the relational contexts in which they exist. This is not to imply that those cannot be identified, critiqued, resisted, and changed. They can. In fact, when practiced well, circles provide means by which misrecognition can be named, challenged, and altered. The methodical, painstaking contribution of each circle member to naming and cultivating consensus on the grounding values and guidelines from their own perspective, and in the full particularity of their own voice, is a way for participants to claim the kind of relational agency that each is due, but that some may have previously been denied.

In taking responsibility for the values, norms, and guidelines of the circle, participants institute ethical practices that can overcome what may appear to be ironclad forms of misrecognition. The agency they claim in circle enables them to innovate with norms and commitments that challenge these cultures. This empowers them to evolve new instances of justice that move beyond the retributive one they are familiar with from the criminal justice system.

At Precious Blood, circle processes openly and intentionally name and reject the purposes with which they sometimes get associated by people in the justice system. These purposes include disciplining and training people who presumably "tend toward delinquency" to "behave better," whatever their alleged "individual choice-making procedure" may be. Circle keepers at Precious Blood forthrightly point out that circles are not for training or conditioning people or for "crime reduction." Circles cannot be a covert "policing strategy" without betraying what they are and disempowering the people and relationships they intend to cultivate.[1] This sometimes generates tensions with the power holders in the justice system and related systems (such as the school system).

To participate in circles that aim to repair harm (or achieve consensus on a formal "repair of harm agreement") is to engage in a practice of justice. Among other things, this practice asks how those who have done harm came to be characterized as "wrongdoers," or "delinquent," or "criminal" in the first place. It invites people to ask themselves how this was laid on them, or when and how they internalized it. It asks the group to reflect on how this happens, and how to challenge and change this framing. This is what it means to care and be compassionate within restorative justice. The stories that participants in the circle share—through which they weave new relationships and build up or repair the fabric of community—name part of the complex circumstances in which they find themselves, and that are thrust upon them. Many of the "choices" they make in their daily lives are not abstract choices at all, but instead reflect an option taken out of an exceedingly limited set of responses available to them. The course of action some follow may be the most industrious or entrepreneurial available to them within a landscape of structural violence, even if that entrepreneurship, for example, runs afoul of the draconian laws and policing practices that emerged in the course of the multidecade "war on drugs." Likewise, as we saw above, people in Back of the Yards as elsewhere have needs for safety and to provide for their friends, families, and loved ones.

Circles that share these stories are not about promoting "better behavior," "self-help," and/or "moral improvement" so that those who have done harm will "make better choices" in the future. They are instead about cultivating practices that make explicit the relational nature of personhood and community in full recognition that individual agency always happens in contexts and circumstances with particular histories, and in common life together. Circles enable the resources available in and through those relationships to inflect the actions and the overall praxis of individuals. They recognize the embeddedness of individual action in the community and recognize the community as a participant in these relational processes. They recognize care and accountability as flowing reciprocally between all of the participants involved in this complex social context.

An Encompassing Account of Deliberation

The form the circle process takes shapes the contents of the sessions. The ritual-like process that brings the circle into being recontextualizes what political philosophers and ethicists refer to as "deliberative democratic exchange." Passing the talking piece means that there is no "cross-talking" in the circle. There is, thus, no direct "back-and-forth," like a verbal tennis match, that could constitute the kind of straightforward "giving and asking for reasons" that is often construed by political theorists as the heart and soul of "deliberative democratic exchange."[2] This does not mean that giving and asking for reasons are irrelevant to the circle. They are vital to it. However, the form of the circle process constrains—and thereby diffuses—any particular back-and-forth that might, however inadvertently or gently, come to monopolize or dominate the process. As a result, "exchanging reasons" becomes a decentered feature of the expansive, expressive relationality that the circle facilitates. Participants who may be especially adept at deliberative back-and-forth, and those who may be less adept or less comfortable but still have much to contribute, are brought into equilibrium by the passing of the talking piece. The talking piece redistributes contribution and reception—speaking and listening—more equitably around the circle.[3]

By carving out a consensus-oriented space of shared values and mutually held guidelines for sharing, participants build relationships and articulate, process, and facilitate the repair of harms. They begin healing by sharing stories, sometimes sharing silence, and observing and responding to nonverbal gestures. Restorative justice instantiates its relational conception of personhood and human flourishing through the relationally derived practices of mutual recognition, reciprocal accountability, care, and repair of harm that persons are due in virtue of being persons. This is the very core of what makes the peacemaking circle an ethical practice of justice. In the chapter that follows we will see how the moral and spiritual dynamics of circles, understood as an ethical practice, can lead seamlessly into transformational action and community empowerment.

11

Justice That Heals and Transforms

Accountability, Forgiveness, and Nondomination

The United States is the only country that imposes life sentences on juveniles with no possibility of parole. Julie Anderson did not know this until her family got caught up in the criminal justice system. When I met Julie at Precious Blood, her son, Eric, was thirty-six years old. He was serving a life sentence for a crime he committed when he was fifteen. In the intervening decades, Julie has become well-versed in the legal minutiae surrounding her son's case and others like it. She has become an advocate and organizer for families whose children have been imprisoned for life.

In her "day job," Julie worked as a real estate agent. Her husband is now a retired Chicago police officer. They live in a blue-collar, mostly White neighborhood on the Southwest Side of Chicago. Julie and her husband grew up there and married immediately after high school. Eric is the oldest of their three children. They sent their children to Catholic grammar school. It was a heavy financial burden, Julie tells me, but they believed that it was worthwhile for the discipline, the moral instruction, and the academics.

Eric's early years in school were largely uneventful. His biggest infraction was not doing his homework. He chose to attend Mount Carmel, an athletics-focused high school, where his best friend played football. Eric, by contrast, was small for his age—five feet three, 110 pounds, not athletic, and as the newspapers would later tell it, "looking for the approval of his peers." On the bus ride to school every day, he met older kids. Eventually, he joined a gang—the Almighty Popes. On December 14, 1995, Eric and four other young men attacked a van as it sat parked on a corner in their neighborhood. Two young men in the van—rival gang members, their intended targets—emerged unharmed. Two thirteen-year-old girls who were also in the van, Carrie Hovel and Helena Martin, were shot dead. Eric had fired the gun. Still a freshman in high school, he was convicted of the double murder.[1]

"Even though my husband was a policeman, I had never really ever been involved with the law and the courts—and I was really under the impression that the whole system worked," Julie tells me. "Come to find out that it was really slanted because prosecutors have all the power. It kind of railroaded me. [Eric] was convicted, ultimately, and sentenced. And we knew if he was convicted, there was only one sentence that he would get—life without parole. And I know a lot of people, they're like, 'What do you mean, without parole?' They didn't realize we don't have parole in Illinois."[2]

As much as a mandatory sentence of life with no possibility of parole for her fifteen-year-old son terrified her, the process of trial and sentencing was even more degrading. Julie described her experience of shame and stigma as a mother who was also losing her child to a double-murder conviction:

> When we went to court, the victims were there. Obviously, you have a tremendous amount of sympathy [for them]. They lost their children. It was so horrible to sit there, across from them, knowing that they hated us—and still do. You build up a little bit of resentment to them, which you shouldn't as the offender's family. But you can't help yourself. They get special parking passes. They get brought into a special office before court. They get breakfasts. If the judge is going to be late, they're notified. Even now, we are at resentencing, we've been there twice when the judge just didn't show up. The victim's family members weren't there because they were notified. But as an offender's family member, you're just shuffled into this automatic second-class citizen status. So it's really hard not to be resentful in some manner or way, because there isn't some relative mercy. You can't talk or ask for forgiveness. And they go through the trial with the state's attorney holding their hand. Of course, we had to pay for our attorney. So we were terrified to call him because every phone call is two hundred dollars. And you're thinking, they're not paying for any of this and they're getting all of this special treatment. And obviously they had a huge amount of resentment towards us. And I will say this about the girls—and they wouldn't put them on trial, of course not. They were two thirteen-year-old girls in a van with two nineteen-year-old guys. Gang-

bangers. So everybody there was doing stuff that they shouldn't have been doing. They were all a bunch of kids playing a very deadly game, with disastrous results.[3]

The trial and sentencing process was not kind to the victims' families, either. The state's attorney was awarded the life sentence he sought, and sent the victims' families on their way at the end of the trial. "He was like, 'You have a life sentence. You can go live your life knowing that that person will be locked up forever—so this will heal you.' There are programs for victims . . . and I was kind of out there on my own. You live in shame. You don't tell anyone you know," Julie tells me. "And no one helps them. As if a life sentence was enough for them? It doesn't honor their daughters. It doesn't do anything. And I realized that the state just uses that. But it took a long time [for me to] recognize it. It took talking to victims' family members."[4]

For the first ten years, Julie says, she lived in a haze of shame and silence. She raised her two younger children and arranged visits to Eric in prison at every opportunity. Beginning in 2005, with her son's fate decided, Julie did the only thing she knew to do. She devoted herself to advocating for his plight, and with it, the plight of other young people subjected to one of the most gruesome facets of US mass incarceration—life imprisonment of adolescents.

Julie began working as a volunteer with Restore Justice Illinois and the Campaign for Fair Sentencing for Children. At Precious Blood in Back of the Yards she helped to found Communities and Relatives of Illinois' Incarcerated Children (CRIIC), a support and empowerment group for families who have lost their children—eighteen or younger when sentenced—to long-term (forty-plus years) or life prison sentences. She also participates in a monthly peace circle meeting, kept by Sister Donna Liette, for mothers who have lost their children to gun violence, prison, or the streets. These circles brought her into face-to-face conversations with victims' families. They transformed her understanding of victims' experiences. "I just thought that everyone would have all this sympathy [for the victims] and we had kind of the opposite, shame and guilt," she explains. "And then I realized that they carry around all that guilt too. 'Why did I let them hang out with those people? I shouldn't have let them out that day.' Because you think you're the only one to have all of that."[5]

Members of the CRIIC group come together to share their stories. They write to, visit, and support each other's incarcerated children. They visit other incarcerated people who have no one to visit them. The mothers' circle promotes healing by cultivating relationships among a group of people who share similar struggles and loss. The circles nurture a sense of safety and acceptance that enables mutual understanding, vulnerability, truth telling, and empathy. "I remember there was this one lady who said, 'I never realized White people had these kind of problems.' And I thought, 'Wow, we really understand each other, we have this great bond.'"[6] Julie also has recognized that her situation was far from as bad as it might have been, or as bad as many others are. She has recognized that the way the different treatment plays out is very much along racial lines. "As I heard some of these moms, I thought, 'Wow, I thought I was bad, but your kid never stood a chance.' Once they brought them into jail, they were gone. The system is not set up to help you at all."[7]

Julie organized families to support one another.[8] Eric has been permitted five family visits per month over the course of his incarceration, and Julie and her husband have taken advantage of each of those opportunities. Like her son, the children of many of the family members she works with across Chicago are incarcerated in prisons across the state of Illinois. It makes visiting extremely difficult. Julie began coordinating trips for families to Menard Correctional Center, 365 miles from Chicago, a six-hour drive that requires a hotel stay. "That's far. There's nothing there, except for the Sisters of Precious Blood. They have a retreat center twenty-five miles away from Menard. So they host us, which is pretty awesome." She continues, "Sometimes when I bring those family members down, they haven't seen their sons in eight years. A lot of them struggled, either with bus fare or [other expenses]."[9]

Even once they reach the facility, families may still be denied visitation. Jobi Cates, the executive director of Restore Justice Illinois, describes the kinds of arbitrary treatment visiting families are subjected to. "I've witnessed countless incidents where a person comes in to see their loved one," she recounts. "But because somebody rubbed somebody the wrong way in the check-in area or they don't understand the rules or they aren't fluent in English or not feeling respected, things get completely blown out of proportion, and the person is told they have to leave. And they have absolutely zero recourse."[10]

CRIIC and the Peace Circle for Mothers also enable participants to organize for policy and legislative change.[11] For example, the members of CRIIC fought to change the number of visits for which all persons interned in Illinois prisons are eligible (they achieved seven visits per month, uniformly across the state of Illinois). They successfully resisted a proposal to replace in-person visitation with video conferencing visits. They successfully fought to change the prohibitive vending machine prices charged for food during visitations, and the arbitrary exclusion of family visitors. They made regular visits to their legislators in Springfield—giving "a face to the families of these [so-called] 'monsters' you're locking up"[12]—to support legislative efforts to raise the age at which juvenile offenders can be considered for transfer into the adult criminal justice system in Illinois. They supported the successful effort to eliminate the sentence of life "without the possibility of parole" altogether in Illinois.[13]

Julie had organized a community gathering a couple of days prior to my meeting with her—an "RJ Café" event in the Art on 51st gallery that Precious Blood has fashioned from an old vacant row house it raised money to buy, then remodeled through its carpentry apprenticeship program. The art gallery frequently hosts open houses and community conversation gatherings. It displays the artwork of people who are serving time in prison, are formerly incarcerated, or are family and friends affected by incarceration. Paintings, drawings, self-portraits, poems—each is positioned next to a photo and brief bio of the artist.

Julie had organized an exhibit of artwork specifically by people who had been sentenced to life without parole as juveniles in Illinois. She sat at a table beside Chicago police officers who attended the event as part of a community policing initiative to develop relationships with people living on the South and West Sides. Julie found herself in an unexpected conversation with the officer sitting next to her. "We talked about automatic transfer [of juvenile defendants] to the adult [criminal justice] system. [I said that it] was the very first thing we needed to stop." She continued,

> My son was fifteen; he was an automatic transfer. It used to be, [if you were] fourteen and under, you would get a hearing [in court to determine whether the transfer into the adult system was justifiable]. Now it's

fifteen- and sixteen-year-olds get a hearing before they're transferred. It's not perfect, because they shouldn't be transferred at all. Anyone under eighteen shouldn't be in the adult court or adult system at all. . . . Now, if you're sixteen or under, you get a hearing. Seventeen-year-olds? Automatic [transfer]. . . . So this police officer looked at me and he said, "Well, you know, I think you have to transfer those kids into adult court. If somebody did something to *my* kids, I would want them locked up forever." I looked like a deer in headlights [*laughs*]. I didn't know what to say to that. . . . I must've said something because [the officer] came and apologized to me [later]. . . . I talked to my son the next day and I told him about this. . . . [Eric] said, "Well, why didn't you say, 'What if your son was on the *other* side of it? If *he* was locked up forever?" And I was like, "Wow! So easy, so brilliant." So I'm ready for the next time. But I realized that's right. Everyone always imagines that their kid [is the victim]. . . . We can always empathize with the victims. Always, "If someone did that to my kid, my mother . . ." But we can never [imagine from] the other side. We can never perceive that someone we know could be involved in something like that. That must be it. You never think, "Oh, my kid could be on the other end of that." That's one of our big problems, probably. People don't think that way.

Numerous people I encountered in the wider Chicago restorative justice community tell me that the restorative justice movement is driven by precisely that: What would you want for your own child? How would you hope for your own child to be dealt with?

Nondomination and the Needs of the Responsible Party

Restorative justice views destructive conflict as a tear in webs of relationships. It seeks to repair and put right, as much as possible, the harms and destructive effects that have occurred in a context of destructive conflict and violence. We have seen how this focuses on the needs and healing of the survivors of destructive conflict and harm, and for the community in question. But restorative justice also focuses on the needs of the person who caused the harm. In this, it deviates drastically from contemporary forms of retributive justice as practiced in the US justice system.

This may be the most controversial aspect of restorative justice. Why should we care about the "needs of the offender," the one who caused the harm, the perpetrator? From the vantage point of many strictly retributive approaches to justice, this is precisely the point at which restorative justice ceases to be justice. These critics see it as ultimately unconcerned that each party to a circumstance of harm, violence, or crime actually receive "what is due to them." Because it is concerned with healing all the people in a given circumstance who have experienced harm in any way, it is (allegedly) altogether different.

Contrary to popular perception, restorative justice is not about amnesty for "offenders". It does not focus on exonerating the wrongdoer or aim to let a person who caused harm off the hook. Accountability is essential to restorative justice. Such accountability asks the one who caused the harm to take responsibility, and commit to putting right and repairing that harm as much as possible. At the same time, accountability also requires recognizing that more basic background conditions often set the stage for wrongdoing.

From the perspective of restorative justice, a person is never a person in isolation. The violence, harms, or unmet basic needs that precipitate wrongdoing may emerge from structural violence suffered by a community. This is one of the ways that the New Jim Crow, the prison-industrial complex, and hyper-incarceration perpetuate themselves. People who enter the criminal justice system are frequently further harmed and traumatized in ways that provoke additional destructive relationships and actions. People who "serve their time" and in theory have been released from the system often return more deeply isolated, distressed, and incapacitated. One of the reasons that recidivism in the United States is so severe is precisely that people returning from incarceration are so frequently left without any social support network. Further, the harm, trauma, and incapacitation of the criminal justice system are perpetrated upon their communities and families as much as or more than on incarcerated individuals themselves. The criminal justice system dominates the individuals, families, and communities caught in it. These realities are central to how the contemporary retributive justice system—designed, allegedly, to contain and deter wrongdoing and crime—in reality perpetuates and frequently exacerbates the very thing that it is supposed to stop.

Irreducibly Social Justice: Beyond a Zero-Sum Equation

As you will recall, Ubuntu names a worldview that social harmony, care, compassion, and generosity in community constitute a shared or "common" highest good. This is a good that can only be realized to the extent that it comes to life in the practices of relational justice. To say that the "highest good" toward which restorative justice aims is "irreducibly social" (or a "common good") is to say that it is alive only as much as it spreads. The more broadly it is shared between people, the more its constituent elements increase as more people come to be included in it. The just relations and humanizing treatment—the common good—at which restorative justice aims is not a "zero-sum game." It is not the case that acquisition of those goods by one person means less (or none) for others. In fact, the opposite is the case.

Retributive justice, by contrast, presents a zero-sum equation of justice. Retribution sees harm or wrongdoing as creating a deficit or debt on one side of a two-sided equation. The deficit created by the wrong must be paid back in a common or similar currency in order to rebalance the relation between offender and victim. Indeed, conceptions of justice as "payback in kind" pervade human cultures and run deep in world history. One frequently cited example is the ancient Mesopotamian Code of Hammurabi (c. 1750 BCE), which contains one of the earliest known injunctions to repay "an eye for an eye." According to this belief, the loss incurred by the harmed party can be repaid by the wrongdoer when he or she undergoes a similar harm. This then resets the balance between the two parties at zero. Retributive theories of justice typically conceptualize retribution as punishment. One person caused pain and harm; for justice to be done, that person must suffer pain and harm.[14]

Modern liberal societies prohibit a direct transposition of bodily harm for purposes of retributive punishment (eye = eye). Instead, someone convicted of causing harm usually pays what they "owe" to society through punishment in the form of confinement, which erases freedom and often constricts their basic status as a citizen in other ways, such as removing the right to vote. Punitive societies often explain retributive justice through harsh punishment as compensation for the one who has been harmed, as the state's attorney did when he told Carrie Hovel's and

Helena Martin's families that the life sentences he had obtained should heal the loss of their daughters. Harsh punishment may also seek to deter future wrongdoing and/or promote the general security of society by making clear the state's power to enforce law. Far less common is a goal of rehabilitating the offender. Instead, harsh punishment aims to diminish the one who caused the harm. This equation is "zero-sum": repayment to one requires deduction from the other. If Eric took the lives of Carrie and Helena, then righting the balance of justice requires that he spend the remainder of his life in prison.

The intrinsically relational and shared character of the goods at which restorative justice aims, by contrast, avoids this zero-sum equation. The more restorative justice is shared, the more it multiplies. It tries to address the needs of the harmed party and repair the harm to the extent possible while also simultaneously respecting and restoratively engaging with the one who caused the harm, rather than extracting and transferring value from that person in the currency of punishment. Moreover, both of these actions occur with careful attention to the context of the community in which the harm occurred and through engagement with members of that community. This requires encouraging the one who caused the harm to embrace opportunities for dignified and dignifying acceptance of responsibility. It requires the community to provide opportunities for the person who caused the harm to fulfill the reparative obligations of accountability. It requires opportunities to be made available to repair the harm one has caused, to the extent that this is possible. These must be forms of repair that are proportional and tailored to the circumstances and the nature of the harm, and to the needs of the harmed parties and community in question. At the same time, it requires that the community attend to and work to correct the structural causes and conditions that precipitated those harmful actions.

Restorative justice does not seek to "restore" in the sense of re-creating the conditions that existed prior to a conflict or harm. In fact, it would be disregarding the impact of harm to claim that one could ever "return to" prior conditions. There can be no reconstructing or "going back to the way things were before" after harm or destructive conflict. And the use of the word "restore" in restorative justice indicates no such thing. Rather, it views destructive conflict, harm, and violence as tears in the web of relationships that can be rewoven by direct interpersonal connection and by attention to the broader relationships in which communities and societies exist.

The image of the web conveys a conception of "interrelatedness" of the many stakeholders, even if at a distant remove. One way their interrelatedness can be revealed is when a tear in the web occurs by way of destructive conflict, violence, and/or crime, and via the effects of such damage. Restorative justice "restores" in the sense of mending the social fabric of damaged relational strands by striving to meet basic needs, foregrounding accountability, facilitating repair and healing, building resilient, healthy relationships across community, promoting restitution, and addressing the structural causes and conditions that precipitated the harm, conflict, and violence in the first place.

If this is true, then responses that frequently emerge from the experience of harm, destructive conflict, and violence—such as resentment and a desire for "payback in kind" (retribution) or revenge—are destructive of the common good. Typically, they extract compensation not merely through the retributive harm of the wrongdoer. They also harm, collaterally, the family and community of the wrongdoer. As Julie Anderson says, the family is punished along with their child. If harm, destructive violence, or crime tears the webs of relationships, then retributive punishment tends to only increase and expand the damage the original tear caused. This occurs through the likelihood of repeat offending, but also through the fragmentation, shame, and stigma that haunt the family and community of the retributively punished party.

The Paradox of Accountability

Critics of restorative justice allege that it promotes disregard for law. If people see that there is no punitive repercussion for wrongdoing, these critics argue, they will have no deterrent against engaging in such actions or behavior. Yet numerous studies indicate that the "deterrent" function of punishment is self-defeating. These studies consistently demonstrate that, rather than deterring crime, the more severely wrongdoers are punished, the higher the rates of recidivism.[15] As an industrial complex, US mass incarceration has proven its systemic genius in perpetuating and expanding itself. The United States not only hosts the highest rates of incarceration in the world, it also has extremely high rates of re-arrest and re-incarceration of the people it punishes.

Accountability is a nonnegotiable feature of restorative justice. If a person who has caused harm is to participate in restorative justice processes, they must accept responsibility for the harms their actions have caused.[16] Paradoxically, justice systems that emphasize retributive punishment frequently incentivize the denial of responsibility—and refusal of accountability—for those accused of causing harm. The retributive legal frame positions a defendant as an opponent to a prosecutor. This creates an adversarial orientation that incentivizes the diminishment of accountability. Within this framing, denying culpability (maintaining one's innocence) is strategically advantageous. Maintaining a claim of innocence at least forces a prosecutor to prove (win) his or her case. As a result, the goal of a criminal trial often has very little to do with establishing an accurate account of what occurred through information sharing and truth telling. In a trial, the primary goal is to win. The prize is either the ascription of guilt to the accused, followed by punishment, or a declaration of "not guilty"; neither of these possible outcomes, however, may represent the actual truth. Moreover, a prosecutor may or may not represent the needs and concerns of the harmed party, as the central purpose of criminal prosecution is to emphasize the power of the state to enforce law and make society secure. The well-being of victims is frequently an afterthought.

Paradoxically, then, retributive punishment within an adversarial legal framework tends to promote the opposite of what it sets out to accomplish: it promotes the denial of responsibility and the refusal of accountability. This constitutes a kind of impunity. That is, it discourages and disincentivizes intentional efforts at truth telling, making oneself accountable, accepting responsibility, working to change by listening and responding to the needs of those one has harmed, and putting right the wrongs that one's actions caused with the victim/survivor's, and the specific community's, needs in view. The system discourages and obstructs, if it does not prohibit, the substance of accountability—bringing truth to light, accepting responsibility, and listening to, answering, and responding to those who have been harmed. The retributive frame marginalizes the importance of identifying and meeting the needs of stakeholders in the context of harm and ruptured relationships. As such, it often dehumanizes all the parties in question. It discourages the possibility of contrition, apology, efforts to repair harm, and forgiveness, all of which have proven to be effective in promoting healing, empowering victims and communities (including responsible parties), and transitioning from a violence-torn society to a sustainable and just peace.

If retributive justice systems often incentivize the denial of responsibility, meanwhile, they also incentivize false confession in the form of plea bargaining. Plea bargaining is a practice in which a defendant agrees to plead guilty to a lesser charge in exchange for a reduced punishment from the prosecutor. It is another area where the United States leads the world.[17] This establishes a model of accountability that risks both becoming arbitrary and even incentivizing false acceptance of responsibility by the accused, who is sometimes told that there is no way he will win at trial even if he is innocent, and is encouraged to "plead out" rather than receive an even harsher sentence. This produces a sham "accountability" whose only virtue is that it "keeps the system functioning" by reducing the number of cases that go to a full jury trial.[18] Moreover, it is a practice that is isolated from, and unaccountable to, the community and most of the stakeholders who are directly affected by it. Truth telling is an integral part of justice. The adversarial, retributive criminal justice system that prevails in the United States disincentivizes—and even disadvantages—truth telling. In so doing, it promotes a state of affairs that falls well short of justice.

Is Forgiveness Necessary for Restorative Justice?

Many restorative justice theorists conceptualize forgiveness as a victim's decision or effort to release the negative effect that the actions of the wrongdoer have imposed. Because restorative justice often emerges from particular religious traditions, some versions espouse forgiveness as important for restorative justice. Critics often protest that restorative justice urges victims to forgive those who have harmed them, pressuring victims to do something they may not want to do. It may also pressure them to embrace a practice or value that is specific to a religious tradition that is not theirs. For these critics, when restorative justice promotes reconciliation, and more specifically, the victim's forgiving of the offender, it exemplifies the hazard of imposing religion-specific values such as forgiveness on practices of law and public justice.

For example, when working explicitly within a Christian "peace church" (Mennonite) tradition, Howard Zehr invokes the New Testament teachings and story of Jesus as a basis for promoting a forgiveness facilitated by lament and prayer. He argues that, properly understood, forgiveness empowers victims by releasing them from the hold of the wrongful act and the wrongdoer.[19] In this Christian understanding, forgiving can aid in the reduction of persistent anger, fear, shame, and a desire for revenge. It can enable the victim to move forward in ways that are not oriented by or tethered to an experience of harm and the actions of a wrongdoer. As such, forgiveness is a process of self-empowerment that "allows one to move from victim to survivor."[20] Zehr offers this description in the broader context of an explicitly Christian account of the character and origin of restorative justice values and practices.

Yet Zehr himself points out that religious-tradition-specific notions of forgiveness are not *essential* to restorative justice. Restorative justice practices provide contexts and practices within which forgiveness and interpersonal reconciliation may organically emerge. However, by no means is forgiveness a prescribed goal toward which all restorative justice practices and encounters must aim. People find different ways of relinquishing anger, processing the effects of pain, or working through and recovering from harms they have experienced. In the general understanding of restorative justice, then, following a particular religious or ethical prescription to "forgive" or to reconcile with a wrongdoer is not essential. It is a decision left to the participant. "There should be no pressure to choose to forgive or to seek reconciliation," Zehr concedes.[21]

Consistent with this stance, restorative justice researchers Marilyn Armour and Mark Umbreit conducted a broad study of the effectiveness of restorative justice initiatives.[22] They looked at self-reported reduction in anger, anxiety, and feelings of shame and fear, as well as these initiatives' impact on participants' understanding of the wrongdoers. They discovered what they describe as a *paradox* of forgiveness in restorative justice practice. The more that initiatives prescribed forgiveness as a goal of restorative justice, the more likely participants were to report feeling pressured and "preached at." They reported further that this pressure truncated their experience of healing and recovery. This compromised the safety of the space in which they were trying to practice restorative justice.

At the same time, when initiatives *did not* foreground forgiveness as an objective or prescribe it as a value in the process, participants self-reported comparatively higher experiences of safety and healing, reduction of anger and anxiety, the ability to experience empathy, and both an increased sense of agency and the ability to let go of a sense of needing to "get even" or seek revenge. People who had suffered harm more frequently reported a deeper understanding of the person who had harmed them, and vice versa. This often led to a softening or shift in attitude and disposition toward that person.

Paradoxically, then, the less restorative justice initiatives prescriptively pursue "forgiveness" as an explicit goal, the more the practical results they achieve tend to approximate (or organically give rise to) the kinds of relational dynamics that many different religious and moral traditions describe in terms related to "forgiveness" or "reconciliation." These might include mutual understanding through truth telling, responsibility taking, contrition, critical empathy, respect, compassion, and an ability to let go of desire to "get even" or move beyond harms to begin healing.[23]

Whether in the context of a religious tradition or not, explicit forgiveness and/or reconciliation on the part of the victim/survivor is relevant only if the person finds these concepts helpful for addressing their needs, assisting in their healing and recovery, and emerging organically from their informed participation in the process. This paradox suggests that pursuing explicit goals of forgiveness or reconciliation is not essential to restorative justice. But it is also true that these concepts may be pertinent as descriptors of moral or spiritual relational dynamics liable to organically emerge when—or perhaps because—an explicit religious tradition or conception is not formally prescribed or held out as an overarching objective.

Doing Sorry

In 2012, in response to the long-term legal work done by Bryan Stevenson and the Equal Justice Initiative, the US Supreme Court ruled in *Miller v. Alabama* that it is unconstitutional to sentence a juvenile to mandatory life in prison without the possibility of parole. The ruling acknowledged the scientific consensus that the nature of adolescent brain development means that juveniles have limited capacity to recognize the full consequences of their actions. The ruling also acknowledged what Justice Elena Kagan described as adolescents' "heightened capacity for change."[24] According to the ruling, however, *Miller* would not apply retroactively to previous sentences. In 2014 the Illinois Supreme Court countered that, in fact, *Miller* must apply retroactively. The US Supreme Court followed suit in 2016 in *Montgomery v. Louisiana*. Eric Anderson and other juveniles who had been sentenced to mandatory life sentences without parole would be resentenced.

The resentencing hearing was difficult, Julie Anderson tells me. The victims' families were present. The judge acknowledged that Eric had no record of disciplinary infractions over the decades he had already served in prison. He acknowledged that Eric had been what those working in the system call a "model inmate"—he read avidly, learned to paint, and shared the constructive and cautionary messages that he conveyed in his art with the community at Art on 51st in Back of the Yards. Through the work of his mother, Julie, and from other visitors and outreach efforts by CRIIC and Precious Blood, Eric has come to understand the nature of restorative justice and the forms of accountability, truth telling, contrition, and efforts at constructive reparation it requires of him. He has come to understand in a restorative sense what he owes for having taken the lives of Helena Martin and Carrie Hovel. When Eric took the stand at his resentencing trial, he apologized and conveyed his remorse to the families of his victims. Julie and her husband each did the same. They had never had the opportunity to do so before.[25]

The resentencing hearing lasted three days. Large numbers of family and members of the Chicago restorative justice community turned out to support Eric and his family. Only the immediate families and some relatives of Carrie Hovel and Helena Martin appeared on their side of the courtroom. The two girls had been gone for twenty-two years, after all.

The final witness who testified on Eric's behalf was Jeanne Bishop, formerly a corporate attorney who became a public defender in Chicago as the result of her own experience as a survivor of her family members' murder by an adolescent. Jeanne and Julie had met through their respective advocacy work. Their stories resonated. Jeanne's brother-in-law and sister—who was pregnant at the time—had been murdered. Only after many years of grief, anger, and pursuing the harshest punishment possible for the young man who killed her family did Jeanne decide to meet him in person. Gradually, she experienced what she calls a "change of heart."[26]

Jeanne had gotten to know the Andersons well. She visited Eric many times once he was moved to a prison in Cook County to await resentencing. She came to understand his remorse and desire to live a changed life that could honor the lives of the victims he had killed. Jeanne agreed to offer an impact statement as a "victim's family member" from a comparable case. This was someone who had come to a deep understanding of Eric's story and that of his family. The transcript of the hearing chronicles the last question asked of Jeanne: "Do you think it would be *just* to release Eric now?" The record of her response runs as follows:

> In my view, as a victim's family member, this hearing is not so much about Eric Anderson as it is about Carrie Hovel and Helena Martin. Because the question is, we can't bring them back. No matter how sorry [Eric] is, he can't bring them back. As much as we'd all like to turn back the clock—every single person in this room wants to turn back the clock to that day and undo that terrible decision he made, what he did, that terrible deed that he did. Everyone in this room wants to turn back the clock. And we can't. We can't do that. And so, the question is, what can we do?
>
> There's two things that we can do to honor the lives of these young girls, and to honor their memory. One is we can say, we're just going to perpetually punish this person . . . with the life sentence, it would be, you know, forever, until he died . . . as long as possible, right? Within the limits of the law. That's one way to do it. . . . But there's another way to honor their lives, and that is to say that this is a person who is doing good; is trying to do good; is sorry; is remorseful; wants to do good; understands what he shattered when he took part of the family because he is starting to appreciate . . . his own family, and, you know, the people around him.
>
> And so, another way of honoring the lives of Carrie and Helena would be to say, we're going to release this person. When he's done an appropriate amount of time equal to the gravity of taking a human life, and we are going to let him do that good in the world they no longer can, understanding that his life is not his own, and that everything he does from now on is to honor them, to honor their memory and to give to the world

back a portion of what he took when he took their lives. That is the more hopeful, proactive living way, and it is another way.[27]

Jeanne Bishop's testimony captures what I have called the irreducibly social dynamic of restorative justice. It refuses to deprive Eric of life beyond a prison cell in order to achieve a supposed balance with the harm he caused. Instead, it aims to facilitate his making efforts at constructive and beneficial repair, to dedicate his efforts to do good and effect positive change, and to do so as a living tribute to Helena Martin and Carrie Hovel. This is "doing sorry," as Danielle Sered describes the lived practices of remorse and efforts at repair that are intrinsic to the understanding of accountability at the heart of restorative justice.[28]

In the second option Jeanne Bishop describes in her testimony above, Eric's efforts and work have the chance to ripple outward, expand, multiply, and likely touch many more people's lives. This would be much like the ways that his mother's efforts, work, and commitment already have rippled outward and touched the lives of many people over multiple decades. These responses—emblematic of restorative justice—multiply the good and amplify its impact in their efforts to repair the harms Eric's actions caused. The more broadly they are shared, the more they multiply.

Of course, it is not possible to repair the harm done "in kind." The lives of the two young girls he killed are absolutely distinct and irreplaceable. While it is impossible to ever compensate fully or adequately for these lost lives, indefinitely extracting some comparable pain and grief in response to their loss adds nothing positive and creates nothing constructive for the surviving family. Julie Anderson's work, the work of CRIIC and Jeanne Bishop, and the work that Eric has done—and commits to do outside prison if given the chance—can amplify the goods that relate to the survivors' side of the relationship as well. Their actions and efforts can be dedicated to the memory of these two young lives that were unjustly taken. Viewed through a restorative lens, there is a possibility to salvage, and then multiply, some good from an evil situation and tragic loss that cannot be reversed.

"There's a way people react to adverse situations," Eric says. "I've seen the whole gamut of how people react. Some people break. Some people just go down a black hole and never come back. Some people do what my mom did—take it and turn it into as much positivity as can be mustered from a super-horrible situation."²⁹ He continues, "What happened can never be undone. The best I can do is try to do as much good from now on to make any kind of reparations I can for taking those girls' [lives]."³⁰ Eric was resentenced in April 2017. He received a new sentence of sixty years. With "day-for-day" time reductions for "good behavior," Eric was released in 2023. He is a Future Leaders Apprentice at the organization, Restore Justice, and has led circle trainings for men at the Kewanee Life-Skills Re-entry Center, where he was previously incarcerated.

What Happens When a Victim/Survivor Does Not Participate?

Carrie Hovel's and Helena Martin's families desired the harshest possible sentence for Eric Anderson all the way through his resentencing. "I guess it's a blessing," Carrie Hovel's father stated to reporters after the new sentence was handed down. "Because he's getting the most time he can get. I still wish he was staying behind bars for the rest of his life."³¹ It is wrong to find fault or to blame them for this response. The losses they suffered are incalculable. Danielle Sered powerfully makes the point that every survivor deserves the validation that what they suffered was wrong, that their pain is being taken seriously, and that they are not being blamed in any way for what happened to them, no matter the particular circumstances. Survivors need information, to have voice and agency in the process, and to have an assurance that the person who harmed them will not harm anyone else.³² At the same time, the experience of each victim/survivor will be distinct, and each must grapple with grief and loss as best they can. To vilify survivors for their responses would amplify the harm by finding fault with a person who already has been victimized.

Yet such responses prompt a further question for an intrinsically relational restorative justice: What happens when a party to the harm chooses not to participate? A person who experienced harm may not wish to—or, perhaps, not be able to—sit face to face with the person who harmed them or their loved ones. Restorative justice is centered on the needs of the people who are harmed. However, it is not the case that refusal by a victim/survivor to participate (or refusal by any stakeholder, for that matter) short-circuits the possibility for restorative practices. A "survivor-centered system is not a survivor-ruled one," Sered points out. "Valuing people does not mean giving them sole and unmitigated control."³³

Sometimes the person who caused harm, too, refuses to participate. One way of dealing with either absence that is consistent with the values and practices of restorative justice is to have a surrogate participant fulfill the open role. In other words, in a situation where a victim/survivor elects not to participate, but other stakeholders are willing, a victim/survivor from another circumstance who has suffered a similar harm, and is willing to help facilitate the restorative justice practices, can provide a substitute for that role.

In Eric Anderson's case, Jeanne Bishop has provided a surrogate presence as a person whose family members were also senselessly murdered by a juvenile offender. As the excerpt from her testimony above conveys, she was able to contribute invaluable wisdom to the restorative dynamics of the process on the basis of her own experience as a victim/survivor of a similar situation. In my earliest interview with her, Julie Anderson named Jeanne Bishop as a person who helped her and Eric understand and develop deeper empathy for the kinds of experiences that the Hovels and Martins likely were suffering, and the responses that prompted.

In this case, Jeanne's turn toward restorative justice in response to her own situation provides another example of how restorative justice multiplies the more it is shared. Jeanne Bishop's restorative response to the wrongdoer she confronted "rippled outward" from her own circumstances, spilling over into the circumstances of Eric, Julie, and the Anderson family. In a specific way, because of her testimony during Eric's resentencing trial, it even rippled toward the families of Helena Martin and Carrie Hovel.

Conclusion: Restorative Justice as Transformational Critical Praxis

Circles, restorative practices, and restorative values all cultivate relationships that can facilitate mourning, generate and sustain solidarity, and aid healing. They can also enact forms of critical praxis that cultivate critical consciousness, providing platforms to organize, resist domination, and empower action for transformational change. Each of these levels is interrelated.

The mothers' peacemaking circle kept by Sister Donna Liette at Precious Blood brings together mothers who are grieving, usually isolated, frequently living in shame and silence. CRIIC does the same. As we have seen in the story of Julie Anderson, these restorative practices consist of sharing stories, cultivating relationships of mutual support, and turning grief into organized action. How might this lead to transformation?

Julie's story demonstrates the isolating, fragmenting, and silencing effects of shame and stigma. These are forms of domination the system inflicts upon the people and families caught up in it. Working in restorative ways builds relationships that aim to generate and sustain solidarity. This solidarity promotes healing by cultivating and reinforcing forms of connection, self-respect and respect for others, and self-love that can neutralize the silencing and isolating acids of shame and stigma of being a family member or friend who "does the time" along with an incarcerated loved one. As these effects began to dissipate through restorative practices and the "co-creation of community," the support groups were able to organize, target specific forms of unaccountable power exerted on them by the system, and mobilize to change those.

The participants supported each other, and each other's children, through letter writing. They organized and facilitated cross-state trips and visited each other's children. These actions further nurtured sprouting tendrils of agency and self-empowerment through the relationships they were cultivating. They gave rise to hope for both mothers and their children, and thereby promoted better emotional adjustment and mental health for their incarcerated loved ones.

As the individuals and the group began to experience some degree of healing and empowerment, the group further moved into a position where the women could work together to consolidate their strength and bring its power to bear for purposes of policy and even legal change. Their experience of solidary mutual care, healing, and hope placed them in a position to critically reflect together on the ways that they and their loved ones have been disempowered and dominated by the criminal justice system.

They worked to raise awareness about particular issues and policies, and then to focus their efforts in ways that resisted domination, as we have seen in their efforts to change how families and loved ones of wrongdoers, as well as those imprisoned, are treated by the system. At a higher level, their solidarity and organizing enabled them to challenge and seek to transform arbitrary forms of state power by engaging them democratically. For example, they organized in order to alter legislation. In concert with legal organizations like Restore Justice Illinois, the women and families who gathered at Precious Blood concentrated their collective power to support legislative change by petitioning, organizing letter-writing campaigns, and lobbying their state representatives in Springfield. They successfully supported legislation to abolish mandatory life sentences without the possibility of parole for juveniles, and then successfully fought to have that retroactively applied. They were also successful in raising the age at which juveniles would automatically receive a hearing to determine whether their case should be transferred to the adult correctional system. They supported the legislative effort to abolish life sentences without the possibility of parole for all offenders under the age of twenty-one in Illinois.[34]

These different levels of engagement are all emblematic of the critical praxis of restorative justice and its ability to resist the domination of the contemporary justice system. This is yet another example of the way that the care, empathy, compassion, and meaning making that Michelle Alexander prescribes at the conclusion of *The New Jim Crow* form the very heart of actual practices of restorative justice. In the context of Chicago's restorative justice hub network, these are not disparate or even merely coordinated practices of moral and spiritual relationality. These are community-based, community-led, individual actors tapping into and consolidating their relational power and doing so together. In the process they become agents of their own critical awareness of, resistance to, and liberation from arbitrary treatment by forms of unaccountable power. This transformation becomes possible and occurs *in and through* practices of restorative justice. This story demonstrates that restorative justice at its best promotes modes of moral and spiritual association that give rise to transformational critical *praxis*.

I have argued that restorative justice is properly an account of justice because its understanding of what it means to give people their due fosters forms of association between people that are moral and spiritual. Moreover, when properly implemented, these give rise to transformational critical praxis. This does not negate concerns raised by those who think that associations with "justice" render it more prone to be co-opted by the retributive criminal justice system. Those risks of appropriation are real, especially in practice. Such challenges must be constantly navigated by restorative justice practitioners. In the chapter that follows, we will examine the risks and liabilities of insufficiently critical interaction with the criminal justice system. We will see how people and initiatives in Back of the Yards navigate the necessities of interacting with "the system," exploring what is required to maintain a critical orientation to that system and therefore a potentially transformational approach.

12

#LaquanMcDonald

Resistance and Compromise in Lawndale

The following post surfaced in my Facebook feed on November 25, 2015, the morning after the release of the dashcam video footage of seventeen-year-old Laquan McDonald being shot to death by Chicago police officer Jason Van Dyke:

SARAH STAUDT

November 25 at 10:22am   Edited

#LaquanMcDonald

I haven't been much of a facebook poster recently. It's because much of what I want to say, of what I witness daily as a lawyer for kids here on the West Side are things that no one would believe. And 90% of the craziness I see is the product of the Chicago Police Department, and until yesterday, until the video, I felt that no one would believe me. In this feeling, I join "my kids"—the young men and women of the West Side, who know that they are facing down a hateful gang disguised as a uniformed police force, and that they are powerless to stop it, because they are not in power, and they do not have proof, and their lives, and their truths, do not matter to anyone who matters.

 I sometimes explain what is going on here—and this is an explanation I normally use with privileged white people because, really, could I GET any nerdier a reference—is what Matilda says about Ms. Trunchbull in Roald Dahl's famous children's book [*Matilda*]. When one of her new friends, Lavender, tells her that their grammar school principal tortures children by swinging them over fences by their hair and sticking them in Iron Maidens, and gets away with it every time, Matilda explains Ms. Trunchbull's secret. She says it's not that the kids don't tell their parents—they do. But Matilda says, Ms. Trunchbull knows the secret, the secret that oppressors know when they're dealing with the weak, and the powerless:

'Never do anything by halves if you want to get away with it. Be outrageous. Go the whole hog. Make sure everything you do is so completely crazy it's unbelievable. No parent is going to believe this pigtail story, not in a million years.'

So often, I have no proof. I'm in the process of working on three police brutality cases as I write this. I'm trying even more cases—indeed, I struggle to think of a case on my caseload where this is not the case—where police have outright lied about what happened in a drug bust, a robbery, an identification procedure, an interrogation. In the police brutality cases, I see in each what happened to Laquan—police reports say he 'lunged' at officers. Lunged, refused to cooperate, jerked away—these are words that litter my kids' cases who are charged with aggravated battery of a cop, like #MalcolmLondon was last night. They are what justifies force. Guns shoved down throats. Children's heads kicked at with steel toed boots. I've seen the black eyes, the stitches, loss of hearing from the kicks in the head. I've seen the fear in my teenagers' eyes. And now, we have seen with our own eyes what I already knew to be true; it is these lies that are used to justify cold-blooded murder. Laquan did nothing to threaten officers. He was shot and killed for being black and high, because his life does not matter to anyone who matters.

The problem extends, though, beyond the brutality realm. In drug busts, kids are 'dropping' drugs in police reports when they were really just walking home from the store. In robberies, kids are 'fleeing' the area when they're sitting on their porches. And regularly, heartbreakingly, I have to sit down with kids, innocent kids, and tell them that it's not smart to take their case to trial. Because without proof, the cop's word is sacrosanct in the halls of justice. My kids' truth is never enough. They will not be believed. It is in those conversations that I feel most powerless as a lawyer, ally, and human being. Because it is in those moments that I am breaking to them a horrific truth that their lives, their truths, do not matter to anyone who matters.

When they want me to, I bring my kids' truths into court. I test the system. My kids sit tall in their school uniforms on witness stands, speaking in public for the first times in their lives, and proclaim that they are innocent. That they have been brutalized, lied about, hurt. They have had guns and drugs planted on them, starved and threatened into confessions. My heart swells with pride that they are brave enough to stand up. And then it is broken again, because I have yet to win such a case. Indeed, judges stop just short after my closings from laughing in my face. My kids' truths about the CPD matter to me. But not to the people who matter.

Laquan's truth was not enough. His family's truth was not enough. He no longer had a voice to share it, but you can be sure that if he had lived, he would never have been believed. Because the CPD—the organization, the system, not some rogue individual cop—is in the habit of what they did here. They have it down to a science. Lie, coverup, perjure themselves, convict. Rinse and repeat. I have been talking to people about mass incarceration, sentencing, big issues because I knew that no one would believe me that here, in my own city, a system so corrupt was really operating. It wasn't even worth my breath.

Please. Believe my kids now. Believe their truths. The Chicago Police Force is an orchestrated oppressive regime that is corrupt from root to branch. From the lowest untrained beat officers who bust down doors, harass families, intimidate witnesses, and lie, lie, lie on paper and on the stand, up to Gary McCarthy who knew that one of his officers had murdered a teenager and kept giving him a gun to carry with him at all times on the streets of Chicago, the CPD is as corrupt as they come. In this case alone they erased video, ignored 17 previous reports of Van Dyke's police brutality and racism, gave hush money to a needy, grieving family. I won't even touch the fact that they now are trying to claim the moral high ground because they've arrested Van Dyke. They are a third-world style oppressive police state operating down the street from you. It is worse than you think. March until it is torn down from the top down. Do not be pacified by making Van Dyke and Servin scapegoats. March until we have a city that believes our children's lives have meaning.

SOURCES: For every accusation I have made here, I have a story that I have personal knowledge of to back it up. Some I cannot share as an attorney with open pending cases; others I will not share publicly as they are not my stories, but would be willing to share privately if I can talk to my kids first about it. I'm always willing to be a conduit of information. Just ask me.[1]

The case of Laquan McDonald's murder resolved in 2018. It resulted in the conviction of police officer Jason Van Dyke, the first conviction in decades of a Chicago police officer for killing while on duty.[2] The murder had occurred in 2014.³ It was initially covered up by the Chicago Police Department, which paid his family a five-million-dollar settlement. Later investigation by independent journalist and civil rights activist Jamie Kalven led to the release of the dashcam footage of the shooting.⁴ The footage revealed that, contra the police claims and doctored reports, McDonald was walking *away* from officers when Van Dyke arrived on the scene, emerged from his squad car, and shot him sixteen times in ten seconds.

When the dashcam footage was finally released just before Thanksgiving in 2015, Chicago community organizers took to the streets. They conveyed their rage openly and publicly. They occupied and shut down stretches of the "Magnificent Mile" retail district along North Michigan Avenue on Black Friday. This prompted some shoppers there to vocally—and forcefully, in several cases—assert their "right to shop."⁵ Activists marched and rallied on numerous other occasions, as well, and at one point occupied City Hall.

Chicago community organizers spoke openly and unapologetically of the community's rage about Laquan McDonald's murder and the cover-up surrounding it. They pointed out the historical and structural conditions that precipitated it, and the numerous other instances of police abuse of force of which it was emblematic. Crucially—and strategically—they managed to quell the compulsion to react violently and to transform that compulsion into nonviolent, direct action. A coalition of Chicago community organizer groups demanded that mayor Rahm Emanuel, the police commissioner, and the county state's attorney resign, and that a citizen review board for police be launched.

The Monday following the release of the police dashcam video, Mayor Emanuel fired Chicago police chief Gary McCarthy, and initiated a civil police accountability council. Organizers spurred the ouster of the county attorney, Anita Alvarez, at the next election. They prompted a federal investigation by the Department of Justice of abusive policing patterns, which resulted in a consent decree.⁶ Van Dyke was tried and convicted. Mayor Emanuel did not seek reelection.

What immediately followed Laquan McDonald's murder was a campaign of nonviolent direct action that brought to light and dramatized the severity and depth of the injustices at stake.⁷ Community organizers pursued concrete goals as part of a negotiation strategy, but also sought a larger institutional correction of the domination of local communities by law enforcement and city government. To this day, activists and residents across South and West Side Chicago neighborhoods persist in their outrage that the city and the police continue to operate arbitrarily and with impunity.[8]

In Chicago, the division between law enforcement and residents runs deep. In some ways it has become even more entrenched following the murder of Laquan McDonald. This is because his murder brought numerous forms of structural violence to the surface. Many of the patterns of abusive policing cited in the Facebook post I initially saw, and by many other community organizers, persist. What could restorative justice look like in this context? What difference could it make? This chapter and the next explore the depth and severity of policing and police abuse of force in Chicago communities. However, they also document and assess the ways that several police and court initiatives are using restorative justice practices to spur change and revitalize community policing in Chicago neighborhoods.

As we have seen, a holistic vision of restorative justice can marshal its transformational potential in virtue of being based in, and led by, the communities most directly affected by unaccountable and arbitrary forms of power. The work of groups like Precious Blood and those they serve offers an example of what a holistic approach to restorative justice practices in the midst of persisting conflict must look like. At their best, such initiatives bring to light the historical and present systemic roots of injustice. They move to the center the voices of the victims and marginalized and amplify their agency in processes of response and recovery. They can uncover the extent and severity of violence and facilitate reparation, restitution, and apology to those who have been harmed. They can alter cultures of conflict by promoting community building and healing. Even now, forms of relationship building and repair are occurring with actual police officers—although in unsystematic, small-scale ways—through local neighborhood restorative justice initiatives across Chicago. "Repair" in this context requires a broad array of tools, processes, and conceptions of sustainable relationship building that include—but are far from exhausted by—the kinds of "depolarization" between opponents that community organizers employ at the conclusion of a campaign.

If restorative justice practices are to be transformative, they will need to participate in the critical praxis that illuminates the need to, and facilitates the practices of, taking back and reconfiguring power structures. Restorative justice, as I have argued, goes beyond interpersonal repair, and seeks to change the policy, laws, and processes by which destructive systems impose themselves. Initiatives need to provide platforms from which to build sustainable alternatives to contemporary policing and justice system practices.

Any such transformation will occur through complex processes of resistance to, but inevitable critical negotiation with, realities that already exist. These efforts to collaborate bring risks for these restorative justice initiatives. Does formal cooperation and/or collaboration with the contemporary criminal justice system (such as police and judges) place restorative justice initiatives at risk of perpetuating previous structural injustices? It is clearly possible for a set of counter-practices to be co-opted by the current criminal justice system. Is it possible for restorative justice to respond at the systemic level without being compromised in this way?

There are several inherent risks for those committed to restorative justice who have close interaction with the criminal justice system. Such risks include the possibility that restorative justice practices and initiatives will be captured and assimilated into a violent system that protects and preserves itself through *appearing* to effect change, while in fact only altering the status quo at its surface-level operations. How does this impact the ability of restorative justice to counter and transform the structural dynamics of abusive policing? To answer these questions, I spent several days exploring how people implement restorative justice practices in North Lawndale, a neighborhood on the West Side of Chicago.

Resistance and Compromise

I met Sarah Staudt, the author of the Facebook post that opened this chapter, during my first visit to the Lawndale Christian Legal Center (LCLC) in Chicago's North Lawndale neighborhood. At the time of our interview, Sarah served as a lead staff attorney there for youth and young adults. Her own desk was at the head of the room, while several attorneys and law school students worked at tables that lined both walls on either side of the cramped, elongated office. These were attorneys Sarah worked with and mentored, all providing legal services to court-involved youth and young adults at the center.

North Lawndale is a West Side community that is widely known across the city as one of the most justice-system-enmeshed neighborhoods in Chicago. Sarah explains that LCLC was founded with the recognition that youth and young adults in North Lawndale needed far more than standard legal representation. So, while LCLC specializes in legal support and services, as a founding member of the restorative justice community hub network, it also works collaboratively with the other hubs across the city to provide mentoring, job training, social work support, and guidance for families. In all of this, it strives to be sensitive to and oriented by the experiences and developmental needs of young people.

LCLC seeks to embed everything it does in a holistic vision of restorative justice. It integrates its formal legal support and restorative justice conferencing with an aim to increase community access to mental health services, special education services, drug counseling, and mentoring and tutoring. Its primary aim, however, is to be in relationship with youth and young adults in North Lawndale. The objective, as Sarah described it to me, is to accompany them in becoming "justly treated youth who are embraced by their families and communities, restored from trauma, empowered to lead, and permanently free of the criminal justice system."[9]

The configuration of the hub means that each young person Sarah is defending in court also has a case manager and a social worker, who work on site at LCLC. The young people are invited to participate in athletic programs, tutoring, mentoring, and community-building exercises that help form the heart of the LCLC community. The staff work with them to understand how their particular circumstances may have led them to engage in harmful or actually criminal actions. In many cases, they guide the young people in understanding and responding to an accusation of doing something they did not do—a kind of event that can derail or cause problems in itself.[10] "We do a huge amount of work in . . . explaining to judges what the whole picture here is so that our children aren't viewed in the court system as just a number or just another face, but as somebody that has potential and an ability to succeed," Sarah told me. "We seek as much as we can to do circles with our kids, but even when we're not doing circles, we do active listening. We don't practice this sort of conditional love approach, of 'you have to do what I tell you to do, or else.' We appreciate our children as people, and in doing so attempt to restore them to become better citizens. Whereas the system sees them as worthless, frankly."[11]

LCLC is one of the oldest and most innovative members of the network of restorative justice hubs in Chicago. In August 2017 it helped to launch a "restorative justice court." Opened by the Circuit Court of Cook County in collaboration with LCLC, and funded by a major federal grant, eighteen- to twenty-six-year-old people accused of nonviolent felony and misdemeanor offenses in Lawndale can apply to participate in the restorative justice court as an alternative to the standard justice system. This court is an example of a diversionary initiative, as discussed earlier; the Cook County state's attorney's office diverts eligible cases from the Cook County juvenile justice system into the restorative justice court.[12]

In order to be eligible, the accused must have a nonviolent criminal history (if they have any such history at all). They must be willing to accept responsibility for the harm they have caused. The person who was harmed must be willing to participate in all the restorative processes as well. If there is not a "traditional" victim—as is the case for many crimes involving drug use or sales—the court seeks a "surrogate victim" volunteer from the community, often someone who was previously impacted by a similar infraction. In fact, the restorative justice court relies on participation and cooperation from community stakeholders, including business owners, community representatives and activists, school administrators, teachers, and church leaders and their congregants from across the Lawndale community.[13] It also relies on cooperation and collaboration from the Cook County justice system. The stakeholders sit together in circle. "The goal is to reach an agreement where both the accused and the victims feel 'restored' to the community: that might include a defendant doing community service work, accessing social services (like counseling, drug treatment, or job training) and/or paying restitution to victims."[14] If the repair of harm agreement is completed, a person who caused harm can ultimately have their nonviolent felony or nonviolent misdemeanor charges dismissed and their criminal record expunged.

Initially, the members of the hub network who participated in its formation proposed that the restorative justice court convene at Saint Agatha Catholic Church, roughly a mile east of LCLC. This would have housed it in a community-based organization located within the North Lawndale neighborhood. The sheriff's office refused, however, saying that Saint Agatha was insufficiently secure. In order for it to be an independent facility, member organizations who helped launch the court had to agree to have a sheriff present, and thus the facility needed to be secure by standards acceptable to law enforcement. The members agreed to instead house the restorative justice court at UCan, a therapeutic youth home situated near Homan Square, about a mile north of LCLC, that helps young people recover from trauma. But several members of the restorative justice hub leadership circle expressed concern that this moved the initiative fully into the orbit of the Chicago criminal justice system. It risked loss of the independence necessary for a genuinely holistic vision and practice of restorative justice. Following this decision, the community restorative justice court increasingly came to replicate—even to feel like and give the impression of—a facility and process "in the system."

"That was a red flag for me right away," Father Kelly says. "It's taking on the guise of a court if you have a sheriff [present]. The other thing that really concerned me was there was too many in-roads back to the [Cook County] court." He continues,

> Once [a young person's case] was given to the community, if the repair of harm agreement wasn't lived up to . . . there was always a threat of "if you don't do it, you're going through the normal criminal justice system [path]." In my mind, once it's given to the community, it's the community's obligation and responsibility to ensure the repair of harm agreement is [fulfilled]—not relying on the courts to be the "big brother" or the one with the stick. So we, as elders of the community, have to wrestle with, you know, "Johnny's not doing what he said he was going to do. What, then, do *we* do?"[15]

The restorative justice court model has multiplied as of this writing. Such courts have opened in the Englewood and Avondale neighborhoods of Chicago. Father Kelly is emphatic that courts of this kind are far better than the standard path through the Cook County criminal justice system. He sees them as a specialty court—comparable to, say, a drug court, but for low-level, nonviolent harms, and taking a rehabilitative and repair-centric focus. It is far better that some system-involved youth and young adults can have nonviolent felonies and misdemeanors expunged from their records through restorative mediation processes. Yet he recognizes that this model exemplifies a diversionary, rather than a holistic and thus potentially transformational, approach to restorative justice. It works within the Cook County criminal justice system, and the system sets the terms by which it operates.

The implications of Father Kelly's assessment here are crucial. If a community-led restorative justice initiative is going to collaborate in any way with the system and still remain potentially transformational in its approach, it must be based on the system giving respect, trust, and autonomy to the restorative justice initiative. If the initiative is to avoid capture by that system—despite the best intentions—the relationship must be structured to recognize, empower, and sustain the independence of the restorative justice initiative. Restorative justice initiatives in the neighborhood hub network do not request that system powers such as judges, DAs, or school principals accord them final decision-making power, and responsibility for following up—they insist on it.

Consider, for example, Precious Blood's "Saturday Sanction" program facilitated by Jonathan Little, discussed earlier. The center started this program at the request of the Cook County juvenile justice system. Probation Department representatives asked them for a place and program to refer young people in the system to fulfill their community service sentences. Indeed, the name "Saturday *Sanction*" was assigned by the Probation Department. It intended to convey an alternative form of punishment (diverting offenders from jail time). Yet Precious Blood runs the program as anything but a "sanction." From the start, staff members were forthcoming that providing a program that "sanctions" young people is something they would not do.

The program, recall, is devoted to restoratively oriented relationship building with youth and young adults. The group integrates circles, but also takes the young people on day trips across the city and region (canoeing, sailing on Lake Michigan, movies, sports events, museums, activities all across downtown, and field trips around broader "Chicagoland"). In fact, Jonathan's description of the group's activities was so antithetical to "sanctions" that I worried I might have misheard or mistranscribed the name of the program during my discussions with him. In following up, I asked Father Kelly whether the program was actually named "Saturday *Sanctuary*." I thought that perhaps the name was actually meant to convey that the group meetings and activities were a shelter and refuge from the difficult circumstances and various forms of violence that the young people in group were dealing with. "No," Father Kelly replied, "but [sanctuary] would be a good name for it. It was named by Probation so it was designed [to be a sanction]. But we never used it that way. And we were very forthcoming in telling them, 'We won't do that.'" He continued,

> For us it's Saturday "engagement." It's a chance for us to get to know these young people more, and to do something outside of our community. So it would broaden their world. . . . But it's interesting because . . . the word ["sanction"] was overwhelmed by what it became. So it's like "sanction" didn't mean "sanction" anymore. It was something that kids said, "Can I go?" "Can I do that?" So it wasn't punishment, even though the words, by definition . . . that's what they called it. . . . And I told [the Probation Department representatives] right from the very beginning, because the idea was that rather than locking somebody up, they would send these kids to the hubs and the organizations would have them paint, or clean, or something. I said, "I'm not interested in that. But I will take that young person and strive to build a relationship with them and strive to make them feel like they're part of the community, and take them out of the neighborhood to let him experience something beyond their ghetto. I will do *that*." And they didn't buck that. They just said, "Okay, well, it's your program. Do what you want with it."[16]

Father Kelly describes an opportunity that Precious Blood embraced to matter-of-factly resist the punitive orientation of the Cook County criminal justice system. It implemented an altogether different and transformative engagement with youth and young adults caught in the system—quite literally *transforming* the very meaning of the word "sanction" in this context and circumstance. Yet, for this opportunity to present itself in the first place, Precious Blood and the other members of the community restorative justice hub network had to be in relationship with actors in "the system" (in this case, the Probation Department). They had to be willing to talk and work with them, rather than maintain a strictly rejective, oppositional stance toward the state. It is, however, in their clear, firm, refusal to cooperate with the punitive interests and purposes of the system, their insistence that they remain free of dictates from the system, and their creative commitment to a holistic vision of restorative justice, that resistance and constructive transformation could merge. Indeed, it was the trust and reliability that certain system representatives felt in their relationships with Precious Blood that led Probation administrators to hand the program over entirely to the discretion of Precious Blood.

Conclusion: "In Schoolyards, on Street Corners, and, Yes . . . in Courthouses"

Another example of the fight to make restorative justice practices in Chicago remain free from encroachment and capture by the system is the fight for restorative justice conferences to have the legal protection of "privileged communications." Such "privilege" protects words that are spoken or written from being admissible in court proceedings; the most common example is what's known as attorney-client privilege, where anything a person tells their lawyer is protected from use in court. Such a privilege, applied to restorative justice conferences, would give legal weight to the value and practice of confidentiality in circle—the guideline "What's said in circle stays in circle."

This basic guideline for peacemaking circles is not a literal prohibition. It does not seek to turn the circle into a secret ritual. The lessons learned, wisdom shared, and agreements reached can all be referred to outside the time and context of the circle when they are relevant. The norm, rather, aims to assure a proper confidentiality. Such confidentiality is essential for the circle to operate as a safe space, as it is intended to. If the conversations in, for example, a conflict or repair of harm circle are to be honest, based on vulnerability and truth telling, the members of the circle must be free to speak openly about their experiences. Responsibility and accountability require that they be able to discuss what they may have done without fear that what they say might be held against them in a legal context or for punitive purposes. In fact, it has been common for defense attorneys to discourage their clients from participating in restorative justice practices for fear of "self-incrimination." Legal authorities must therefore recognize circle processes as private, protected relationships. Otherwise, the vulnerability and truth telling that they facilitate—and that are their animating force—could be weaponized against participants.

In 2015 Father Kelly and the Catholic Lawyers Guild of Chicago drafted legislation that would formally recognize peacemaking circle processes, and conflict mediation processes in restorative justice practices more generally, as privileged communication. It took six years and multiple attempts to finally get the legislation (Senate Bill 64) signed into law on July 15, 2021. The result, however, is groundbreaking in its breadth and scope. Other jurisdictions had previously set forth limited protections of confidentiality or privilege for restorative justice programs and practices. Illinois SB 64 diverged radically from those in its range of applicability. As one commentator described, SB 64 "broadly applies privilege to all restorative justice practices—practices convened in schoolyards, on street corners, and, yes, in courthouses. . . . As the new law states, the hope is that 'residents of this State [will] employ restorative justice practices, not only in justiciable matters but in all aspects of life and law.'"[17] In other words, the vision orienting this legislation is not only to safeguard the power and enable the full effectiveness of restorative justice practices as they might be implemented throughout the life of Chicago neighborhoods and communities. It is also to promote an expansive vision of restorative justice. It aims to grow and expand restorative justice practices throughout the daily life of local communities—to cultivate restorative justice by facilitating it as widely as possible—even in informal and ad hoc locations and circumstances.

In fighting for and achieving such an encompassing application of "privileged communication" for all restorative justice practices, the Catholic Lawyers Guild shared the vision that orients the community restorative justice hub network. This is a vision of restorative justice that not only challenges and offers practicable alternatives to the criminal justice system and its impact on communities, but moves in the direction of transforming those systems and communities. These practices of restorative justice strive to remain apart from control by the justice system itself, yet position themselves to work with actors in that system who are willing to engage restoratively and to recognize and respect the integrity of restorative justice norms and practices. Indeed, it is through the relationships they maintain with people in the system that they position themselves to resist the system itself.

13

Can Policing Be Restorative Too?

Critical Praxis and the Dilemma of "Restorative Policing"

Many Chicago police officers, and some juvenile court justices as well, have come to recognize the unsustainability of the current rates of arrest and incarceration and the dehumanizing impact of the general hyper-punitive model of justice deployed there. They cooperate with various restorative justice initiatives as a means to address both the destructiveness of the current system and the harms the police themselves have suffered working in violent neighborhoods. They see these practices as vital to healing damaged relationships with the communities where they work and transforming policing culture more broadly.

As challenging as it may be, there are signs that officer participation in community-based restorative justice initiatives and practices can begin to identify harms and repair relationships that have become toxic and destructively oppositional ("community versus police"). They can help build community in more positive and self-sustaining forms. Yet the *transformational* potential of such processes is obstructed by the depth and pervasiveness of the corruption from which the Chicago Police Department suffers. Systemic transformation is required. Is it possible for the juvenile justice system and law enforcement to reform themselves in line with restorative justice in ways that do not merely preserve oppressive dynamics?

"It Helps People See Each Other as People"

What would it look like for Chicago officers to participate in restorative justice practices, however small in scale such participation might be? I caught a glimpse of an answer to this question when I participated in a four-day peacemaking circle training at Precious Blood that included CPD officers.[1] The circle participants were divided nearly evenly between younger activists, organizers, social workers, and youth ministers in nearby communities, and middle-aged adults who turned out to be plainclothes officers.

One of the civilians was a youth minister from a church in Oak Lawn. He sought to incorporate peacemaking circle processes into his youth meetings and outreach to the community. Another participant was a social justice community activist, a young woman of color who was also an undergraduate student at a university in Chicago. There was an older African American woman from Back of the Yards who was a mother of several children, including an oldest son who was incarcerated. Her family was active in the Precious Blood center. Another community person in the training was a White man in his late twenties who had spent the previous years working as a union organizer. He specialized in "salting"—getting hired at hotel chains in order to help organize workers there to unionize. He confessed to being completely burned out. Community organizing had incorporated "circles," but mainly for what he came to experience as "destructive" purposes. Lead organizers would convene circles in order to place people they thought were not doing their jobs well enough onto the "hot seat" and "tear them down." They would then build them back up in the ways that the lead organizers desired. The work involved no self-care and placed intense pressure upon himself and others. The young man said he sought out the peacemaking circle training with Community Justice for Youth at Precious Blood as a way of healing from that and moving forward in a more constructive way.

Ice Breaking

The first day of the training was devoted to laying the foundation of the circle as a practice and process. We spent the morning hours exploring the role of the opening and icebreakers for cultivating a sense of "who we are in this circle." One icebreaker used a bag of wooden blocks. The blocks were spread out on the floor around the base of a small table placed in the middle of the centerpiece. As the talking piece passed, each person took a turn adding to, subtracting from, or otherwise altering the sculpture that gradually emerged and evolved there over the course of multiple rounds. No one was allowed to speak.

The sculpture took on a life of its own. It grew into a tall tower until one circle member knocked that over. A flat structure—less liable to be toppled, I figured—then began to emerge. Some of the flat quadrilaterals fanned out around the base in a beautiful but persistently changing pattern. After roughly forty-five minutes, the circle keeper invited us to reflect and debrief the exercise. She passed a talking piece and invited us to consider the effect that the activity had on each of us. What did we think was going on? What was our experience of the process? What did we perceive in ourselves? About others in the circle? Did we accomplish something together? If so, what? Were we trying to? What was good? What was not?

At the most basic level, the purpose was to overcome the social stiffness and trepidation that typically accompany sitting down together with a group of strangers by focusing on a shared task. Not allowing anyone to speak—to explain or justify their contributions to the block sculpture—deepened that focus. There were moments of humor and playful curiosity. At times we broke out into collective laughter. This indeed broke the ice in ways necessary for us to build our own relationships with one another in and through the circles that unfolded over the days that followed. But it also involved us in an absorbing object lesson, we discovered, as the circle trainer led us in rounds of debriefing.

One circle member pointed out that prohibiting verbal communication gave us no choice but to "trust the process." This meant allowing the sculpture to unfold naturally and experience ourselves as one part of that spontaneous flow of the activity. It was impossible to direct our collective efforts at achieving a coordinated or shared objective. We were all forced to let go of any specific, goal-directed efforts to organize, and just allow the changes to happen. No one of us was in control. Some members of the circle admitted that, at certain moments, they were pleased with what the sculpture had become. But that inevitably changed. One woman expressed her disappointment that the formation she created—which she considered beautiful—had been undone by the participants who took their turns immediately after her, instead of their tweaking or adding to what she had sculpted.

One key takeaway from the morning's work was that an effective icebreaker and rounds of check-in are fundamental elements in initiating a peacemaking circle. They enhance the circle's capacity to become a space and a time for relationship building and generate a sense of ease and comfort from which "who we are in this circle" can gradually emerge and grow.

Values and Guidelines

We spent the second half of the first day discussing the values our circle should embody, and then the guidelines we would all agree to follow based on those values. The discussion of what it means that the circle is a "values-based" practice—and that those values should emerge through group consensus—generated controversy. The university student suggested that "centering the oppressed" should be the central value that orients the circle. That raised questions from several participants. Was the idea to privilege the voices of certain people, determined in advance? Would that require that others deemed non-oppressed remain silent during circle rounds, or speak less? How would we decide whose voices to privilege? Several in the circle expressed skepticism. They questioned the prior privileging of voices deemed to be marginal. The purpose of the circle, they thought, was to treat every participant with equal dignity and equal respect, facilitating "equal voice."

The circle, some argued, must be a safe space where every member can contribute without fear of judgment or disapproval, whether that contribution is based on their identities or on something they have done. In effect, the circle is designed to facilitate each person's participation. This requires more than eliminating constraints or inequalities that would limit certain persons' participation. It means, rather, constructively developing conditions so that each member has what they need to be able to fully participate. This means, for example, maximizing the comfort level and cultivating warmth and familiarity between the members of the circle so as to minimize reticence and hesitation. It means that each round affords multiple opportunities for participants to share or pass. It means that the particularities of each member's identity, history, and personal story are invited in and foregrounded as a part of cultivating a community of mutual recognition and equal, reciprocal respect in the circle. The talking piece and rounds of the circle apportion the contributions people make in their own, distinct voices, and attune the circle's attention exclusively on the person who holds the talking piece. The aim, again, is to lay the foundations for and build relationships. The only "mediator" is the talking piece. This was the understanding that gradually emerged from the circle that day, at least.

Sharing Our Stories

Our second day focused on building trust throughout the circle by sharing our stories of where we came from, and how and why we came to the circle. We shared introductions through another icebreaking activity in circle. With crayons and a piece of construction paper, we each drew a picture of some place that we considered to be a safe and welcoming space. We then sent the talking piece around the circle for each person to share their drawing and the ways and reasons why that space was distinctly welcoming. The exercise was intended to make us individually reflect on, and then share with the group, how we understood the concept of a safe and welcoming space. Ultimately, it was meant to help us identify the present time and space (the circle) with welcoming and safety for sharing and relationship building. I drew a picture of my grandparents' kitchen table, where I spent countless hours in conversation growing up and as an adult.

Each member of the circle checked in, and then we turned to sharing our stories with the group. During the individual introductions it came out for the first time "in circle" that seven of the people participating in the training were plainclothes officers from the Chicago Police Department. "No one told me there were going to be cops here," one young woman stated sharply when the talking piece made its way to her. She explained that she had been a victim of police brutality. The woman had helped organize and participate in a nonviolent protest during which she and her fellow protestors had sat down to block a sidewalk on a public street. When the police gave the order to clear out, they refused to move. One officer had grabbed the young woman by her hair and dragged her across the street prior to arresting her. The experience had traumatized her. She was not certain that she was going to be able to sit in an extended peacemaking circle training with CPD officers. She did not return after the second day of the training.

As we told our stories of where we came from, one of the officers—a longtime restorative justice practitioner who was working as an assistant circle keeper for the circle—explained that she was a lead officer for the Bridging the Divide initiative of the community policing program that CPD had started back in 1993. The purpose of that program was to build relationships through circles and community-based activities (dialogue sessions, collective art projects, sports events) conducted largely between police and young people.

Another of the officers said that he had been working in violent neighborhoods. He said that his heart had always gone out to the victims of the crime and violence he encountered there. Then he was transferred to the Cook County jail, where he worked for eighteen months. During that time, he slowly built relationships with people who were incarcerated, including some in maximum security. Through that experience he came to recognize the impact of trauma on the young people in many of the neighborhoods he had policed. Many of those who ended up incarcerated had acted out of their own pain and the desperation of their circumstances. But he also pointed out the impact of trauma on police.

Several of the officers in the circle went on to speak of their own experience of trauma—harm done to them or their partners—and their experience of deep hatred from the communities they police. By the time the talking piece got around to someone I will call "John," I had begun to see why and how restorative justice peacemaking circles could also be vital to police officers. His job, he said, was to respond to "hot calls," which usually meant that he would end up locking someone up in order to "make peace." He and his partner were assigned the night shift in Englewood, a neighborhood to the immediate south of Back of the Yards. It is one of the Chicago neighborhoods most riddled with gang conflict. John spoke about the impact of the alienation and anger officers experience from the communities where they work. He told the story of driving his squad car slowly down a block, smiling and waving hello to a little boy—five years old or so, he thought. The boy looked at him from the sidewalk. As he passed by, the boy raised his hand in a fist, and very slowly and deliberately extended his middle finger. John said that the boy held it aloft, aimed directly at him, until he was out of sight.

John claimed that his experiences in Englewood had desensitized him to trauma. In sharing his story, however, he portrayed the opposite. One night while he was off duty, his partner responded to a "shots fired" call at an address in West Englewood. As his partner and another officer investigated outside the residence, they were both shot dead from a moving car. John's partner was survived by his wife, who was pregnant with their first child at the time. The loss was devastating for everyone involved. John took it especially hard.

As John shared this story, tears began to flow from his eyes. He went on to share that another officer and friend who knew and worked with John's murdered partner was a combat veteran from the war in Iraq. This officer suggested that they adopt the practice that he and his fellow soldiers had observed in Iraq—wearing a black wristband in honor and remembrance of their fallen fellow police officer. They did. Less than a year later, this officer was robbed while off duty. When he identified himself as a police officer and drew his service weapon, he was shot in the abdomen and died.

John gathered himself and explained that he had internalized the pain of losing two partners and close friends. He recognized that bottled-up anger had negatively impacted how he interacted with the people he encountered while working in Englewood. He also said that in recent years, opportunities for community interaction between police and local neighborhood young people had helped him process and let go of some of that anger. These were events of the kind that Sarah Staudt had mentioned—many associated with the Bridging the Divide encounter and dialogue initiatives of the CAPS (community policing) program. LCLC and Precious Blood spent much time and effort planning to bring youth and neighborhood CPD officers together to play basketball, cook out, and hold listening sessions.

Another officer in the circle, a Black woman, shared her concern for her son. She explained how difficult it is to be the mother of a young Black man in Chicago. She feared both that he might have a deadly encounter with violence in their neighborhood and that he might have a deadly encounter with police. The fact that she was a CPD officer offered no protection for her son. He was aware of that as well, she said. She and her husband had bought him a car for his sixteenth birthday. It was red, as he had asked for. Within a year, he requested that they have the car painted a different color. He had come to fear that the red color—which he loved—was too likely to attract attention from the police.

What was clear was that many of the police sitting in circle were suffering. Their alienation from the communities where they worked—and in some cases those where they lived—harmed them. As people, they were themselves suffering from the demands, the vulnerabilities, and the violence of policing. They acknowledged the impact that the circle training had in helping them process these harms and heal through building relationships.

A Conflict Circle as Critical Praxis of Awareness and Transformation

On the final day of the training we moved into breakout groups. Each group of four people was tasked with designing, preparing for, and then facilitating a circle for the final hours of the training. It was not a "mock" exercise. Rather, we would all actually participate in each of the circles, although the four circles were abbreviated due to time constraints.

Participants for each group were randomly chosen. Each group developed the purpose, theme, and elements of its circle (opening, icebreaker, closing, and so forth). My group chose to do a conflict circle. We planned to address the conflict that arose on the second day of the training around police brutality and its effect on the training. We would focus on what led the young university student to express her abiding distrust toward the police in the circle and then withdraw from the training altogether.

After our circle moved through the opening, icebreaker, and check-in, we began addressing this issue. One officer raised the issue of accountability. He suggested that, in the context of a conflict circle, the young university student should be held accountable for what he considered to be her "bias" regarding police, and her refusal to even engage them in the training. The officer who treated her abusively—dragging her across the street by her hair when she didn't comply with his order to disperse—was just one officer, he suggested. Perhaps he was a bad cop. But his abusiveness should not be held against the officers who were participating in the circle training that week. Yet she did just that. Most of the other officers in the circle agreed with this.

Another officer offered a response. She was serving as assistant to the circle keeper for the week. She pointed out that what they considered accountability for the woman's attitude toward policing, and thus, the police sitting within that circle, must take a secondary role to the circle being a safe place where that woman—and any participant in a peacemaking circle—can honestly speak from her experience, that is, "speak her truth" without the fear of being judged and treated negatively as a result.

The rounds of the circle allowed the other members to express concerns about the officers' emphasis on "holding the young woman accountable." Some speakers made the point that the abusive treatment experienced by the student who left the circle was far from an isolated incident across Chicago, and that officers who had been identified and named as "bad actors" could not be dismissed as "a few bad apples." There were systemic issues and recurring patterns in the culture of policing in the CPD that needed to be addressed, and that culture had to be changed in fundamental ways.

The former union organizer pointed out that the officers in this circle were in a unique position to be catalysts for change in the CPD. He noted that each of the officers there had supervisors and colleagues who were likely curious, perhaps perplexed, about why they were taking part in a restorative justice training as part of their career in the CPD. The young man posed a question to these officers: "What does it mean to change the profession that seven people in this room inhabit? People are trying to change it from the outside. What does it look like to challenge it from the inside?"

The conflict circle that we held for the final afternoon of the training could easily have gone much deeper into the causes and conditions of the persistent conflict between communities across Chicago and the CPD. We were constrained by the time limit. But a powerful, if fleeting, lesson emerged from the process. Together we recognized and named some of the systemic issues that perpetuate police overuse of force and that promote abusive policing and brutality. The circle discussion emphasized that the fundamental issues were systemic, and not a problem of a few individual bad actors in the CPD. The circle pointed to the need for greater police accountability to the community. Police are equipped with the use of lethal force and are authorized by the power of the state to use that force as they deem necessary. Further, they are protected by such state provisions as "qualified immunity" when they use force. We insisted that the changes needed to be systemic—changes like demilitarizing policing as a whole, reducing the size and scope of CPD, and redirecting newly available funds back into community-based programs and services that promote community-led public safety. At present, police are charged with handling a wide range of issues, though they often do not have the necessary training to handle them.

To be frank, I expected the conflict circle to devolve into a shouting match once the criticisms of policing emerged as its primary focus. To my surprise, the officers responded receptively to the emerging consensus of the circle. The encounter over a conflict had moved from their collective effort to hold the (now absent) young woman accountable for her view of police, to understanding the personal and structural reasons she held those views, to raising awareness of their responsibility, as police, to spur broader awareness and change in the harmful culture and violent structures of policing. Their ability to listen, to receive these concerns and assertions that were challenging, and at moments were quite analytically sharp and critical, was surely a result of the many hours we had devoted to relationship building and trust building together over the previous several days. They knew our stories and struggles, just as we knew theirs. We had cultivated a mutual vulnerability, just as we had cultivated a mutual recognition and reciprocal respect.

At the same time, those of us who were civilians also became acutely aware through our time in the circle that police officers are also in a position of vulnerability. We heard firsthand accounts of the harms that many of them had suffered as police officers. We learned of the pain that many of them felt over their alienation and as a result of the violence they had experienced.

The police in our circle training were almost all people of color themselves. They had witnessed their own family members, loved ones, and neighborhoods subjected to the very forms of racism that the structural and cultural violence of policing perpetuates. They expressed fears and a sense of vulnerability about the forms of violence perpetuated by the culture of policing and mass incarceration. It dawned on me that, each in different ways, these individual police officers were themselves victims of the violence inscribed in the structures, culture, and practices of contemporary policing.

The conflict circle enabled us to reflect on, make explicit, and critically sift through numerous causes and conditions underlying the specific incident of conflict that occurred on the second day of the training.

It enabled us to understand each other's stories, backgrounds, and circumstances in much more depth. It enabled us to be vulnerable with each other, even as we spoke honestly—and at times critically—of the reasons that conflict between police and local neighborhood people runs so deep. The police officers in the circle agreed to the need for increasing intentional efforts to build constructive relationships between police and members of the community, for the sake of their own well-being as well as for the people living in those communities across Chicago. And they recognized the role that restorative justice practices could play in those efforts.

This peacemaking circle training, and the conflict circle in which it culminated, was at most a tiny step in the direction of relationship building, healing, and potential transformation between Chicago police and local community people there. This was only a minuscule sample of CPD officers, and moreover, these were officers who were already involved in the Bridging the Divide community policing initiative. They were perhaps already inclined to build the kind of relationships that could effect some constructive change in community relations. Even so, the training demonstrated a peacemaking circle's ability to function as a form of critical praxis—raising awareness and spurring some effort to change.

Importantly, its critical effectiveness, and the transformational potential of the practical implications toward which the circle pointed, came in and through the cultivation of relationships of mutual recognition and reciprocal respect. This recognition and respect were manifest in the methodical building of trust and the cultivation of care and empathy over four days. This situation then opened possibilities for vulnerability that enabled "deep truth telling." Then, and only then, could we move toward accountability in the form of critical reflection and critical awareness, with an eye toward transformational practice. The extended relationship building we did over the course of that week helped the officers name the harms they had suffered. It enabled them to reflect on how the fear and vulnerabilities they experienced informed their approaches to the communities in which they work. That relationship building enabled us all to speak forthrightly to one another, to challenge one another regarding how "the system" must change in a fundamental way, and how they might play parts in that.

People who work in law enforcement are part of the community as well. Any true transformation of the prison-industrial complex ultimately will have to include them. While this liberation will look different in its particulars for different people, the liberation of each is bound up together with all others'. The processes and practices by which critical awareness and transformation occur will not leave the structures and cultures the same as they were.

Conclusion: The Dilemma

To many restorative justice practitioners, "restorative policing" is nonsensical. I propose instead to see any attempt to place restorative justice and policing into conversation as a dilemma. The first part of this dilemma is that a holistically restorative approach to policing ultimately entails the community reducing, to the greatest extent possible, any reliance upon police. There are many situations for which police are frequently the first called, though they may be the least well-suited or trained for such situations. Mental health crises, medical emergencies, family crises, dire financial situations, situations arising around lack of housing and substance abuse/addiction, or circumstances best addressed by a social worker all come to mind as situations where an armed officer of the state on hyper-alert is not a good responder. Reducing—or eliminating—reliance on policing as we know it requires that communities build capacities and locate resources that can more directly and effectively respond to many difficult situations that arise. These are precisely the kinds of initiatives and resources that the members of the restorative justice hub network are building up and spreading in their collaborations across Chicago.

At the same time, many of the communities I observed and followed in Chicago have minimal control over the level of policing they experience. They are policed. This reality, shaped, as we have seen, by classist and racist histories, requires relentlessly calling this to attention and challenging it. Many of the "crimes" named as such because of these racist and classist histories and structures will have to be decriminalized (drug use, homelessness, "quality of life" offenses, among others). Government resources and programs will have to be reappropriated and restructured in order to address these issues in constructive and life-affirming ways. And groups of people will also have to be "decriminalized." This must occur, for example, through implicit bias training on the part of law enforcement, and the examination, unlearning, and transformation of dominant cultural scripts. This is especially true for the Black and Brown youth and young adults whom police (and many White people in general) implicitly or explicitly—and erroneously—presume to be, perceive, and fear as "dangerous" or "criminal."[2]

At the same time, reducing policing and the community's reliance on policing as much as possible—and exposing and challenging unjust profiling, criminalization, and policing strategies that target poor and communities of color—cannot simply altogether eliminate efforts to cultivate relationships with police. Within a holistic restorative justice framing, such relationship building may hold out a hope for change in community-police relations as one avenue to changing policing practices and strategies. This can occur, for example, when police perceptions of Black and Brown young people are altered through stereotype replacement, counter-stereotypic imaging, individuation, perspective taking, and increasing opportunities for positive contact with people of color.[3] On a practical level, it is also necessary since restorative practitioners will, for the time being, inevitably continue to have contact with police and the rest of the criminal justice system. This horn of the dilemma is that community members must remain vigilant that any such interaction, relationship, and trust building not be perceived as diminishing the need for systemic transformation of the criminal justice system and reduction of policing institutions as they currently exist.

When I asked Sarah Staudt, the attorney at Lawndale Christian Legal Center, whether the community restorative justice hub network could work restoratively with the police, her response was cautious. "As a defense attorney, I know that there are systemic problems that you can't solve by having individual cops be invested in restorative justice, as great as that is," she explained. While willing to hope for and imagine possibilities of systemic change in the Chicago Police Department, she was more than a little skeptical of the likelihood of this actually occurring in the near future. The possibilities of such developments contrast starkly with the daily realities she faces around policing and its effects on the young people she works with in Lawndale. Sarah spoke to me of frequent incidents of police officers arresting kids for things they did not do, and of police brutality—which, she says, many of the young people at LCLC experience regularly.

> There are things that can be fixed and healed in circle. But unless you're going to get every single possible police commander and police officer in circle, I just don't think . . . Personally, [I think] there are bigger things that need to happen about the culture of the Chicago Police Department before we will see a restorative justice approach create meaningful large-scale change. Now, it has a meaningful effect on the kids that are involved, and probably the officers that are involved. Most of those officers, though, are not "beat officers,"[4] they are not "undercover buy"[5] officers, they're CAPS [community policing] officers. They are the people who are already invested in community growth. It's going to have to run deeper than that. It's going to [have to] reach officers who are beat cops, who are going to have regular interactions with our kids. So far, I have not seen a program like that. I would love to, but I haven't seen one yet.

I asked her whether she sees interaction with CPD officers in restorative justice settings making specific differences to the youth and young adults whom she works with in North Lawndale. Her answer was, again, ambivalent. Referring to a Chicago Police Department Bridging the Divide dialogue between local Lawndale youth and police from the community policing initiative, she explained,

> It gives our youth an outlet to talk about what's going on in their lives and what's going on in their interactions with police. It gives the police a chance to hear what they are seeing, but it also does what restorative justice does—it helps people see each other as people. It was a great conversation and a turning point for some of our kids, having a little bit more of a nuanced view of the Chicago police, whether any individual officer they encounter may or may not be out to get them. Unfortunately, as a lawyer, given the systemic problems in the Chicago Police Department, I haven't seen the systemic changes yet. When I do, I think as that happens I really hope that restorative justice is part of it. As we address as a city what is wrong with the CPD—and *everything* that is wrong with the CPD—[I think I hope for] reconciliation [like] in South Africa, [that] kind of major large-scale healing. . . . I hope that we *really* do that in our

communities. So far, we are doing piecemeal, little things. But if it was part of *systemic* change, I'm all in.[6]

Two things became clear to me about the possibility of a restorative approach to policing during my days in Back of the Yards and Lawndale. The first is that restorative justice can make positive and powerful interpersonal impacts on individual community-police relations, on the basis of which broader changes gradually can be built. Numerous officers have trained in peacemaking circles and incorporated what they learned into their work in communities, as well as into their approach to policing through "officer only" circles.[7] The second is that culture and practices of policing in Chicago must transform at a fundamental level in order to be compatible with a holistic approach to restorative justice. On this, there was uniform agreement among the community practitioners across Chicago whom I interviewed. Such a fundamental change would have to occur through systematic transformation from within the CPD culture and institution itself.

14

The Price of a Powerful Slogan Is a Concrete, Constructive Alternative

Transformation beyond the "Abolition versus Reform" Dichotomy

To this point, I have gradually built the case that a holistic account of restorative justice can be a theory of justice and can form concrete justice practices because it fosters modes of association between people that are moral and spiritual. My central contention is that the transformational power of restorative justice depends on understanding and developing these often implicit moral and spiritual dynamics. This chapter and the next work in tandem to further illuminate the religious and ethical dimensions of restorative justice initiatives and practices. They also respond to key objections to this way of understanding restorative justice.

It is especially important to assess how restorative justice ethics and practices reflect various elements of commitment, self-understandings, relationality, and motivations sometimes considered to be "religious." Doing so responds to two high-stakes questions for the restorative justice movement as it has unfolded in the United States from the 1970s to the present. First, what does it mean to resist mass incarceration in ways that can concretely challenge and actually transform its causes, conditions, and impact, rather than merely reconfiguring its surface-level features while (however inadvertently) perpetuating the deeper forms of violence it effects? Second, what difference does it make to rail against the system with utopian demands to "abolish it all now"? These questions ask about the viability of the movement for "prison abolition" in the United States and the roles that restorative justice can (or cannot) play within that movement.

Assessing and explicating restorative justice practices through lenses of everyday or lived religion should enrich our understanding of their critical and transformational potential. These categories highlight the moral and spiritual dynamics in the forms of association that restorative justice promotes, and that make possible the transformation of structural injustices. Moreover, they do this by helping us see how concrete social practices of restorative justice move through and beyond the two poles of an alleged "abolition versus reform" dichotomy, incorporating the strengths and best insights of each while overcoming their respective weaknesses.

In terms of scholarly discourse, this argument dislodges restorative justice from its placement within a polarized framing of "the secular" versus "the religious," as currently forwarded by some religious studies scholars.[1] In so doing, it challenges portrayals of the religious dynamics of restorative justice as a vacuous "spirituality." It further challenges the claim that this (allegedly) vacuous spirituality, in fact, is evidence that restorative justice has become a vague "nonreligious" form of religion that is permitted by the secular state. As this account would have it, the state permits restorative justice to exist as diversionary practices that can only leave intact the systemic injustices of mass incarceration by which the (White, settler colonial, carceral) state imposes and reinforces its power.

Abolition and Its Temptations

Prison abolition is a movement that seeks to eliminate the prison system and criminal justice system as they have emerged in the United States since the 1960s. It is a loosely grouped coalition of affinity organizations and figures. In the details, their agendas vary. They find common cause in three central demands: (1) "moratorium" (stop building prisons), (2) "decarceration" (remove people from prisons), and (3) "excarceration" (divert people away from the prison-industrial complex to begin with). Self-described abolitionists demand structural and cultural changes in how we think about and respond to "crime" in the United States. They point out that incarceration ultimately perpetuates the very condition it purports to address. Another point on which abolitionists tend to converge is that reducing and ultimately eliminating incarceration and policing will require transforming its causes and conditions through policy and countermeasures. These include eliminating poverty, homelessness, substance abuse, and addiction; combating the criminalization of these conditions; and providing adequate education, health care, and mental health care. Further, prison abolitionists reframe the discussion by instead posing the question, How do we create a society that has no need for prisons and policing? Generally, they organize and advocate for societal conditions that would make policing and incarceration obsolete (for example, redirecting policing and prison funding to provide the kinds of health care, housing, education, and good jobs that would promote such conditions).[2]

Certain streams of the contemporary prison abolition movement have deeply religious roots and emerge from religiously identified quarters.[3] Many people in this part of the movement hold up restorative justice as part of the alternative that will replace the criminal justice system and mass incarceration. This sets up a series of challenging and highly contested questions about how restorative justice ought to be conceived and how such practices and initiatives must be implemented in order to alter current conditions. These claims risk dividing the ranks of both restorative justice practitioners and prison abolition activists.

Some critics claim that, because restorative justice is primarily or exclusively concerned with healing and various forms of reconciliation, it can be "justice"—the virtue according to which each person receives what is due them—in name only. Insofar as its goal is reconciliation or forgiveness between victims and the person who caused the harm, these critics claim, restorative justice illegitimately imposes a religious vision (whether explicit or tacit) on any who participate. Thus, they argue, restorative justice might be appropriate for certain private and religiously identified contexts such as churches, mosques, synagogues, temples, religious community settings, or societies sharing broad consensus on specific religious practice. However, the religious dimensions of restorative justice present a liability that makes it unfit for a public life as religiously diverse and morally plural—and, at times, religiously contentious and conflicted—as that of the United States. For these critics, if restorative justice is to be workable in public life, civil society, and justice system settings, it must sublimate any explicit religious dimensions.[4]

Other critics, by contrast, celebrate the claim that restorative justice is religious in its history and character. Indeed, they claim, it is religious at its core. To deploy it in ways that obscure or play down its religious identification is to capitulate to secularism—whether militant or creeping. This is secularism understood as the sequestering of religious belief and practice to the personal and interior. Further, according to this concern, the "secular" lays claim to a legal-political and cultural regime where an allegedly religiously neutral state determines what counts as "religion." It then determines which religions, and which of their forms, get recognized as legitimate or illegitimate in state-sanctioned public, political life (and sometimes even in matters of private—or "sincerely held"— belief).[5] To deploy restorative justice authentically, then, one must refuse to dilute or weaken its religiousness. It is in its unapologetic religiousness that restorative justice can stand starkly over against (can "confront and refuse") the essential violence of the US prison-industrial complex.

According to these voices, erasing the essential religiousness of restorative justice domesticates it. It breaks off its critical edges. It does so most insidiously through appeals to the bland, reformist "spirituality" permitted by the secular state, and cultural secularity more generally. In numerous contexts around the world, such appeals to the "spiritual" qualities of restorative justice allegedly invoke and camouflage themselves in indigenous peoples' justice and peacemaking practices, the trimmings of which then get amalgamated with New Age "self-help" jargon and sensibilities. As a result, restorative justice practices that are authentic—whether cast in an originary biblical language of peaceableness such as Jewish or Christian conceptions of Shalom,[6] or in terms of some other substantial religious tradition—must "enact a higher law diametrically opposed to the myopic and violent law of the state."[7]

This either/or framing of restorative justice, as I have summarized it here, presents a dichotomy that I argue is both theoretically problematic and likely to be self-defeating in practice. This framing presents "the state" as the realm of secularity, violence, and oppression, and religion as the purveyor of a "higher law" that underwrites a genuine restorative justice that can altogether abolish and replace, as opposed to reform, the violent laws of the state. Such a vision claims that restorative justice must formally declare its religious sources in order to maintain a genuinely oppositional, card-carrying abolitionist integrity. Otherwise, restorative justice becomes a domesticated, "spiritualized" (and thus secular) reformism that leaves intact and subtly perpetuates the violence intrinsic to the secular state.[8]

As a historical matter of fact, restorative justice is neither essentially rooted in a single historical religious tradition nor necessarily religious or theological. At the same time, versions of restorative justice that do emerge from religious or theological traditions need not be transposed into an allegedly secular (nonreligious or anti-religious) register in order to contribute to practices that can transform structural violence and systemic injustice.[9] The either/or framing positions religion, as bearer of a "higher law," against an intrinsically violent secular statecraft. Such a framing is likely to be self-defeating precisely because it overlooks the ambivalences, partialities, and messiness of the sometimes explicitly theological but often informally lived religion and ethical humanisms in and through which the halting, piecemeal, but genuine resistance to—and transformation of—the structural and cultural violence of the US prison-industrial complex sometimes occurs. To claim that commitment to an explicitly religious "prison abolitionism" is the only position for authentic restorative justice is as one-sided as the corresponding claim that secularity is intrinsically violent. This argument mistakes the correct identification of the US criminal justice system as "a system that is broken and cannot be fixed" (and that, therefore, must be challenged and transformed) for a categorical rejection of "secular state law" as "myopically" violent. The latter does not necessarily follow from the former.

It is true that the modern state is an entity identified, in part, by its capacity to legitimately deploy coercive physical force. As Max Weber put it, for example, the modern state simply is that institutional and bureaucratic apparatus that establishes "a monopoly on the legitimate use of physical force within a particular territory."[10] This includes the use of physical force to administer its laws and maintain the integrity of its borders, among others. The state can wield coercive and deadly force through its military and police. It deploys force (or the threat of it) through numerous administrative means as well. Moreover, manifestations of state institutions can be (or become) structurally violent. The US prison-industrial complex is surely an example of both the direct and structural violence of the state run out of control.

At the same time, for Weber, the state has as its basis a *human* community—a community of people and citizens—that constitutes and administers it. In a constitutional, liberal-democratic state, the state's operations are accountable to the rule of law, constitutional principles, and a range of checks and balances on both state uses of coercive force and the conception of justice these purport to entail. The state's uses of coercive force are, in principle, subject to measures of legitimacy as well as moral and legal constraints. The citizens of a democratic polity share the responsibility of holding the state accountable for illegitimate or abusive uses of physical force, the passage and implementation of unjust laws, and other forms of violence perpetrated by the state and state actors. At times, citizens of a democratic polity will need to resist and work to change the state. They may appeal to supernational measures of legitimacy such as human rights norms or international institutions and conventions to do so.

At its best, the restorative justice movement in the United States is an example of resistance to both structural and direct forms of state violence, as well as the private corporate and economic interests that interweave with these and the deformed cultural norms of retributive justice that underwrite them. It is a movement to transform the causes and conditions of all these forms of violence. And while organized religious traditions and resources can and do contribute powerfully to this movement, they do so no more than do the forms of lived religion, spirituality, and ethical humanisms that restorative justice norms and practices also embody.

Rather than mere piecemeal reform, the US prison-industrial complex as it currently exists and operates must be changed at a fundamental level. However, to be other than utopian, any talk of "abolishing" the current system must coincide with constructive, practicable alternatives that form the actual work of dismantling. Otherwise, the relentless criticism of things as they exist risks miring the movement for substantial, constructive change in terminally deconstructive, wishful thinking—purporting to somehow altogether leap outside the context of the modern state or "the secular" via "the religious." The rhetoric of such relentless criticism tends to be broadly unpersuasive to many people working in local communities—or, if received as persuasive, then it tends to be terminally wistful precisely because it is self-styled as "truly radical." (This is often a luxury of academics, among other privileged peoples.)

Rallying resistance around the demands to immediately and altogether abolish status quo conditions and institutions brings with it the risk of losing sight of the everyday struggles and commonplace steps, sometimes grinding and mundane, that are necessary to achieve the goals in question. Keeanga-Yamahtta Taylor powerfully captures this caution against downplaying or refusing concern for gradual reforms attainable in the present in favor of calls to radically change the very character of American society: "Demanding everything is as ineffective as demanding nothing, because it obscures what that struggle looks like on a daily basis," she writes, referring to the Movement for Black Lives. "It can also be demoralizing because when the goal is everything, it is impossible to measure the small but important steps forward that are the wellspring of the movement."[11]

Transformation beyond Abolition versus Reform

Restorative justice need not lock itself into an abolition/reform dichotomy to effectively challenge and, over time, transform in practice the structural and cultural violence of the prison-industrial complex. But the abolitionists are correct to point out the risks of co-optation present in "reform." To avoid this, restorative justice advocates must integrate critical analysis with constructive and pragmatic counterproposals, practices, and initiatives, and they must identify, critically assess, and practically and transformatively address the very causes and conditions of the prison-industrial complex—the elements that enabled its emergence and perpetuate it even now. Otherwise, changes become surface-level alterations by which, under a new guise, previous dynamics of social control, exclusion, and humiliation persist, and even become worse. If the movement is to successfully build itself, restorative justice initiatives must intervene *transformationally* in the violence and injustice that the contemporary justice system perpetrates. Transformation is key to mediating the abolition/reform dichotomy.

What goes into "transformation"? Restorative justice, as should be evident from the stories in this book, does not suggest a "one size fits all" approach to change. Transformation is radical in that, to the degree that it occurs, it reconceives the institutions of justice in US society, implementing alternate practices in their place. Yet what this actually looks like will vary on a case-by-case basis. At times transformation may look like "abolition," in the sense of replacing state programs and institutions as they currently exist with community-based and community-led alternatives. For example, Precious Blood Ministry of Reconciliation piloted neighborhood response teams in Back of the Yards (as alternatives to direct notification of police) in 2021. A similar example is the successful effort to pass legislation that protects restorative justice conferences (of whatever form or location) with legal "privilege," so that anything communicated during the practice is confidential, and cannot simply be appropriated and used by the criminal justice system.

At times, transformation may look like relentlessly critical collaboration with an organization and/or actors within it (perhaps a state organization or specific judges) who are willing to reorient and guide their own practices and understandings according to the substantive norms and practices of restorative justice. In some cases, it takes the form of a creation of networks of initiatives and practices that operate alongside—in simultaneous critical collaboration with *and* selective refusal of—state operations.[12] At times, it will require a separate set of community-based practices and institutions in contrast to those of the state. Instead of proposing a single type of practice, I think it is better to do what I have done in this book: to engage with particular contexts, cases, and ends in view. I examined what works—and what does not—for the purposes of criticism, resistance, and transformation. What each of these variations will share is their participation in the cumulative and overarching abolition of the US prison-industrial complex.

Such claims are not foreign to the broader movement for prison abolition. As prison abolitionists of the 1970s saw, abolitionism is not about moral posturing, absolutist refusals, or top-down utopian revolutions. It is always a ground-up project of organizing communities at the grassroots and building a sustainable, broad-based movement for societal transformation. It occurs through the cultivation of resilient relationships of compassion and care. This is especially true in communities that have been decimated by the prison-industrial complex.[13] However, if this is the case, then the theoretical arguments for "prison abolition" that are put in terms of religion over against secularity and state violence must, instead, assume a stance of teachability. Those advocating such positions must seek to self-reflexively accompany everyday people in their efforts at resistance and transformation, to listen and learn from them rather than force what they encounter there into prefabricated scholarly schemes. Researchers, activists, and scholar-practitioners must seek to reinforce and amplify the voices of the people who live in places most affected by mass incarceration—who are, tragically, most directly experienced in these matters. For these everyday people are also best positioned to help articulate what resistance can and must look and feel like. They are equipped to guide the rest of us in resisting the local variations of the US prison-industrial complex because they struggle with its realities daily.

As we have seen in the details of my observations and encounters with community actors across Chicago in previous chapters, *accompaniment* embodies ("puts into practice") the central dynamics of the relationality intrinsic to restorative justice, holistically understood. Accompaniment is an ethical practice of "walking alongside" in a spirit of teachability, solidary resolve, and making oneself available to learn from and actively support others. We have seen that many of the people enmeshed in the US prison-industrial complex already know what they need. The imperative for those wishing to alleviate their suffering, and to alter its causes and conditions, is to recognize and then amplify what people in these communities are expressing. As is often the case, it is the people with power whose mentality and culture most need to be changed. "Prison abolition" must be conceptualized from the perspective of, and in dialogue with, those most affected by it.

Any form of praxis that can cut to the level of structural violence and contribute to systemic transformation is *critical* praxis. This, again, is a theoretically informed diagnostic reflection on practice in light of continually unfolding experiences and engagement with practical challenges. Critical praxis does not merely ask, "What is to be done?" in light of "what we know" and "what we have and are experiencing." It also examines the processes and categories by which knowing occurs. It interrogates the presuppositions behind what we claim we know, which often appear to be self-evidently certain. Moreover, it does so with attention to how this kind of knowledge may itself hide, or participate in, the forms of violence and injustice that infect the system against which everyday people are struggling.

Engaging in critical praxis to investigate transformational possibilities requires that we further consider lived religion and the ways this concept takes us beyond an alleged dichotomy between religion and the secular. This means that working toward transformation is not anti-intellectual, anti-theoretical, or anti-"expertise." It is, rather, a task dedicated to *dialectically integrating* experience-tested practice and implementation with a theoretically informed (and self-reflexive) reflection upon those experiences and practices, and then moving to further action. In such an integrative dialectic, which we could also call a transformative dialogue, each learns from, and is refined by, critical engagement and collaboration with the other. This is critical praxis.[14]

Carving up these processes in terms of "religious" versus "secular," and construing them as examples of retrievals (or resurgences) of the religious and/or theological over against secular state violence and/or "the secular" more generally, shoehorns a diverse array of community-based, on-the-ground realities into a prefabricated scholars' schema. It forces lived practices of restorative justice initiatives into the confines of abstract discourse (religious versus secular). The categories of this discourse not only deviate widely from the realities of everyday people and restorative justice practitioners, they also tend to be tone-deaf about the complex—and sometimes ambivalent and conflicting—motivations, interests, and purposes of particular people and groups. Perhaps most significantly, they also wash out the ways that even the most self-identifiably religious initiatives and efforts are shot through and intimately interwoven with many different motivations and collaborating partners, including so-called secular ones. Even the most relentless "abolitionist" efforts interweave with—much as they attempt to resist and alter—institutional and everyday realities of government and law.

To engage communities relationally over time, and through critical participatory action research, is to open oneself to possibilities of radical transformation that look markedly different from what the terms of the scholarly debates anticipate or permit. The practices and initiatives I encountered across the South and West Sides of Chicago are sometimes halting and partial. They may take on—at times, unavoidably—work that engages government actors and institutions, even as many espouse radically transforming the criminal justice system as it currently exists in favor of a vision centered on restorative justice ethics and practices. These practices and initiatives attend to the messy complexities best understood in terms of lived religion as much as lived politics—and the ways these intermingle—in local community settings. These require flexible, multidimensional lenses of analysis, rather than overdetermined categories that have fixated scholars of religion for the past generation. So, what do I propose?

15

Everyday Religion in Unexpected Places

Restorative Justice through Lenses of Lived Religion

Lived religion refers to the practical, daily understandings and sensibilities that might be thought of, broadly, as religious. The practices of lived religion, through which we can often identify corresponding beliefs and commitments, often do not explicitly identify with the "official" teachings or institutionalized practices of organized religious traditions. These everyday features of religion might, therefore, elude attention and analysis if we attend only to traditional, institutional, or expert-oriented accounts of religion. Lived religion, in contrast to institutional religion, can refer to meaning making that takes place through ad hoc practices of piety, reverence, devotion, and informally (or perhaps formally) ritualized action. It may include intentionally "cultural," "nontheistic," or "naturalist" engagement in informal and perhaps even unintended forms of spirituality and commitment.[1] Using the category of lived religion necessitates thickly describing practices and understandings that at first often appear prosaic and mundane.

The key to understanding the significance and power of lived or everyday religion is to begin by, first, taking it on its own terms rather than as a deviation from (or perversion of) a supposed normative "organized," "traditional," or "institutional" religion. When we ask more critically about what we mean by "religious" and "spiritual" practices and understandings, we may find such practices of meaning making, and their impact, in places and in forms that are unexpected. Such forms would not be illuminated by the categories of "organized religion" or "the religious" (as counter to "the secular").

Lived religious practices tend to complicate and sometimes challenge institutionalized, "official," and "expert-authorized" accounts of religion. It is nonetheless important to emphasize that there are not hard-and-fast dichotomies between these categories. Lived religion directs attention to "institutions *and* persons, texts *and* rituals, practice *and* theology, things *and* ideas—all as media of making and unmaking worlds."[2] The study of lived religion positions "being religious"—that is, religious practice and conceptualization—as cultural work.

The work of lived religion is "cultural" in several ways. First, it is always historically situated and socially embodied in specific times and places. As such, it is located within the commonplace affairs of people's ordinary lives rather than set apart from them as an alternative. It is "cultural work" in that particular people's ways of encountering, coping with, and acting on the world around them are usually developed in dialogue with cultural idioms and practices. Through these, people make sense of their world and engage in meaning making that filters and shapes their experiences; the idioms and practices are then often further shaped by these emerging experiences and meanings, and so on.

The critical tendencies facilitated by attending to lived religion often gesture in the direction of religious innovation, imagination, and creativity. Focusing on lived religion, however, also foregrounds messy partialities, ambivalences, and perhaps even errant inventions that follow from the ordinary experiences, understandings, sense making, and coping of everyday people. Attending to this aspect of "religious experience" requires the kinds of descriptive analyses of restorative justice ethics, practices, and initiatives that I undertook across Chicago.

Restorative justice has an array of historical origins and sources, is conceptualized in manifold ways, and is implemented in a variety of configurations. It is constituted by a historically instituted set of practices that are as dynamic as the communities in which they developed. It is precisely this internal diversity that affords restorative justice ethics and practices a hybridity and flexibility that can accommodate numerous specific religious and moral traditions, as well as ethical humanisms and nontheistic philosophies. For many of its current practitioners, it is a mode of finding a deeply religious form of relationality and community in and through which healing, repair, and resilience—relationally conceived—become possible. For others, it is a means of sustaining practices they describe as "spiritual." Indeed, restorative justice practices and understandings give tangible content to what some people mean when they depict their participation in these initiatives as "spiritual but *not* religious."[3]

Restorative Justice as "Spiritual but Not Religious"

The claim of an increasing number of people to be "spiritual but not religious" has vexed scholarly assessment of contemporary US religiosity in recent decades. Customarily, sociologists and political scientists deposit such self-characterizations in the catch-all category of "none" or "no religion" ("religious nones"). The "nones" are survey respondents who, when presented with the standardized slate of survey or polling questions, check the box "none" when asked to identify their religious tradition or denomination.[4] From time to time, appeals to "spirituality" get altogether dismissed. At other times, they are characterized as vague and indeed vacuous sensibilities.[5] "Spiritual" (allegedly) intimates a generic divinity or source of values—that is to say, people who claim to be spiritual have a notion of God, "the divine," or "the spiritual" that is particular to no religious tradition, but that is selectively amalgamated using traits from several. Christian Smith's popular formulation "moralistic therapeutic deism" establishes the spiritual but not religious person as one who has some notion of a God who wants people to be happy and nice to each another, and as further believing that spirituality's main purpose is "therapeutic"—promoting personal development and self-satisfaction, perhaps combating addiction or otherwise offering coping mechanisms in the face of personal challenges, and offering calm in the face of anxieties.[6]

Some political-theological accounts see the so-called spiritualization of restorative justice (where, for example, practitioners recognize early versions of restorative justice values and practices in various indigenous peoples' concepts and practices) in differently pejorative terms. These critics see such spiritualization as the process of diluting and secularizing authentic religion, and thus (however inadvertently) allowing it to be obscured if not co-opted by secular state violence. As noted in the previous chapter, this carves out dichotomous categories of "religious" and "secular," and shunts "spirituality" into the secular. "Spiritual but not religious" then becomes a covert operating term by which the violence intrinsic to secular state justice bends to its own purposes the authentic opposition and resistance afforded by the genuinely religious origins and core of restorative justice.[7]

Many of the restorative justice practitioners we encountered in previous chapters describe their work as "spiritual." Some anchor that description in the spiritual practices and understandings of a specific religious tradition or affiliation. Others do not. Indeed, some contrast their work in restorative justice with organized, institutional religion altogether, but may still describe it as having "spiritual" qualities. In this way, restorative justice demonstrates the flexibility and dynamism of lived religion, even while participants may avoid the characterization of their practices as formally inspired by, or an extension of, a religious tradition. They report instead, simply, that these are the values and understandings they employ to engage the world around them. These values and understandings enable them to develop and sustain durable relationships and communal bonds, and to withstand and constructively counter multilayered forms of violence that assail their communities. These restorative justice values and practices, as they tell it, are "spiritual" in the sense that they allow for the intentional cultivation and rehabilitation of resilient interpersonal bonds and communities decimated by the violence of the prison-industrial complex.

Sometimes participants who invoke the word "spiritual" gesture toward "something more" or "bigger" that occurs in this.[8] Sometimes they do not. Nonetheless, in practice—and even among those who do not invoke the word at all—there is consistent agreement that restorative justice is a way of building and sustaining relationships of trust and practices of mutual care, compassion, respect, critical empathy, accountability, and repair. Practitioners identify these as constituent features of the "co-creation of community" that promotes the flourishing of all the people involved, and that would not be available to them otherwise. Practitioners I encountered all across Chicago associated these with the so-called spiritual dynamics of restorative justice. A perception of "more" may occur when the slow and sometimes arduous cultivation of relationships, and the manifold practices of striving to "co-create community" through a holistic vision of restorative justice, engender some sense of a "whole greater than the sum of its parts"—that is, individuals participating in something larger than themselves, though each person remains individual and distinct. This is the case whether or not participants are willing to invoke—or conversely, intentionally avoid—a notion of "God" or "religion" alongside that claim.

Just as importantly, these dimensions of practice are motivated by and organized around an ideal vision of justice that is relational and participatory and culminates in what philosophers of restorative justice refer to as "inclusive nondomination."[9] I would describe this as a trust that this vision of the reduction of violence in all its forms and the cultivation of justice most fundamentally consists in ennobling and enabling relationships of mutual recognition, reciprocal respect, compassion, and accountability. These values and practices are oriented by and aim toward a (sometimes tacit) conception of human dignity and thriving.[10] Clearly, accountability, compassion, and substantive relationship building for the purposes of creating a justice that heals, resists, and counteracts violence in all its forms make restorative justice a form of moral practice. How might it be described as "spiritual" in anything more than a vague and domesticating sense? Here the concept of lived religion becomes helpfully illuminating.

Varieties of "Spiritual"

In the context of her broader work on lived religion, Nancy Ammerman has challenged the disparaging dismissal of everyday or vernacular uses of the term "spiritual" by developing a taxonomy of common uses of the word.[11] She found that people often use the term "spiritual" in meaningful ways across what she calls four broad "cultural packages."

The first of these ways of using the word "spiritual" conveys an explicitly theistic association. In these contexts, "spirituality is about God; spirituality is about practices intended to develop one's relationship with God; and spirituality is about the mysterious encounters and happenings that come to those who are open to them."[12] Those that fall in the second group use "spiritual" in a way that is not grounded in theistic belief but instead invoke "a different kind of transcendence, of experiences 'bigger than me' and beyond the ordinary."[13] This second range of uses portrays "spiritual" as some sense of the person, in effect, pulled out of a self-focused individuality and toward recognition of the importance of one's interrelatedness and mutual interdependence with others. This sense of "spiritual" may also point to awe-inspiring encounters with nature and various forms of beauty that evoke acknowledgment of human dependence on the natural world. Such experiences transcend a narrow self-focus, but not necessarily in ways reliant on belief in divinity or anything supernatural.

A third "cultural package" of vernacular uses of the word "spiritual" revolves around various ethical senses of the term. Here people use the word to refer to efforts to live "a virtuous life, one characterized by helping others, transcending one's own selfish interests to seek what is right."[14] This way of speaking uses the word "spiritual" as a catch-all term covering sensitivity to the needs of others, compassionate responsiveness, and an ensuing effort to strive for meaning and significance in helping others and seeking justice as a central part of living a good life. This sense of "spiritual" as "striving to live a good life" by seeking the good of others is, in Ammerman's study, often simultaneously invoked by those who also fall into the previous two groups (in other words, by theists and nontheists alike).

Finally, the fourth "cultural package" she identifies includes those who describe as "spiritual" their association with the values, teachings, and/or culture of a religious tradition or group, even if this has no explicitly theistic significance for the person—for example, the "spiritual" sensibility of someone who adheres to "cultural (nontheistic) Judaism" or "cultural Catholicism," Buddhism, and so forth.

The nontheistic, humanistic, or moral senses of "spiritual" that some practitioners ascribe to restorative justice do not stand at odds with practitioners who associate the term with an explicit religious tradition. Indeed, some think that it is precisely the expansive sense of the moral and spiritual dynamics of restorative justice ethics that enables its practices to work within and alongside various religious traditions and different conceptions of justice and mercy.[15] For these practitioners, the spiritual ethos of restorative justice ethics and practices marks out a space in which particular religious traditions and/or philosophical conceptions of personhood can find some degree of overlapping consensus.[16] People coming from different starting points can therefore find important points of agreement in theory and practice without claiming that they share an identical core, that their respective motivating commitments are ultimately the same, or that they can be reduced to a single, shared religious common denominator. As a result, even practitioners who do not identify with a particular religious worldview or tradition can enter into the relational framework that fits with restorative justice ethics.

For Ammerman, this taxonomy suggests conceptual coherence in the range of ways that the word "spiritual" is used both by people who self-identify as "religious" and by those who describe themselves as "nonreligious." She challenges presumed and fairly rigid definitional binaries of "the religious" versus "the spiritual." Understanding this spectrum of coherent and meaningful uses cuts against the grain of prevailing treatments, which construe the term "spiritual" as vacuous, if not altogether incoherent, or, at best, code-speak for self-help therapy.

Rather than a fixed typology or a description of unchanging essences,[17] Ammerman's study provides a helpful heuristic tool. Its range can help us understand sometimes pronounced and sometimes subtle differences and a range of family resemblances that occur across the array of uses of the word "spiritual" in the contexts of the restorative justice practices that I describe in this book.[18] I encountered variations of each of these uses of the word "spiritual" at some point among the different people I interviewed. Sometimes there was more than one sense present in a given case. Which one(s) may be most pertinent depends upon the person and circumstance.

As I mentioned earlier, I observed two senses of the word "spiritual" as used by restorative justice community members who disavow being "religious." The first coheres with the sense of "spiritual" as some "sense of transcendence," understood as moving "beyond the ordinary," often in relation to a community with a shared sense of interrelation and mutual interdependence (Ammerman's "package 2"). This was exemplified in what practitioners refer to as the "co-creation of community." The "co-" prefix here is crucial, for it marks out the presence of the individuals who work together with others to create and sustain resilient community. The creation of "community," as we have seen, does not supplant or dissolve the individuality of particular persons. Quite the opposite. The practices of co-creating community are collaborative, simultaneously illuminating particularity and aiding the individual in developing her distinctiveness and irreplaceability. However, they do so in and through the relationships that are central to who she is becoming.

The second sense I observed is a sense of "spiritual" compassion and care for others that leads people to move beyond a focus on the self. Doing so allows an individual to seek the good of others as part of striving to live an ethical life ("package 3"). Thus, so-called spiritual dynamics occur in the conception of a relational, interdependent account of individual personhood. They also occur through the expression of this relational account in practices of the co-creation of community, and alongside these, emerging forms of accountability, compassion, care, and efforts at healing and repairing harms. These practices generate the senses of "spiritual" with reference to restorative justice, whatever other senses of "spiritual" might be ascribed to it from explicitly theistic and/or religious tradition-based approaches.

The "spiritual" and "moral" dynamics of restorative justice inform and inflect the kind of justice that it conceptualizes, and that its practices seek to embody. These senses of the "spiritual" occur through the relational ethics of restorative justice and the account of justice that this ethical framework entails. Both of these aspire toward an ideal of relational justice. The actual results and achievements of restorative justice practice may be perennially partial compared with this ideal. But achieving some balance between the real circumstances they work within and the ideal for which they strive frames the expansive senses in which the conceptions and lived practices of restorative justice are "spiritual."[19]

Forms of Moral and Spiritual Association in a Framework of Lived Religion

As I observed them, these senses of the moral and spiritual dynamics of restorative justice come into view especially clearly when assessed in terms of lived or everyday religion. Restorative justice practices can be seen, most pointedly, as forms of "meaning making" in the face of nihilism. This is not "nihilism" conceived as a philosophical doctrine according to which values are claimed to have no basis in metaphysical or religious foundations. This is, as Cornel West describes, "nihilism" as a lived reality—the pervasive and persistent experience of "the loss of hope and absence of meaning," and the various attempts to deal with the onslaught of such meaninglessness that harm oneself, others, and the community. These are recurrent dynamics of communities that have been victimized by the forms of violence and marginalization characteristic of the US prison-industrial complex, and the New Jim Crow more specifically.[20] So understood, nihilism is a lived reality of despair and lovelessness, typically coinciding with "a numbing detachment from others and a self-destructive disposition toward the world"—"a disease of the soul."[21] Conceived in this way, nihilism cannot be countered by abstract philosophical arguments. Rather, it must be "tamed by love and care," as West argues, because "any disease of the soul must be conquered by a turning of one's soul . . . through affirmation of one's worth—an affirmation fueled by the concern of others" and equally by the quest for reclamation of community-sustaining, individual-dignifying practices of justice.[22]

To describe restorative justice as a form of "meaning making" that promotes forms of association that are moral and spiritual through everyday practices of mutual recognition, reciprocal respect, critical empathy, compassion, and care is not to reduce it to an introspective, personal, "internal" enterprise. Restorative justice practices are public, shared, organized social practices of community formation and maintenance, as well as individual capacity building and the cultivation of self-reliance. What I identify as the moral and spiritual dynamics of restorative justice occur in the training for such relational—and in some forms, ritual-like and intentional—ethical practices of cultivating compassion, accountability, repair of harm, and the forms of individual agency and community building that emerge from them. Restorative justice thus becomes a purposeful form of meaning making that consists in the cultivation of durable and resilient community relationships that are built on shared dignity and amplify the purposefulness of the individual participants. These are interlocking purposes that are facilitated through the moral and spiritual dynamics of restorative justice practices. The terms "lived religion" and "everyday religion" help highlight these aspects of restorative justice. Just as importantly, they move beyond any counterproductive "secular" versus "religious" dichotomy.

Accordingly, describing the relationality and meaning making of restorative justice as, in various senses, "spiritual" need not be disparaged as diluting or intrinsically at odds with its openly theological or traditionally religious versions. Nor need it be construed as its co-optation by secularism. Ammerman's investigation of how ordinary people use the term sketches the ways that these different senses of "spiritual" have coherent meanings and significant content if we listen carefully. And while different, those senses need not be construed as mutually exclusive or at odds with each other.

Approached as forms of lived religion and everyday senses of "spiritual," these descriptions of restorative justice can be understood and examined on their own terms on a case-by-case basis. For it is the moral and spiritual resonances of its relational dynamics that afford these practices the power to cut against the neoliberal conception of the discrete, rational self whose choosing and acting, if it cannot be disciplined of its own accord, must be disciplined and corrected by the structures and practices of mass incarceration.

Conclusion

In many cases the practitioners, activists, and neighborhood people we have encountered use the term "spiritual" to describe a basic reverence for the interrelationality and communal bonds that are integral to human personhood and to the communities where particular persons are embedded. These values and commitments are indispensable for human flourishing and require intentional cultivation and protection. These are the aspects of individual personhood and community that the prison-industrial complex violates.[23] These practitioners share the view that the violation of relationships is at the heart of harm, destructive conflict, and violence in all its forms. Restorative justice practices are means for cultivating a refusal to dominate (and thereby dehumanize) persons and fragment communities—two pervasive effects of US hyper-incarceration.

Restorative justice offers methodical ethical practices of self-formation and community formation, spiritual sustenance, and care for one another. At their best, the restorative justice practices and initiatives I have encountered in Chicago embody dialogical understanding and critical reflection in the midst of lived experience that issues in transformational action in and upon the world. Reflection on these actions then further expands and clarifies the critical awareness and consciousness of its participants, feeding back into and motivating further action.[24] This complex integration of reflection and action aims to transform structures and cultures, ultimately, for the purposes of liberation.[25]

Restorative justice, thus, opens up highly complex forms of individual and community agency in local, everyday contexts. Properly conceived, restorative justice is not a "more humane," "kinder," "gentler" mode of disciplining and promoting compliance among people who are otherwise (allegedly) likely to "be offenders." These practices do not impose a set of rules for those whose bodies and actions are deemed "unruly," liable to "delinquency," and criminalized by the US prison-industrial complex. Rather, the explicit ethical framework, values, and practices of restorative justice aim to facilitate and amplify the agency of individuals at the same time that they promote the co-creation of a more just community through the building of relationships between individuals. As a critical praxis, it can enable the very people who suffer violence in different forms to achieve a critical understanding of the nature and character of the oppression they confront, and then to speak out, organize, and act to change its causes and conditions.

For all of these reasons, the restorative practices I describe promote modes of association that are moral and spiritual. Indeed, it is the spiritual and moral flexibility, as well as the hybridity, of restorative justice philosophies and practices that makes them able to cut to the root of the structural and cultural violence as well as systemic injustice of US mass incarceration. Further, it allows them to do so in potentially transformational ways. Practitioners are not engaged in sentimental spontaneity, New Age spiritualism, or self-help "navel-gazing."[26] There is always the risk that restorative justice practices might degenerate into rote, formulaic applications for instrumental purposes like reducing recidivism. However, at their best they engage in informal and ad hoc forms of awareness of, critical consciousness about, and resistance to multiple forms of violence as part of promoting a holistic vision of relationality, dignity, and flourishing.

But the constructive purposes of restorative justice are equally essential. Over time, these practices have the capacity to make explicit and actively cultivate capacities for building sustainable relationships of trust and mutual accountability through self-disclosure, truth telling, attuned listening, tailored responsiveness, and repair. Such practices and relationships can prove durable in the face of persisting conflicts and harms. They help illuminate, resist, and transform forms of violence that imbue the structures and cultures of the contexts in which they dwell. In this, restorative justice practices must be situational, organic, dynamic, and bottom-up, rather than top-down, universal, and generic.

Conclusion

How to "Change It All": Small but Important Steps toward a Transformational Social Movement

Throughout this book, I have built the case that restorative justice, holistically construed, is properly understood as a form of justice that emerges from the relational dynamics of personhood and community. Centering these relational dynamics also illuminates restorative justice as an encompassing, coherent range of purposeful ethical practices. I have argued that these can foster forms of association between people that are moral and spiritual. I demonstrated that the character and impact of such forms of association can be helpfully illuminated through lenses of lived or everyday religion. The features of such association include mutual recognition, reciprocal respect, critical empathy, compassion, and approaches to accountability that aim to heal, repair harms, and address needs in ways that promote the well-being of all the people involved in a given circumstance and context. The holistic forms of practice that emerge from this understanding of restorative justice can, both in theory and in practice, address systemic injustices and transform structural and cultural forms of violence.

The chapters build toward the key insight that when approached through a holistic restorative justice framework, illumination of, resistance to, and transformation of systemic injustice does not occur after, separately from, or as an adjunct to the cultivation of relationships that are healthy and just. Rather, these occur *in and through* the cultivation of such relationships and the ensuing self-sufficiency and expanded agency that flow from restorative justice practices. This crucial insight opens up possibilities for restorative justice to present practicable, sustainable alternatives to retributive systems and the structural violence they manifest. The forms of moral and spiritual association its relational practices engender can transform the prison-industrial complex and the New Jim Crow.

The community-based and community-led restorative hubs that I examined promote transformation in several ways. They address the harms and needs of all the people in the community who are enmeshed, at whatever level, in the violence perpetrated by the prison-industrial complex. They develop trauma-informed approaches to harms to promote resilience and repair of harms. I have argued that they must orient those trauma-informed approaches in accord with the distinctive relationality at the heart of restorative justice. This enables them to overcome isolation and experiences of stigmatization to help community members organize and amplify their agency. Through this, they work alongside one another to rebuild neighborhoods and cultivate their communities to promote the flourishing of the people there. In so doing, they facilitate people coming together to challenge, resist, and alter the forms of structural and cultural violence perpetrated and sustained by the criminal justice system.

The restorative justice neighborhood hub organizations work across Chicago by opening up spaces that strive to promote safety within neighborhoods—carving out, and then methodically growing outward, spaces characterized by recognition, mutual respect, and care (where, for example, young people feel less like they need to arm themselves or join a gang for a sense of basic safety). This increased safety may be from street violence or police violence. To do this, the hubs practice radical forms of hospitality. They meet and receive any who turn to them "where they are"—welcoming them, and then conveying their openness to them, again, and again, and again. They elicit the harms, needs, and goals of the people they encounter. Practitioners invite them into a relationship of accompaniment on whatever journey may be necessary to heal those harms, meet the needs, and support the pursuit of achieving their goals. This can mean facilitating their capacities and competencies for school and work, finding and maintaining employment, building and sustaining relationships, investing their labor in the community itself, or cultivating resiliency in navigating, resisting, and overcoming the forms of domination they experience through enmeshment in the criminal justice system, or the prison-industrial complex more broadly. Inevitably, it means that restorative justice initiatives and practitioners relentlessly engage the systems and stakeholders that can afford some of the needed resources. They thus maintain relationships with community-based *and* government organizations that can support the neighborhood people who come to the hub organizations. At the same time, they insist on their independence and autonomy vis-à-vis facets of the system, or third-party funders. They also actively engage the system to make changes in policy and law. Finally, mutually supportive, collaborative, integrative growth is both the immediate process and the overarching objective. This forms and aims to persistently further expand and deepen a "learning community" in a citywide network of restorative justice spaces, initiatives, and co-collaborators.

In 2019 the six community restorative justice hubs worked with over 3,100 youth and young adults across several of the neighborhoods in Chicago most beset by violence. They logged over 105,000 hours of contact with participants, their families, and related community members there. These outcomes for 2019 demonstrate a consistent increase from the years immediately prior (744 participants and 40,000 contact hours in 2016; 1,451 participants and 70,000 contact hours in 2017; 2,043 participants and 80,000 contact hours in 2018). Of these participants, 74.8 percent have successfully sustained or completed connections with educational institutions and programs (for example, re-enrolled in school with academic support and sustained attendance, graduated from high school, or completed their GED). Sixty percent of those participants who conveyed needs for housing support were accompanied to find and secure housing. Eighty-five percent of the total participants were accompanied in locating and accessing some community-based organization support they needed. Eighty-two percent of youth and young adults who expressed a need for help with mental health issues or substance abuse were accompanied to successfully access resources. Each of these reflect a dimension of the holistic vision pursued by Chicago's community restorative justice hub network.

The restorative justice hub network that is emerging across Chicago tracks its "connections" and similar numbers to portray the "impact" of the hubs, and the hub network as a whole. Numbers such as these provide a passing snapshot of the size and scope of their work. The number of community restorative hubs continues to grow, and the number of participants and contact hours as well. Yet, as is clear from the voices, stories, and descriptions that fill the preceding chapters, such metrics convey only a small portion of the effect of these initiatives, the different ways they implement a holistic restorative justice vision, and their results.

What the above numbers and the on-the-ground examples of grassroots organizing and movement building I have described gesture toward is the true work of any movement to abolish the prison-industrial complex. Hope to "dismantle and tear down" prisons, "abolish policing," and create a society that does not need prisons and policing can only be predicated on the treatment and transformation of the causes and conditions that keep prisons seemingly indispensable. It also must be predicated on the construction and expansion of actual working, sustainable, transformational replacements for the prior system and ways of doing things. The causes and conditions that must be addressed include, for example, undiagnosed and unaddressed mental health issues and trained crisis response and care; drug addiction and the criminalization of addiction and drug use; inadequate education and vocational schooling resources and opportunities; the inaccessibility of affordable and dignifying housing; cultural scripts that criminalize people of color and poor people of all colors; targeted law enforcement practices and police unaccountability; and other conditions to which policing and mass incarceration are often de facto—though incorrect and ineffective—responses.

Of course, I have also argued that, rhetorically, the abolition/reform dichotomy itself quickly degenerates into an obstruction. As such, it becomes an obstacle to sustaining transformational practices and initiatives. At worst, fixation on the term "abolition" as a litmus test (for example, refusal to work or collaborate with any who do not embrace the term) degenerates into virtue signaling. This can devolve into divisive, fragmenting forms of dogmatism that obstruct the building of a transformational social movement. In fact, those who commit themselves to the term "abolition" must demonstrate realizable, concrete, constructive paths, institutions, and practices by which to replace what currently exists, as well as paths toward abolishing the status quo that are actually walkable. On the other hand, those who focus on visualizing and working toward "realizable reforms" must remain vigilant against falling into collaboration with the prison-industrial complex, however inadvertently. They must also make sure that reform work remains ultimately devoted to dismantling and altogether replacing the prison-industrial complex.

The fact is that any attempt to actually practice alternatives and implement change brings one into contact with realities that currently exist on the ground.[1] What is clear is that the system of mass incarceration and the "criminal justice" system are broken and cannot be fixed or "made better," "kinder," or "gentler." For these reasons, I argued that transformation, or a transformational vision of restorative justice, is a better framework within which to engage these realities both in critical analysis and in practice. *Transformation* is radical in that, to the degree that it occurs, it must result in implementing alternate practices and justice initiatives in US society. Yet transformation, to be effective in the context of restorative justice, cannot pose a "one size fits all" approach to change. What transformation amounts to in practice will vary on a case-by-case basis. By and large, it will look like what some mean by "prison abolition." It will replace state programs and institutions as they currently exist with community-based and community-led alternatives. In some cases, it may look like relentlessly critical collaboration with parts of "the system" that are willing and able to reorient and guide their work by the norms of a holistic vision of restorative justice. It may require networks and initiatives to work in parallel fashion to state programs (perhaps, simultaneously, in critical collaboration *and* selective critical refusal). At times, it will require an altogether separate set of practices and initiatives that contrast to those of the state. Precious Blood and the restorative justice community hub network across Chicago present concrete examples of what grassroots, bottom-up emergence of community-based, community-led transformational practices and initiative building will look like. They could not (and should not) be replicated exactly elsewhere. They are highly context-sensitive and specific. But as a general model of what implementation and integration can look like, they may afford a valuable example for other contexts.

The controversy invited by the reform/abolition dichotomy generally degenerates into disputes that are, in many ways, verbal. The contesting positions overlap significantly in the actual content of their claims. Michelle Alexander's *The New Jim Crow* is sometimes dismissed as "reformist" by card-carrying "abolitionists" for its focus on the war on drugs in contrast to eliminating mass incarceration more broadly.[2] But

Alexander writes, in a passage worth quoting at length, that "reform work is the work of movement building, provided that it is done consciously as movement building work." She continues,

> The relevant question is not whether to engage in reform work, but how. There is no shortage of worthy reform efforts and goals. . . . If the way we pursue reforms does not contribute to the building of a movement to dismantle the system of mass incarceration, and if our advocacy does not upset the prevailing public consensus that supports the new caste system, none of the reforms, even if won, will successfully disrupt the national racial equilibrium. Challenges to the system will be easily absorbed or deflected, and the accommodations made will serve primarily to legitimate the system, not undermine it. We run the risk of winning isolated battles but losing the war.[3]

To recognize the work of Precious Blood and Chicago's larger community restorative justice hub network as effecting forms of "transformation"—and contributing to a broad-based, sustainable transformational movement—requires moving beyond a dichotomous all-or-nothing conception of what we recognize as transformational. Specifically, it requires moving beyond the claim that if the status quo is not altogether abolished with a wholly different reality put in its place, then there has been no transformation. To the contrary, what I have observed and described in this book requires that we see the gradual, strategic accumulation and maintenance, building up and out, and cross-context connection and integration of small and sometimes halting steps as the primary forms that transformation takes. These are "the wellspring of the movement," as the epigraph to this book suggests. They may be easy to miss as examples of transformational process precisely because they are how the struggle actually occurs on the ground—and builds—on a daily basis, bit by bit, in and through the relationships of everyday people over time.

Throughout this book, I have worked to show that, if we expand what we mean by "transformation" to include sustainable acts and initiatives of resistance that accrue, and constructive initiatives that can be sustained and built outward, we see numerous meaningful practices and paths that have opened up—and are currently opening, or further expanding. Chicago's community restorative justice hub network works collaboratively with similar restorative justice initiatives across the United States, such as Common Justice in Brooklyn, New York. Carefully building up and outward, they resist, alter, and move beyond the status quo of retributive punishment, the community-annihilating effects of mass incarceration and the New Jim Crow, and the US prison-industrial complex.

ACKNOWLEDGMENTS

I owe thanks to many people for assistance in completing this book. Generous colleagues at Notre Dame invited me to present my fieldwork and manuscript-in-progress in their classes over recent years, and they and their students tested the material: Ernesto Verdeja's and Ann Mische's MA Foundations, Emmanuel Katongole's Theology and Peacebuilding, Susan St. Ville's Strategic Peacebuilding, Norbert Koppensteiner's Methods in Peace Research, several iterations of Introduction to Peace Studies led by Atalia Omer and David Cortright, and Christian Smith's workshop in Religion and Society. Special thanks go to George Lopez; as this project evolved over numerous years, I presented excerpts at George's invitation to national and international groups attending Notre Dame's Summer Institute for Peace Studies Faculty. Cecelia Lynch supported this project as an invaluable mentor to me, and more generally through our many shared interests and intellectual friendship. I am grateful to David Anderson Hooker, my erstwhile colleague at Notre Dame, for his persistent suspicion of restorative justice. Conversations with David pressed me, time and again, to sharpen the arguments in this book. I owe a special debt of gratitude to Susan Sharpe, restorative justice advisor at Notre Dame's Center for Social Concerns, for inviting me in to her 2014 seminar. That brilliantly led course first set this project in motion. Invitations from Connie Mick to attend and later present my work at the center's workshops on community-based research and teaching oriented the project in its formative stage.

I am grateful to Anthony Pinn for identifying the rudiments of this book in the earliest public paper that I presented on the subject, and for inviting me to submit it for consideration in New York University Press's Religion and Social Transformation series. Thanks go, as well, to Loren Lybarger, Ellen Ott Marshall, Christopher Tirres, and the manuscript reviewers for NYU Press. Their multiple rounds of meticulous, thoughtful, critical feedback were invaluable, and pushed me to refine the book in crucial ways. My work on the ground in Chicago launched successfully thanks to Loren's invitation to a citywide workshop addressing "Criminal Activity Evictions, Public Housing, and Ex-Offender Reintegration" that he organized as senior fellow at the University of Chicago's Martin Marty Center in May 2015. Thanks to Jennifer Hammer, my publishing experience at NYU Press has been superb (indeed, my best to date by far). I am grateful for editorial support and feedback from Josh Lupo, and for Catherine Osborne's stellar editorial guidance. I am grateful to Tené Morgan for her close, thoughtful reading of the manuscript just prior to its penultimate submission to the press, and for her teaching me from her own work and experience in Minneapolis throughout our semester-long conversations and readings in restorative justice. Mahmoud Youness was kind enough to offer meticulous philosophical feedback on an early draft. The book is much improved because of it.

I launched the field research for the project during a leave funded by the Louisville Institute's Sabbatical Grant for Researchers (2015–2016), and benefited from input I received from my working group, led by Marie Griffith, at the institute's workshop. My fieldwork across Chicago was funded over several years by three Kroc Faculty Research Grants. I delivered the earliest segments of this book as the 2016 George Walker Redding Lecture at Georgetown College and the 2018 Peace Studies Conference Keynote Address at Grinnell College.

As always, I owe special thanks to Atalia Omer, Pnei'el Alois, and Yonatan, my parents, Lance and Kathy Springs (who read and scrutinized every word of the manuscript draft along with Rose Hamblen), and Amanda and Bryan Langlands.

My deepest debt of gratitude goes to the many young people, community elders, and initiatives across Chicago portrayed in these pages—too many to name in the acknowledgments (but discussed in detail in the introduction). I hope that this book does justice to their witness and work to build a world beyond the US prison-industrial complex, from the ground up.

NOTES

INTRODUCTION

1 US mass incarceration is a concrete historical and present-day sociological instance that embodies and institutionalizes what Eddie Glaude calls "the value gap." See *Democracy in Black: How Race Still Enslaves the American Soul* (New York: Crown, 2014), chap. 2. These forms of oppression do not confine themselves to any national boundaries, as they compel forms of solidarity with people who suffer comparable forms of oppression in global and international contexts. For the purposes of this book, I focus on these dynamics as they play out in the United States and especially in regional and local contexts. On the search for international solidarity, see, for example, Angela Davis, "Ferguson Reminds Us of the Importance of a Global Context," and "On Palestine, GS4, and the Prison Industrial Complex," in Davis, *Freedom Is a Constant Struggle: Ferguson, Palestine, and the Foundations of a Movement*, ed. Frank Barat (Chicago: Haymarket, 2016), chaps. 2 and 4.

2 Ethicists, philosophers, and scholars of religion use the term "piety" for this recognition of and appropriate response to our indebtedness to the sources of our life and flourishing. So understood, piety is "a spiritually healthy recognition of dependence," followed by a just and properly proportioned gratitude, attuned responsiveness, and ensuing cultivation of individuality and agency. As a religious and/or spiritual sensibility, piety can take many forms. For example, it may posit either human or supernatural sources of indebtedness (parents, family, friends, community, God). It may take sociopolitical forms as well, such as "democratic piety" (a sense of indebtedness to, empowerment from, and accountability to one's political forebears and fellow citizens, as well as a sense of responsibility for the future of one's society) or respond to dependence upon and indebtedness to nature as a source of life ("natural piety"). The conceptions of piety that best describe what I encountered in the holistic approach to restorative justice are in Jeffrey Stout, *Democracy and Tradition* (Princeton: Princeton University Press, 2004), chap. 1 (esp. 34–41); Henry S. Levenson, *Santayana, Pragmatism, and the Spiritual Life* (Chapel Hill: University of North Carolina Press, 1992), esp. 158–63; and Melvin Rogers, *The Undiscovered Dewey: Religion, Morality, and the Ethos of Democracy* (New York: Columbia University Press, 2008), chap. 3; relatedly, my use of the term "care" as a moral dynamic of the restorative justice practices I encountered in

Chicago gestures to exposition of, and debates regarding, both the value and limits of that concept in recent work on "the politics of care." Discourse on "the politics of care" pushes beyond the "ethics of care" debates of the 1980s and 1990s, and past the temptations of carceral feminism. For orientation to these discussions of "caring" behind my use of the word, see Deva Woodly, Rachel H. Brown, Mara Marin, Shatema Threadcraft, Christopher Paul Harris, Jasmine Syedullah, and Miriam Ticktin, "The Politics of Care," *Contemporary Political Theory* 20, no. 4 (2021): 890–925.

3 Throughout this book I use the term "spiritual" adjectivally, to describe the dynamics, sensibilities, purposes, and effects of restorative justice when those are practiced in what I identify as "holistic" (as opposed to instrumental) ways. I intentionally do not describe restorative justice as "*a* spirituality," which would indicate a fixed essence. What I focus on, rather, occurs in the different ways its practices, understandings, and sensibilities are implemented. The chapters move inductively from the particular cases I encountered to the more general descriptions, expositions, and assessments of the moral and spiritual dynamics of restorative justice I examine. The more theoretical discussions of these dynamics, which engage the relevant scholarly literatures, occur toward the end of the book. Academic and scholarly readers who desire a more formal definition of my adjectival use of the term "spiritual" up front should skip ahead to the final two chapters of the book, where I offer more specific exposition of the "spiritual dynamics" I describe. To interpretively situate, compare, and contrast these, I use Nancy Ammerman's typology of vernacular uses of "spiritual"; see Ammerman, "Spiritual but Not Religious? Beyond Binary Choices in the Study of Religion," *Journal for the Scientific Study of Religion* 52, no. 2 (June 2013): 258–78.

4 For these and other examples, see Priscilla Hayner, *Unspeakable Truths: Transitional Justice and the Challenge of Truth Commissions* (New York: Routledge, 2011), chaps. 4–5.

5 Michelle Alexander, *The New Jim Crow: Mass Incarceration in the Age of Colorblindness* (New York: New Press, 2012).

6 See, for example, Danielle Sered, *Until We Reckon: Violence, Mass Incarceration, and a Road to Repair* (New York: New Press, 2018), 244–45; Angela Davis, *Are Prisons Obsolete?* (New York: Seven Stories, 2003); Margaret Urban Walker, *Moral Repair: Reconstructing Moral Relations after Wrongdoing* (New York: Cambridge University Press, 2006).

7 Alexander, *New Jim Crow*.

8 See Sered, *Until We Reckon*.

9 Paulo Freire, *Pedagogy of the Oppressed*, 30th anniversary ed., trans. Myra Bergman Ramos (New York: Bloomsbury, 2016), esp. chap. 1.

10 Such a formal definition appears most influentially, for example, in the sixth-century systematization of Roman law; see Alan Watson, trans., *The Digest of Justinian* (Philadelphia: University of Pennsylvania Press, 1985). Justinian codified a characterization from the third-century Roman jurist Ulpian.

11 For extensive treatment, see Ryan Lugalia-Hollon and Daniel Cooper, *The War on Neighborhoods: Policing, Prison, and Punishment in a Divided City* (Boston: Beacon, 2019). For a revealing account of corruption that expands through Chicago's criminal courts, see Nicole Gonzales Van Cleve, *Crook County: Racism and Injustice in America's Largest Criminal Court* (Stanford: Stanford University Press, 2016).

12 I have worked to make the main body of this work as accessible as possible to a general audience, especially for the kinds of practitioners with and for whom I have written the book. For this reason, many of the usual scholarly conventions—such as debating scholarly positions and arguments designated by the names of the scholars who hold them, extensive technical exposition of theoretical concepts, or showcasing of scholarly literatures—I confine to the notes. The notes for this book are, as a result, extensive at times, and are aimed at scholarly and academic readers.

13 Notre Dame's Institutional Review Board determined the field research for this project to be "exempt" from IRB review (protocol number 15-04-2503), April 29, 2015.

14 Michelle Fine, *Just Research in Contentious Times: Widening the Methodological Imagination* (New York: Teachers College Press, 2017), esp. 80–82; Michelle Fine and Maria Elena Torre, *Essentials of Participatory Action Research* (Washington, DC: American Psychological Association, 2021).

15 Hilary Putnam, *The Collapse of the Fact/Value Dichotomy and Other Essays* (Cambridge: Harvard University Press, 2002). Putnam demonstrates the old insight from Max Weber that ethical values inform the researcher's decision as to what ought to be (what is worthy of) investigation and research, and why (63). But he pushes the interwovenness of fact/value and description/norm much further than Weber (indeed, correcting him), by demonstrating that the very act of "stating facts" and "making factual claims" is, itself, an intrinsically normative enterprise based on *epistemic* values (norms) such as empirical verifiability, plausibility, coherence, and even the ideal of "impartiality," itself, among others (31). He presses further, pointing out that "the terms one uses even in description in history and sociology and other social sciences are invariably ethically colored," exemplified by Weber's own use of the term "ideal types," of which, for example, "charisma" is "described by him as essentially counter-rational and anarchic, or radically non-epistemic in character." For this quotation, see David Little, "Ethics and Scholarship," *Harvard Theological Review*, January 2007, 5. Putnam points out that the difference between ethical and epistemic values to which the scholar commits themselves is a distinction that is not absolute (as opposed to a dichotomy that presumes a metaphysical structure), and therefore, the scholar's ethical and epistemic commitments, while distinguishable, nonetheless interact and affect one another.

Critical participatory action research approaches instances of injustice, harm, and dehumanization of people and groups not merely to describe them or to neutrally study the causes, character, and effects of such oppression. It is also driven by an ethical responsibility to address these in ways that aid in reducing violence in all its forms, and examines, clarifies, and promotes justice as it pertains to these circumstances. The critical participatory action researcher aims to approach contexts of conflict, violence, and oppression in the ways that a medical doctor aims to approach a patient who suffers from an illness—to understand, diagnose, and address the symptoms of an illness as well as its underlying causes, and further, to identify and promote conditions that open possibilities for and support prevention, resistance, resilience, and flourishing.

16 For a helpful application of Putnam's argument to ethno-national studies and the study of religion—and an insightful chastening of the common reading of Weber's claims that researchers can make explicit and inventory their normative purposes, their commitments and values, in order to then (putatively) set them aside and achieve impartiality—see Little, "Ethics and Scholarship," 1–9.

17 Maria Elena Torre refers to such spaces as "participatory contact zones" in "Participatory Action Research and Critical Race Theory: Fueling Spaces for Nosotras to Research," *Urban Review* 41, no. 1 (January 2009): 106–20.

18 Clifford Geertz, "'From the Native's Point of View': On the Nature of Anthropological Understanding," in *Local Knowledge: Further Essays in Interpretive Sociology* (New York: Basic Books, 1983), 55–70, esp. 57–58.

19 Clifford Geertz, "Thick Description: Toward an Interpretive Theory of Culture," in *The Interpretation of Cultures* (New York: Basic Books, 1973), 23. Many social scientific researchers and ethnographers chafe at the suggestion that their work is "extractive." Here three questions help illuminate the extent to which fieldwork may be extractive. First, who is one's audience and for whom is one writing? If the answer is, first and foremost, one's scholarly peers, then the work will be predominantly extractive. A second question presses further: Who does the scholarship benefit? If the primary answer is something like the researcher's career, the scholarly discussion, or "discourse," or if the researcher rejoins by saying that the research "deliverables" benefit the community in question in so far as its members take the initiative and develop the requisite skills to enter into (or eavesdrop on) the scholarly discussion and see what they might learn from the researcher's analysis, then the research is extractive. Third, in so far as the "researched group's" interests, needs, questions, concerns, and voices do not come to explicitly inform and shape the purpose of the research, if the groups investigated are not reflective participants, represented, and, in effect, co-researchers, then the research is extractive. For work that has influenced my approach in this book, see Chicago Beyond, *Why Am I Always Being Researched? A Guidebook for Community Organizations, Researchers, and Funders to Help Us Get from Insufficient Understanding to More Authentic Truth* (Chicago: Chicago Beyond, 2018), https://chicagobeyond.org. My thanks to Tené Morgan for drawing this instructive study to my attention.

20 Fine, *Just Research in Contentious Times*, 6–7. As such, the participatory component of this approach contrasts starkly with so-called relational ethnography.

In the latter, the researcher cultivates significant relationships with research subjects for purposes of gathering information, and then conducts "relational uncoupling" with those subjects and field sites to "cleanse one's analytical mind" in order to establish "truth" from a more objective and impartial vantage point. The researcher does this, in part, by returning to their academic context unfettered by the research relationships they established (and have now uncoupled from), and by reacclimating to scholarly contexts by giving talks based on their research and presenting that research for feedback from credentialed colleagues and students. From the perspective of critical participatory action research, relational ethnography (so understood) instrumentalizes relationality for purposes of what one might describe as "phenomenological objectivity." Its basic epistemic orientation remains (however tacitly) positivist (i.e., predicating "true" statements upon the correspondence between a researcher's distanced—and putatively impartial—representations of the object in view and the object itself). It remains, thus, beholden to the Eurocentric, Enlightenment epistemology underlying—and privileging—"scientific" knowledge acquisition as necessarily standing apart from what/who it is about, and exclusively the provenance of credentialed experts.

Critical participatory action research also holds itself accountable to norms of scholarly research and rigorous peer review, though not exclusively. It simultaneously strives to make itself accountable to the groups it engages and invites their critical input. It views both as compatible with a sustained dialectical relational dynamic between the person conducting the research and the groups they enter into relationships with for the purposes of their research. Moreover, it sees the cultivation and maintenance of those relationships as necessary for a more thoroughgoing construction of knowledge (e.g., knowledge production that participates in transformational purposes), and strives to be neither exploitative nor instrumental in its treatment of the people, activism, and initiatives that the researcher engages. For an exposition of relational ethnography that provides a succinct point of contrast with the critical participatory approach I describe above, see Robert Vargas, *Wounded City: Violent Turf Wars in a Chicago Barrio* (Oxford: Oxford University Press, 2016), 185–98.

21 My thinking on this point was helpfully guided by Anthony Pinn, *When Colorblindness Isn't the Answer: Humanism and the Challenge of Race* (Durham, NC: Pitchstone, 2017). I had the good fortune to offer in-depth reflections on my participation in Chicago's restorative justice communities in conversation with Pinn in a symposium on his book. See Jason A. Springs, "'He Not Busy Being Born . . .': Solidarity as Sisyphean Friendship, Democratized Discomfort, and the Cunning of White Supremacy," *Political Theology* 21, no. 3 (2020): 262–68.

22 I found this research approach and sensibility of "co-research" captured most helpfully in Orlando Fals-Borda and Mohammad Anisur Rahman, *Action and Knowledge: Breaking the Monopoly with Participatory Action-Research* (New York: Apex, 1991); and Orlando Fals-Borda, "Participatory (Action) Research in Social Theory: Origins and Challenges," in *Handbook of Action Research: Participative*

Inquiry and Practice, ed. Peter Reason and Hilary Bradbury (London: Sage, 2001), 27–37.

23. On object-directed inquiry and its answerability to social and natural phenomena, my thinking has been helped by Jeffrey Stout, "On Our Interest in Getting Things Right: Pragmatism without Narcissism," in *New Pragmatists*, ed. Cheryl Misak (Oxford: Oxford University Press, 2007), 7–31.

24. For "justpeace" as an orienting norm in peace and justice studies—and my genealogy of how the concepts emerged and developed there—see Jason Springs, "'Violence That Works on the Soul': Structural and Cultural Violence in Religion and Peacebuilding," in *The Oxford Handbook of Religion, Conflict, and Peacebuilding*, ed. Atalia Omer, Scott Appleby, and David Little (New York: Oxford University Press, 2015), 146–79.

CHAPTER 1. SOUTH AFRICA TO SOUTH SIDE

1. See Rashied Omar, "Economic Justice–The Fulcrum of Strong Reconciliation: A Muslim Critique of South Africa's TRC," in *Unfinished Business? Faith Communities and Reconciliation in a Post-TRC Context*, ed. Christo Thesnaar and Lee Hansen (Stellenbosch: African Sun Publications, 2020), 125–40; Charles Villa-Vicencio, "Pursuing Inclusive Reparations: Living between Promise and Non-delivery," in *Restorative Justice, Reconciliation, and Peacebuilding*, ed. Jennifer J. Llewellyn and Daniel Philpott (Oxford: Oxford University Press, 2014), 197–213; Charles Villa-Vicencio, "Restorative Justice in Social Context," in *Burying the Past: Making Peace and Justice after Civil Conflict*, ed. Nigel Biggar, expanded and updated ed. (Washington, DC: Georgetown University Press, 2003), 235–50. See also the essays throughout Robert I. Rotberg and Dennis F. Thompson, eds., *Truth v. Justice: The Morality of Truth Commissions* (Princeton: Princeton University Press, 2000). For incisive exposition of the literature and relevant debates on restorative justice dimensions of South Africa's TRC, see Margaret Urban Walker, *Moral Repair: Reconstructing Moral Relations after Wrongdoing* (New York: Cambridge University Press, 2006).

2. Priscilla Hayner provides a meticulous review and exposition of forty truth and reconciliation commissions in her book *Unspeakable Truths: Transitional Justice and the Challenge of Truth Commissions* (New York: Routledge, 2011). Other key studies of international truth and reconciliation commissions that have influenced this chapter include Martha Minow, *Between Vengeance and Forgiveness: Facing History after Genocide and Mass Violence* (New York: Beacon, 1998); and Ernesto Verdeja, *Unchopping a Tree: Reconciliation in the Aftermath of Political Violence* (Philadelphia: Temple University Press, 2009).

3. Restorative justice and political reconciliation are closely related, but not identical. For a helpful account of the ways that these frameworks relate, see Jennifer Llewellyn and Daniel Philpott, "Restorative Justice and Reconciliation: Twin Frameworks for Peacebuilding," in Llewellyn and Philpott, *Restorative Justice*, 14–36.

4 Truth and Reconciliation Commission, *Truth and Reconciliation Commission of South Africa Report* (Cape Town: Truth and Reconciliation Commission, 1998), vol. 1, chap 5., para. 80; see also Jennifer Llewellyn, "Truth Commissions and Restorative Justice," in *Handbook of Restorative Justice*, ed. Gerry Johnstone and Daniel Van Ness (Devon, UK: Willan, 2007), 351–71.
5 Tanya Goodman, "Performing a 'New' Nation: The Role of the TRC in South Africa," in *Social Performance: Symbolic Action, Cultural Pragmatics, and Ritual*, ed. Jeffrey C. Alexander, Bernhard Giesen, and Jason L. Mast (New York: Cambridge University Press, 2006), 169–92.
6 Angela Davis, *Are Prisons Obsolete?* (New York: Seven Stories, 2003), 114–15.
7 Wendy Sawyer and Peter Wagner, "Mass Incarceration: The Whole Pie 2022," Prison Policy Initiative, March 14, 2022, www.prisonpolicy.org.
8 Sawyer and Wagner, "Mass Incarceration."
9 Johan Galtung's definitions of "structural" and "cultural" violence have been influential. Galtung defined structural violence as the ways that "individuals may do enormous amounts of harm to other people without ever intending to do so, just performing their regular duties, as a job defined in the structure.... Structural violence was then seen as unintended harm done to human beings . . . as a process, working slowly in the way misery in general, and hunger in particular, erode and finally kill human beings." For example, "in a society where life expectancy is twice as high in the upper class as in the lower classes, violence is exercised even if there are not concrete actors one can point to directly attacking others, as when one person kills another." Galtung, "Violence, Peace, and Peace Research," *Journal of Peace Research* 6, no. 3 (1969): 171. Cultural violence occurs in "those aspects of culture, the symbolic sphere of our existence—exemplified by religion and ideology, language and art, empirical science and formal science—that can be used to justify or legitimize direct or structural violence." Galtung, "Cultural Violence," *Journal of Peace Research* 27, no. 3 (1990): 291. "Cultural violence makes direct and structural violence look, even feel, right—or at least not wrong.... [It] legitimates violence and the use of violence." For a comprehensive exposition of how these analytical concepts interrelate with religion and peacebuilding, see Jason Springs, "'Violence That Works on the Soul': Structural and Cultural Violence in Religion and Peacebuilding," in *The Oxford Handbook of Religion, Conflict, and Peacebuilding*, ed. Atalia Omer, Scott Appleby, and David Little (New York: Oxford University Press, 2015), 146–79.
10 In chapter 12 I discuss the example of a restorative justice court launched by the Circuit Court of Cook County.
11 Danielle Sered, *Until We Reckon: Violence, Mass Incarceration, and a Road to Repair* (New York: New Press, 2018), 133, citing Mark S. Umbreit, Robert B. Coates, and Betty Vos, "The Impact of Victim-Offender Mediation: Two Decades of Research," *Federal Probation* 65, no. 3 (December 2001); sujatha baliga, Sia Henry, and George Valentine, "Restorative Community Conferencing: A Study of Community Works West's Restorative Justice Youth Diversion Program in Alameda

County," *Community Works Web*, 2017, 6–9. See also Jeff Lattimer, Craig Dowden, and Danielle Muise, "The Effectiveness of Restorative Justice Practices: A Meta-Analysis," *Prison Journal* 85, no. 2 (June 2005): 127–44.

12 For a 2017 meta-analysis of eighty-four evaluations within sixty unique research projects or studies of restorative justice initiatives, see David B. Wilson, Ajima Olaghere, and Catherine S. Kimbrell, "Effectiveness of Restorative Justice Principles in Juvenile Justice: A Meta-Analysis," May 12, 2017, www.ncjrs.gov. See also Lawrence Sherman and Heather Strang, *Restorative Justice: The Evidence* (London: Smith Institute, 2007). Analysts find similar results for restorative justice initiatives in international contexts. A 2011 study by the New Zealand Ministry of Justice found that "offenders who participated in restorative justice conferences . . . had a reoffending rate 20% lower than that of a similar group of offenders who did not receive restorative justice"; see *Reoffending Analysis for Restorative Justice Cases: 2008 and 2009—A Summary* (Wellington: New Zealand Ministry of Justice, 2011). See also Joanna Shapland, Gwen Robinson, and Angela Sorsby, *Restorative Justice in Practice: Evaluating What Works for Victims and Offenders* (Oxford: Taylor and Francis, 2011). John Braithwaite provides a global analysis of indicators of success (to overall positive results) in chapters 3 and 4 of his *Restorative Justice and Responsive Regulation* (Oxford: Oxford University Press, 2002).

13 See, for example, Jeffrey Reiman and Paul Leighton, *The Rich Get Richer and the Poor Get Prison: Ideology, Class, and Criminal Justice*, 11th ed. (New York: Routledge, 2017); Douglas Blackmon, *Slavery by Another Name: The Re-enslavement of Black Americans from the Civil War to World War II* (New York: Anchor, 2009); Michelle Alexander, *The New Jim Crow: Mass Incarceration in the Age of Colorblindness* (New York: New Press, 2012); and Ruth Wilson Gilmore, *Golden Gulag: Prisons, Surplus, Crisis, and Opposition in Globalizing California* (Berkeley: University of California Press, 2007).

14 Nancy Heitzeg, *The School-to-Prison Pipeline: Education, Discipline, and Racialized Double Standards* (Santa Barbara, CA: Praeger, 2016); Sered, *Until We Reckon*; Mara Schiff, "Can Restorative Justice Disrupt the 'School-to-Prison Pipeline'?," *Contemporary Justice Review* 21, no. 2 (2018): 121–39.

15 Jordan Camp and Christina Heatherton, *Policing the Planet: Why the Policing Crisis Led to Black Lives Matter* (New York: Verso, 2016).

16 Devah Pager, *Marked: Race, Crime, and Finding Work in an Era of Mass Incarceration* (Chicago: University of Chicago Press, 2007).

17 Joshua M. Price, *Prison and Social Death* (New Brunswick: Rutgers University Press, 2015); James Forman Jr., *Locking Up Our Own: Crime and Punishment in Black America* (New York: Farrar, Straus, and Giroux, 2017); Donald Braman, *Doing Time on the Outside: Incarceration and Family Life in Urban America* (Ann Arbor: University of Michigan Press, 2004), 219; Todd Clear, *Imprisoning Communities: How Mass Incarceration Makes Disadvantaged Communities Worse* (New York: Oxford University Press, 2007).

CHAPTER 2. RESURRECTION IN BACK OF THE YARDS

1. Jonathan Little, interview by author, Precious Blood Ministry of Reconciliation, Chicago, February 26, 2016.
2. Parish census of 1922, "St. John of God Parish: Its Beginning," St. John of God Church Golden Jubilee, 1907–1957, Chicago, 34–40, http://liturgicalcenter.org (accessed September 6, 2018); for broader context, see Dominic A. Pacyga, *Polish Immigrants and Industrial Chicago: Workers on Chicago's South Side, 1880–1922* (Chicago: University of Chicago Press, 1991), 133–34.
3. For a startling description from that time, see Sophonisba P. Breckinridge and Edith Abbott, "Housing Conditions in Chicago, III: Back of the Yards," *American Journal of Sociology* 16, no. 4 (January 1911): 433–68.
4. Quoted in Walter Rideout, *The Radical Novel in the United States, 1900–1954* (New York: Columbia University Press, 1992), 30. Though not without its problems, Harriet Beecher Stowe's *Uncle Tom's Cabin* had made a revolutionary intervention in resistance to chattel slavery in the mid-nineteenth-century United States with its sentimental portrayals of the horrors of that institution and depictions of the people it enmeshed. The only book to sell more copies in the nineteenth century was the Bible. Both Sinclair's *The Jungle* and Stowe's *Uncle Tom's Cabin* became international best-sellers and were translated into seventeen and seventy different languages, respectively. For a detailed account of *Uncle Tom's Cabin* as an example of moral imagination that amplified and expanded the power and impact of the movement to abolish slavery in the pre–Civil War United States, see Jason A. Springs, "Turning the Searchlight Inward: Cultivating the Virtues of Moral Imagination," in *Healthy Conflict in Contemporary American Society: From Enemy to Adversary* (Cambridge: Cambridge University Press, 2020), chap. 2.
5. Dorothy Day, *The Long Loneliness* (New York: Harper and Row, 1952), 40–45.
6. See Jeffrey Stout, *Blessed Are the Organized: Grassroots Democracy in America* (Princeton: Princeton University Press, 2010).
7. Martin Millspaugh and Vivian Gurney Breckenfeld, *The Human Side of Urban Renewal: A Study of the Attitude Changes Produced by Neighborhood Rehabilitation* (New York: Doubleday, 1960), 177–220.
8. Jane Jacobs, *The Death and Life of Great American Cities* (New York: Vintage, 1992), 271–99.
9. "In 2010, Chicago had the fifth highest combined racial and economic segregation in the nation and the 10th highest Black and white segregation," according to a 2017 study from Chicago-based Metropolitan Planning Council. See "The Cost of Segregation," March 2017, www.metroplanning.org.
10. Douglas Massey and Nancy Denton, *American Apartheid: Segregation and the Making of the Underclass* (Cambridge: Harvard University Press, 1993), 2; see also Keeanga-Yamahtta Taylor, *Race for Profit: How Banks and the Real Estate Industry Undermined Black Homeownership* (Chapel Hill: University of North Carolina Press, 2019), 17–18.

11 Jose Casanova, "Nativism and the Politics of Gender in Catholicism and Islam," in *Gendering Religion and Politics: Untangling Modernities*, ed. Hanna Herzog and Ann Braude (New York: Palgrave Macmillan, 2009), 21–50.
12 Woodrow Wilson, "Final Address in Support of the League of Nations," September 25, 1919, www.americanrhetoric.com.
13 James Baldwin, "On Being White . . . and Other Lies," in *The Cross of Redemption: Uncollected Writings* (New York: Pantheon, 2010), 137.
14 Robert A. Slayton, *Back of the Yards: The Making of Local Democracy* (Chicago: University of Chicago Press, 1986), 100–104. Sylvia Hood Washington provides a meticulous account of Mary McDowell's activism and community organizing in the context of environmental inequalities and racism in Back of the Yards; see *Packing Them In: An Archaeology of Environmental Racism in Chicago, 1865–1954* (New York: iUniverse, 2017), chap. 3.
15 Khalil Gibran Muhammad, *The Condemnation of Blackness: Race, Crime, and the Making of Modern Urban America* (Cambridge: Harvard University Press, 2010), esp. 122–26; Allen F. Davis, *Spearheads for Reform: The Social Settlements and the Progressive Movement, 1880–1914* (New York: Oxford University Press, 1967), 94.
16 See Muhammad, *Condemnation of Blackness*, esp. 6–7; see also Jane Addams, *The Spirit of Youth and the City Streets*, reprinted with a new introduction by Allen F. Davis (1909; repr., Urbana: University of Illinois Press, 1972); and Jane Addams, *A New Conscience and an Ancient Evil* (1912; repr., New York: Arno Press and New York Times, 1972).
17 Charles Richmond Henderson, *An Introduction to the Study of the Dependent, Defective and Delinquent Classes: And of Their Social Treatment* (Boston: D. C. Heath, 1901), 246–47.
18 Daniel Patrick Moynihan, *The Negro Family: The Case for National Action* (Washington, DC: US Department of Labor, 1965), esp. chap. 4, www.dol.gov. For a meticulous, critical exposition, see Daniel Geary, "The Moynihan Report: An Annotated Edition," *Atlantic*, September 14, 2015, www.theatlantic.com; see also Geary's expansive study of the Moynihan Report's origins and background, the controversies it generated, and its present-day impact in *Beyond Civil Rights: The Moynihan Report and Its Legacy* (Philadelphia: University of Pennsylvania Press, 2017). Michelle Alexander describes the circulation of the Moynihan Report as a pivotal turn in the emergence of the New Jim Crow. Alexander, *The New Jim Crow: Mass Incarceration in the Age of Colorblindness* (New York: New Press, 2012), 44–45.
19 Muhammad, *Condemnation of Blackness*; for an extensive account and refutation of culturalist explanations used to underwrite racial differentiations, see William Julius Wilson, *When Work Disappears: The World of the New Urban Poor* (New York: Knopf, 1996).
20 James J. Feigenbaum, Christopher Muller, and Elizabeth Wrigley-Field, "Regional and Racial Inequality in Infectious Disease Mortality in US Cities, 1900–1948," *Demography* 56, no. 4 (June 2019): 1371–88.

21 Davarian L. Baldwin, *Chicago's New Negroes: Modernity, the Great Migration, and Black Urban Life* (Chapel Hill: University of North Carolina Press, 2007), 206–7.
22 Allan H. Spear, *Black Chicago: The Making of a Negro Ghetto, 1890–1920* (Chicago: University of Chicago Press, 1967), 12–21, 208–12.
23 MJS, "Land Contract Sales in Chicago: Security Turned Exploitation," *Chicago Bar Record*, March 1958, cited in Beryl Satter, *Family Properties: Race, Real Estate, and the Exploitation of Black Urban America* (New York: Metropolitan Books, 2009), fn5; see also Arnold R. Hirsch, *Making the Second Ghetto: Race and Housing in Chicago, 1940–1960* (Cambridge: Cambridge University Press, 1983).
24 Robert Loerzel, "Displaced: When the Eisenhower Expressway Moved In, Who Was Forced Out?," WBEZ, n.d., https://interactive.wbez.org (accessed September 27, 2021).
25 CSIL99, "Final Mass at St. John of God–Part 1," n.d., YouTube video, www.youtube.com/watch?v=BZ5criQbOiE.
26 CSIL99, "Goodbye St. John of God Church," n.d., YouTube video, www.youtube.com/watch?v=0exj2XEB_So.
27 Father David Kelly, interview by author, Precious Blood Ministry of Reconciliation, Chicago, February 26, 2016.
28 Little, interview.
29 Little, interview.
30 Little, interview.

CHAPTER 3. PILLARS AND CIRCLES

1 Here I discuss two of the five pillars (accompaniment and radical hospitality). I address the latter three (building relationships, relentless engagement, learning community) in chapter 7.
2 Tina Johnson, Elena Quintana, David Kelly, Cheryl Graves, Ora Schub, Peter Newman, and Carmen Casas, "Restorative Justice Hubs Concept Paper," *Revista de Mediación* 8, no. 2 (2015): 3.
3 Father David Kelly, "Transcript: Stemming Gun Violence in Chicago," *Religion and Ethics News Weekly*, April 7, 2016, www.pbs.org.
4 Sister Donna Liette, interview by author, Precious Blood Ministry of Reconciliation, Chicago, February 8, 2016.
5 This recognition has been substantiated by socio-analytical assessments. See Taylor Jones, Jessica Rose Kalbfeld, Ryan Hancock, and Robin Clark, "Testifying While Black: An Experimental Study of Court Reporter Accuracy in Transcription of African American English," *Language* 95, no. 2 (2019): e216–52.
6 Jonathan Little, interview by author, Precious Blood Ministry of Reconciliation, Chicago, February 26, 2016; Jones et al., "Testifying While Black."
7 "Moes" and "GDs" refer to the Black P. Stones and Gangster Disciples gangs, respectively. Both are major, national street gang organizations that originated in Chicago in the late 1950s and 1960s.
8 Little, interview.

9 David Heinzmann, "Leaderless Chicago Street Gangs Vex Police Efforts to Quell Violence," *Chicago Tribune*, July 29, 2016, www.chicagotribune.com. "With consistent data trends now going back almost a decade, the majority of illegally used or possessed firearms recovered in Chicago are traced back to states with less regulation over firearms, such as Indiana and Mississippi: More than two of every five traceable crime guns recovered in Chicago originate with their first point of sale at an Illinois dealer. The remaining 60 percent of firearms come from out of state, with Indiana as the primary source for approximately one out of every five crime guns." Chicago Police Department, "Gun Trace Report," 2017, 8, www.cityofchicago.org.

10 Discussion group, Chicago Restorative Justice Summit, Chicago Teachers Union, Chicago, August 24, 2018.

11 See Ryan Lugalia-Hollon and Daniel Cooper, *The War on Neighborhoods: Policing, Prison, and Punishment in a Divided City* (Boston: Beacon, 2018), esp. 63–66. Linda Lutton submitted a sobering report for a five-month assignment covering Harper High School in Englewood, the neighborhood immediately to the south of Back of the Yards; see Ira Glass, "Harper High School: Part One," *This American Life*, February 15, 2015, www.thisamericanlife.org.

12 Focus group, Precious Blood Ministry of Reconciliation, Chicago, May 18, 2016.

13 Johnson et al., "Restorative Justice Hubs Concept Paper," 2.

14 Jonathan Little, focus group, Precious Blood Ministry of Reconciliation, Chicago, May 18, 2016.

15 Little, focus group.

16 For detailed historical and conceptual exposition of how rudiments of restorative justice peacemaking circles emerge, to consider one example, from Afrocentric justice practices, see Morris Jenkins, "Gullah Island Dispute Resolution: An Example of Afrocentric Restorative Justice," *Journal of Black Studies* 37, no. 2 (2006): 299–319; see also Morris Jenkins, "Afrocentric Theory and Restorative Justice: A Viable Alternative to Deal with Crime and Delinquency in the Black Community," *Journal of Social and Societal Policy* 3, no. 2 (2004): 17–32. For a broader account of the indigenous origins of restorative justice and the difference this makes in overcoming the weaknesses of the "Western legal tradition," see Fania Davis, *The Little Book of Race and Restorative Justice: Black Lives, Healing, and US Social Transformation* (New York: Good Books, 2019), chap. 2.

17 Father David Kelly, Zoom interview by author, January 9, 2023.

18 Barry Stuart and Kay Pranis, "Peacemaking Circles," in *Handbook of Restorative Justice*, ed. Dennis Sullivan and Larry Tift (New York: Routledge, 2008), 125.

19 See, for example, Carolyn Boyes-Watson, *Peacemaking Circles and Urban Youth* (St. Paul, MN: Living Justice Press, 2008), 84–86.

20 Hannah Stanley, "The Promise of Restorative Justice, Part 3: Interview with Fr. David Kelly," *On Social Health and Change*, WGN Radio, February 17, 2016 (13:30–14:22), https://wgnradio.com.

21 Little, interview.

22 Father Kelly has recounted this story on multiple occasions. I have altered the names of participants to preserve anonymity. Father David Kelly, "Global Issues Plenary Discussion," Precious Blood Ministry of Reconciliation, Chicago, July 20, 2018; Kelly, "Global Issues Plenary Discussion," Precious Blood Ministry of Reconciliation, Chicago, July 19, 2019. The story also features in Michelle VanNatta and Mariame Kaba, "'We're in It for the Long Haul': Alternatives to Incarceration for Youth in Conflict with the Law," *Project Nia*, n.d., https://project-nia.org (accessed June 15, 2023).

CHAPTER 4. THE POWER OF A CREDIBLE MESSENGER

1 Orlando Mayorga, interview by author, Precious Blood Ministry of Reconciliation, Chicago, August 5, 2018.
2 Orlando Mayorga, "The Long Term with Orlando Mayorga," video interview, March 20, 2019, 10:08–10:53, https://vimeo.com/325575065.
3 Mayorga, interview.
4 Mayorga, interview.
5 Mayorga, interview.
6 Mayorga, interview.
7 Officer Andrew Washington, interview with Linda Lutton, "Harper High School: Part One," *This American Life*, February 15, 2015, www.thisamericanlife.org.

CHAPTER 5. RESTORATIVE JUSTICE AND THE NEW JIM CROW

1 Wendy Sawyer and Peter Wagner, "Mass Incarceration: The Whole Pie 2022," Prison Policy Initiative, March 14, 2022, www.prisonpolicy.org.
2 Michelle Alexander, *The New Jim Crow: Mass Incarceration in the Age of Colorblindness* (New York: New Press, 2012).
3 Marie Griffith, *Moral Combat: How Sex Divided American Christians and Divided American Politics* (New York: Basic Books, 2017), 84–120.
4 Equal Justice Initiative, "Lynching in America: Confronting the Legacy of Racial Terror," 2017, https://lynchinginamerica.eji.org; "Map of 75 Years of Lynchings," *New York Times*, February 9, 2015, www.nytimes.com.
5 My account here largely follows Alexander, *New Jim Crow*.
6 Jeffrey Reimann and Paul Leighton, *The Rich Get Richer and the Poor Get Prison: Ideology, Class, and Criminal Justice*, 11th ed. (New York: Routledge, 2017).
7 E. Ann Carson, "Prisoners in 2014," US Justice Department, Bureau of Justice Statistics, 2015, www.bjs.gov. As Human Rights Watch reported in a 2009 report, "Although Blacks comprise only 13% of the general population, 33% of all drug arrests are of Blacks, and they are more likely to be incarcerated upon conviction for drug offenses." Jamie Fellner et al., "Decades of Disparity: Drug Arrests and Race in the United States," Human Rights Watch, March 2009, www.hrw.org. Ojmarrh Mitchell and Michael S. Caudy summarize: "Blacks' likelihood of being arrested for drugs at ages 17, 22, and 27 are approximately 13%, 83%, and 235% greater than that of whites. While some have suggested that such disparities can be explained

by differences in drug use, drug offending, or neighborhood residence, a recent study examining these severe racial disparities in drug arrests found that the disparities cannot be accounted for by differences in such factors. Specifically, the study found that 87% of Blacks' higher probability of drug arrests is in fact not attributable to differences in drug use, nondrug offending, or neighborhood context, but instead due to racial bias in law enforcement." Ojmarrh Mitchell and Michael S. Caudy, "Examining Racial Disparities in Drug Arrests," *Justice Quarterly* 32, no. 2 (2013): 19–20.
8   Dan Baum, "Legalize It All," *Harper's*, April 2016, https://harpers.org.
9   Violent Crime Control and Law Enforcement Act of 1994, HR 3355, 103rd Congress (1994).
10 United States Sentencing Commission, "Cocaine and Federal Sentencing Policy," May 2002, www.ussc.gov.
11 Critics sometimes diminish the impact of the war on drugs by pointing out that people convicted of violent crimes are a far larger share of the prison population than people convicted of drug crimes. Alexander responds, "About five per cent of people who are arrested every year have been convicted of violent crimes or charged with violent crimes. People who have been convicted of violent offenses typically get much, much longer sentences than people who have been convicted of nonviolent crimes like drug offenses. And, therefore, they comprise a much larger portion of the prison population. However, ninety-five per cent of those who are arrested and swept into the criminal-justice system every year have been convicted of nonviolent crimes. And the largest category of arrests are drug arrests. That was true in 2010, and it's true today." Cited in David Remnick, "10 Years after *The New Jim Crow*," *New Yorker*, January 17, 2020, www.newyorker.com.
12 See Marc Mauer and Meda Chesney-Lind, eds., *Invisible Punishment: The Collateral Consequences of Mass Imprisonment* (New York: New Press, 2002), 5.
13 This is the thesis at the heart of Alexander's *New Jim Crow*.
14 The "broken windows" strategy was formulated most famously in George L. Kelling and James Q. Wilson, "Broken Windows: The Police and Neighborhood Safety," *Atlantic*, March 1982, www.theatlantic.com.
15 Taahira Thompson, "NYPD's Infamous Stop-and-Frisk Policy Found Unconstitutional," Leadership Conference Education Fund, August 21, 2013, https://civilrights.org.
16 John A. Eterno and Eli B. Silverman, *The Crime Numbers Game: Management through Manipulation* (Boca Raton, FL: CRC Press, 2012).
17 American Civil Liberties Union, "The War on Marijuana in Black and White," 2013, 17–22, 90, 11, www.aclu.org.
18 Reiman and Leighton, *Rich Get Richer*, chap. 1.
19 This is the sketch that Zehr offers in his *Little Book of Restorative Justice*, rev. ed. (New York: Good Books, 2014), 20–22. I expand upon Zehr's sketch here in light of Dan Van Ness and Karen Strong's account of the three basic concep-

tions that different definitions of restorative justice center around (encounter, repair of harm, and transformation). See Daniel W. Van Ness and Karen H. Strong, *Restoring Justice: An Introduction to Restorative Justice*, 5th ed. (New York: Routledge, 2015), chaps. 2–3 (esp. 43–45). For an exposition of the array of family resemblances that span restorative justice approaches, see also Gerry Johnstone, *Restorative Justice: Ideas, Values, Debates*, 2nd ed. (New York: Routledge, 2011).

There are important points of complementarity between retributive and restorative frameworks. As Zehr has it, "Both acknowledge the basic moral intuition that balance has been thrown off by wrongdoing and that . . . the victim deserves something/the offender owes something. Both agree that there must be a *proportional* relationship between the act and the response. They differ in the currency that will fulfill the obligations and right the balance." Zehr, *Little Book*, 52. Retributive justice responds through inflicted pain; restorative justice deploys an active effort to encourage those who caused the harm to take responsibility and make right the wrongs, and for both those who cause harm and communities to identify and address the causes of the actions that caused the harms. By addressing the need for vindication in a positive way, restorative justice has the potential to affirm both victim and offender and to help them transform their lives.

20 Tina Johnson, Elena Quintana, David Kelly, Cheryl Graves, Ora Schub, Peter Newman, and Carmen Casas, "Restorative Justice Hubs Concept Paper," *Revista de Mediación* 8, no. 2 (2015): 3–4. These authors are drawing on an account of power as an intrinsically social and collectively shared good of the community. Kay Pranis, Barry Stuart, and Mark Wedge articulate this view of restorative justice practices (peacemaking circles in particular) in *Peacemaking Circles: From Crime to Community* (St. Paul, MN: Living Justice Press, 2003), esp. 211ff.

21 "Restoring relationship" does not imply an attempt to return to a status quo ante, nor does it presume that the victim and offender were interpersonally related prior to the crime. I refer to healing and repairing harms within a web of relationships. The image of the web conveys the "interrelatedness" of the many stakeholders whose lives are interwoven (even if at a remove from one another), and whose interrelatedness is illuminated in and through the effects of violence and/ or crime.

22 For a detailed treatment of this challenging point in restorative justice, and an overview of the wide variety of ways that "reparation" is conceived of and deployed in practice, see Susan Sharpe, "Reparation," in *Handbook of Restorative Justice*, ed. Jerry Johnstone and Daniel Van Ness (Portland, OR: Willan, 2007), 24–35.

23 For powerful examples, see Susan L. Miller, *After the Crime: The Power of Restorative Justice Dialogues between Victims and Violent Offenders* (New York: New York University Press, 2011).

24 See Van Ness and Strong, *Restoring Justice*, 160.

25 Here Van Ness and Strong add the proviso, "Based on crime seriousness, assumptions might be established concerning the parties that must be included in the decision about which approach to use in handling the matter. For example, in the most serious crimes, the government would play a role in making this decision in addition to the victim, offender, and community." *Restoring Justice*, 160.

26 When victims and offenders are not willing to participate, stakeholders may use a "reparative model" in which "court proceedings focus on identifying and taking steps to repair the harm caused by the crime. This conception would not describe something as restorative if it did not provide some sort of redress to direct victims and, perhaps, communities and offenders as well." Van Ness and Strong, *Restoring Justice*, 42. One example is New Zealand's juvenile justice system, which operates an exclusively restorative justice program.

CHAPTER 6. RESTORATIVE JUSTICE *IS* "TRANSFORMATIVE JUSTICE"

1 See, for example, Bonnie Price Lofton, "Does Restorative Justice Challenge Systemic Injustices?," in *Critical Issues in Restorative Justice*, ed. Howard Zehr and Barb Toews (Monsey, NY: Criminal Justice Press, 2004), 381–89.

2 See the conclusion of chapter 3.

3 For example, Ruth Morris, "Not Enough!," *Mediation Quarterly* 12, no. 3 (1994): 284–91; Ruth Morris, *Penal Abolition: The Practical Choice* (Toronto: Canadian Scholars Press, 1995); Donna Coker, "Transformative Justice: Anti-Subordination Processes in Cases of Domestic Violence," in *Restorative Justice and Family Violence*, ed. Heather Strang and John Braithwaite (Cambridge: Cambridge University Press, 2002), 128–52.

4 Like restorative justice, transformative justice is a much-debated concept, as is the relationship between the two. The degree to which transformative justice is intrinsically "anti-state" (even anarchic) will need to be assessed on a case-by-case basis. For a succinct argument that its anti-state and anti-authoritarian (anarchist) tendencies and commitments are essential features that distinguish transformative justice from restorative justice, see Peter Kletsen, "Revolution and Restorative Justice: An Anarchist Perspective," *Abolition Journal*, May 9, 2017, https://abolitionjournal.org. For a claim that restorative justice can take sufficiently anti-state and anarchist forms from an abolitionist perspective, see Duane Ruth-Heffelbower, "Anarchist Criminology: A New Way to Understand a Set of Proven Practices," 2011, 6–7.

5 Mia Mingus, "Transformative Justice: A Brief Description," TransformHarm.org, January 11, 2019, https://transformharm.org. See also Mariame Kaba, *We Do This 'til We Free Us: Abolitionist Organizing and Transformative Justice* (Chicago: Haymarket Books, 2021), 149.

6 See, for example, Andrew Woolford and Amanda Nelund, *The Politics of Restorative Justice* (Boulder: Lynne Rienner, 2020), 195–220.

7 For a succinct overview of these claims, see John Washington, "What Is Prison Abolition?," *Nation*, July 31, 2018, www.thenation.com.

8 Coker, "Transformative Justice," 137–38.
9 This transformational component is central in Zehr's *Little Book of Restorative Justice*, rev. ed. (New York: Good Books, 2014), 28–31. Fania Davis also highlights the transformative component of restorative justice in her *Little Book of Race and Restorative Justice: Black Lives, Healing, and US Social Transformation* (New York: Good Books, 2019), 35. For helpful exposition of the encounter, repair, and transformative dimensions of restorative justice, see Gerry Johnstone and Daniel Van Ness, "The Meaning of Restorative Justice," in *Handbook of Restorative Justice*, ed. Gerry Johnstone and Daniel Van Ness (Portland, OR: Willan, 2007), 5–23.
10 See Daniel W. Van Ness and Karen H. Strong, *Restoring Justice: An Introduction to Restorative Justice*, 5th ed. (New York: Routledge, 2015), chap. 3.
11 Van Ness and Strong write, "[Transformation] addresses not simply individual instances of harm but goes beyond to structural issues of injustice such as racism, sexism, and classism. . . . Restorative justice is therefore a way of life because it addresses all of our relationships, and it offers a way in which broken relationships can be repaired (often through challenging existing societal injustices). This conception would not describe something as restorative if it did not address structural impediments to wholesome, healthy relationships." *Restoring Justice*, 44.
12 I have developed these claims about the nature and character of human freedom and the role of exemplars in expanding and enriching such forms of freedom in *Healthy Conflict in Contemporary American Society: From Enemy to Adversary* (Cambridge: Cambridge University Press, 2020), chap. 6, esp. 169–91.
13 Paulo Freire, *Pedagogy of the Oppressed*, 30th anniversary ed., trans. Myra Bergman Ramos (New York: Bloomsbury, 2016), esp. chap. 1.
14 Jeffrey Reiman and Paul Leighton, *The Rich Get Richer and the Poor Get Prison: Ideology, Class, and Criminal Justice*, 11th ed. (New York: Routledge, 2017), 12–49.
15 John Braithwaite and Philip Petit, "Republicanism and Restorative Justice: An Explanatory and Normative Connection," in *Restorative Justice: From Philosophy to Practice*, ed. Heather Strang and John Braithwaite (Aldershot: Dartmouth, 2000), 155. Again, I owe thanks to Susan Sharpe for pushing me to be increasingly precise in articulating this. I also note that I delineate reciprocal accountability as a feature of relationality. Each is accountable to the other in virtue of the basic form of relationality in which persons, as persons, are caught up together. Reciprocal accountability does not entail *parity* of accountability between partners to specific interpersonal relationships vis-à-vis circumstances of harm. For example, a survivor of harm by no means shares parity of accountability (or any accountability) with the responsible party regarding the harms done to them. However, reciprocal accountability still inheres in the basic form of relationality in such circumstances, and, as a result, in the nature and character of the respect that each party to the circumstance (survivor or wrongdoer) deserves. For an example of reciprocal accountability that illuminates the non-parity between a victim and a responsible party in circumstances of harm, see Danielle Sered, *Until We Reckon:*

Violence, Mass Incarceration, and a Road to Repair (New York: New Press, 2018), 115–18.
16. Galtung, "Cultural Violence," *Journal of Peace Research* 27, no. 3 (1990): 294.
17. Braithwaite and Petit, "Republicanism and Restorative Justice," 152.
18. Michelle Alexander, *The New Jim Crow: Mass Incarceration in the Age of Colorblindness* (New York: New Press, 2012), chap. 3.
19. This notion was disseminated in perhaps its most influential form in the Moynihan Report (see chapter 2). For a historical account of the emergence and development of such cultural perceptions, see Keeanga-Yamahtta Taylor, *From #BlackLivesMatter to Black Liberation* (Chicago: Haymarket Books, 2016), 21–50. Alexander counters, "The absence of black fathers from families across America is not simply a function of laziness, immaturity, or too much time watching Sports Center. Thousands of Black men have disappeared into prisons and jails, locked away for drug crimes that are largely ignored when committed by Whites." *New Jim Crow*, 175.
20. Galtung, "Cultural Violence," 294.
21. Alexander, *New Jim Crow*, 196.
22. Galtung, "Cultural Violence," 299.
23. Martin Luther King Jr., *Where Do We Go from Here: Chaos or Community?* (Boston: Beacon, 1968), 90–95.
24. This is a central thesis of Michel Foucault's *Discipline and Punish: The Birth of the Prison* (New York: Vintage, 1995), part 3.
25. Alexander, *New Jim Crow*, 172.
26. Indeed, care, compassion, and love are recurring elements of the remedy that Alexander thinks is necessary. In the final portion of the book, Alexander confronts her readers with a stark choice: "We could choose to be a nation that extends care, compassion, and concern to those who are locked up and locked out or headed for prison before they are old enough to vote. We could seek for them the same opportunities we seek for our own children; we could treat them like one of 'us.'" Alexander, *New Jim Crow*, 206.
27. Freire, *Pedagogy of the Oppressed*, 51–55.
28. James Baldwin, *The Fire Next Time* (New York: Dial, 1963), 22–23.
29. For a sharp example of the ways peacemaking circles can illuminate and challenge "White advantage," see my article "'He Not Busy Being Born . . .': Solidarity as Sisyphean Friendship, Democratized Discomfort, and the Cunning of White Supremacy," *Political Theology* 21, no. 3 (2020): 262–68.
30. This is not an exhaustive list of the forms of structural and cultural violence or the ways that restorative justice practices and initiatives resist those dynamics. I focus my treatment on these because these are the most relevant to the communities I engage.
31. Alexander, *New Jim Crow*, 243.
32. Michelle Alexander, "The Newest Jim Crow," *New York Times*, November 8, 2018, www.nytimes.com.

CHAPTER 7. RESTORATIVE JUSTICE WITH A HAMMER?

1 In 2016, 4,368 people were shot in Chicago, 764 of whom were killed. Of those, 80 percent were Black, and over 50 percent were Black males, ages fifteen to thirty-four. See Max Kapustin et al., "Gun Violence in Chicago, 2016," University of Chicago Crime Lab, January 2017, https://urbanlabs.uchicago.edu.
2 Madeline Buckley, "74 People Shot, 12 Fatally, in Chicago over the Weekend," *Chicago Tribune*, August 6, 2018, www.chicagotribune.com.
3 Pamela Purdie, interview by author, Precious Blood Ministry of Reconciliation, Chicago, August 6, 2018.
4 Elena Quintana, "Keeping Kids Safe in a Violent Society: Understanding ACES and Trauma-Informed Care," 2003 YNAN Conference, YouTube video, https://www.youtube.com/watch?time_continue=7&v=7w3Qx_re85k (accessed February 4, 2019).
5 Ellen McGrath, "Recovering from Trauma," *Psychology Today*, November 1, 2001, www.psychologytoday.com.
6 Dr. Elena Quintana, interview by author, Adler University, Chicago, May 18, 2016. Researchers in PTSD refer to the dynamic Dr. Quintana describes as the role that "interpersonal neurobiology" plays in healing the effects of trauma (see, for examples, work by Janina Fisher, Bessel van der Kolk, Pat Ogden, and Dan Siegel). As children learn to regulate their emotions through the caring and nurturing relationships through which they grow into independent individuals, so survivors of trauma can heal and recover through the cultivation of caring and nurturing relationships post-trauma. The problem, as I argue in this chapter, is that trauma discourse tends to undercut the very modes and means of relationality that make healing from trauma possible.
7 See Bessel van der Kolk, *The Body Keeps the Score: Brain, Mind, and Body in the Healing of Trauma* (New York: Penguin, 2014), esp. chap. 4.
8 Michael G. Vaughn, Matthew O. Howard, and Lisa Harper-Chang, "Do Prior Trauma and Victimization Predict Weapon Carrying among Delinquent Youth?," *Youth Violence and Juvenile Justice* 4, no. 4 (2006): 314–27.
9 See the discussion on these points by Ryan Lugalia-Hollon and Daniel Cooper, *The War on Neighborhoods: Policing, Prison, and Punishment in a Divided City* (Boston: Beacon, 2018), esp. 69–74.
10 Purdie, interview.
11 See, for example, Richard D. Lane et al., "Impaired Verbal and Nonverbal Emotion Recognition in Alexithymia," *Psychosomatic Medicine* 58, no. 3 (1996): 203–10; Henry Krystal and John H. Krystal, *Integration and Self-Healing: Affect, Trauma, Alexithymia* (New York: Analytic Press, 1988); and van der Kolk, *Body Keeps the Score*.
12 Howard Zehr identifies the September 11, 2001, terrorist attacks as pivotal in prompting restorative justice practitioners to integrate trauma healing discourse. See "Doing Justice, Healing Trauma: The Role of Restorative Justice in Peace-

building," *South Asian Journal of Peacebuilding* 1, no. 1 (Spring 2008); see also Howard Zehr, "The Intersection of Restorative Justice with Trauma Healing, Conflict Transformation and Peacebuilding," *Journal for Peace & Justice Studies* 18, no. 1 (2009): 20–30, https://doi.org/10.5840/peacejustice2009181/23.

13 See, for example, Barry Hart, ed., *Peacebuilding in Traumatized Societies* (Lanham, MD: University Press of America, 2008).

14 Melanie Randall and Lori Haskell, "Trauma-Informed Approaches to Law: Why Restorative Justice Must Understand Trauma and Psychological Coping," *Dalhousie Law Journal* 36, no. 3 (2013): 501–33.

15 In his later work, Zehr himself has come to treat "trauma" as ubiquitous, stating that "an experience of victimization and even trauma is involved in most situations of conflict and wrongdoing." Zehr, "Intersection of Restorative Justice," 23.

16 This conceptualizes trauma as "complex" or "developmental." In this view, being trauma-informed means "being psychologically literate in a sophisticated way, one which is cognizant of the trajectories and complexities of human development and the ways in which abuse, neglect, violence, and other traumatic experiences interfere with and constrict human relational capacities and human neurobiology." Randall and Haskell, "Trauma-Informed Approaches to Law," 521.

17 Zehr, "Doing Justice, Healing Trauma," 10.

18 Caroline M. Angel et al., "Short-Term Effects of Restorative Justice Conferences on Post-Traumatic Stress Symptoms among Robbery and Burglary Victims: A Randomized Controlled Trial," *Journal of Experimental Criminology* 10 (2014): 291–307; Ana M. Nascimento, Joana Andrade, and Andreia de Castro Rodrigues, "The Psychological Impact of Restorative Justice Practices on Victims of Crimes—a Systematic Review," *Trauma, Violence, and Abuse* 24, no. 3 (2022): 1–19, esp. 12–13, https://journals.sagepub.com/doi/pdf/10.1177/15248380221082085.

19 National Scientific Council on the Developing Child, *Supportive Relationships and Active Skill-Building Strengthen the Foundations of Resilience*, Working Paper 13 (Cambridge: Harvard University Center on the Developing Child, 2015), www.developingchild.harvard.edu.

20 Joshua Dubler and Vincent Lloyd, *Break Every Yoke: Religion, Justice, and the Abolition of Prisons* (Oxford: Oxford University Press, 2019), 136–38.

21 Focus group interview by author, Precious Blood Ministry of Reconciliation, Chicago, May 18, 2016.

22 Adler University is not a restorative justice hub per se, but is a collaborative partner that has "a seat at the table" in the hub network leadership circle.

23 Father David Kelly, interview by author, Precious Blood Ministry of Reconciliation, Chicago, February 26, 2016.

24 Kelly, interview.

25 Quintana, interview.

26 Quintana, interview.

CHAPTER 8. WHAT DOES "SPIRITUAL" GET YOU THAT "TRAUMA" DOES NOT?

1. Hannah Stanley, "The Promise of Restorative Justice, Part 3: Interview with Fr. David Kelly," *On Social Health and Change*, WGN Radio, February 17, 2016 (2:36–3:18), https://wgnradio.com.
2. Orlando Mayorga, interview by author, Precious Blood Ministry of Reconciliation, Chicago, August 5, 2018.
3. Father David Kelly, "Global Issues Plenary Discussion," Precious Blood Ministry of Reconciliation, Chicago, July 19, 2019.
4. John Paul II, *Laborem Exercens*, www.vatican.va (accessed March 9, 2022).
5. Father David Kelly, interview by author, Precious Blood Ministry of Reconciliation, Chicago, February 26, 2016.
6. Bessel van der Kolk, *The Body Keeps the Score: Brain, Mind, and Body in the Healing of Trauma* (New York: Penguin, 2014), 13.
7. Dr. Elena Quintana, conference presentation, University of Notre Dame, November 9, 2019.
8. Again, I unpack the senses in which practitioners describe restorative justice as "spiritual" in detail in chapter 15.
9. Group presentation, Precious Blood Ministry of Reconciliation, Chicago, July 19, 2019.
10. Cornel West, *Race Matters* (1993; Boston: Beacon, 2017), 13–15.
11. West, *Race Matters*, 19.
12. Michelle Alexander, *The New Jim Crow: Mass Incarceration in the Age of Colorblindness* (New York: New Press, 2012), 225–26.
13. See David Kelly, discussion Q & A, "Responding to Violence: A Restorative Justice Approach," conference presentation, "Dialogues on Religion and Nonviolence," University of Notre Dame, October 25, 2017.
14. Father David Kelly, "Global Issues Plenary Discussion," Precious Blood Ministry of Reconciliation, Chicago, July 20, 2018.
15. Father David Kelly, group discussion, Precious Blood Ministry of Reconciliation, Chicago, July 19, 2019.

CHAPTER 9. BUT IS IT *REALLY* "JUSTICE"?

1. See Mara Schiff and David Anderson Hooker, "Neither Boat nor Barbeque: In Search of New Language to Unleash the Transformative Possibility of Restorative Justice," *Contemporary Justice Review* 22, no. 3 (2019): 219–41.
2. My general claims about the nature and character of justice here have been aided by Nicholas Wolterstorff's meticulous critical exposition of justice and rights in *Justice: Right and Wrongs* (Princeton: Princeton University Press, 2008).
3. See, for example, Dennis Sullivan and Larry Tift, "Needs-Based Justice as Restorative," in *The Restorative Justice Reader*, ed. Gerry Johnstone (London: Routledge, 2003), 208–16.

4 For a systematic exposition of the Aboriginal or First Nations roots of restorative justice ethics and practices in Canada, see Rupert Ross, *Returning to the Teachings: Exploring Aboriginal Justice* (Toronto: Penguin Canada, 2006). For a more expansive overview, see Daniel W. Van Ness and Karen H. Strong, *Restoring Justice: An Introduction to Restorative Justice*, 5th ed. (New York: Routledge, 2015), chap. 2, esp. 33–38; A. P. Melton, "Indigenous Justice Systems: Tribal Society Is a Way of Life," *Judicature* 79, no. 3 (November–December 1995): 126–33; and Gerry Johnstone, *Restorative Justice: Ideas, Values, Debates*, 2nd ed (New York: Routledge, 2011). See also Laura Mirsky, "The Wet'suwet'en Unlocking Aboriginal Justice Program: Restorative Practices in British Columbia, Canada," International Institute for Restorative Practices, October 21, 2003, www.iirp.edu; H. Eagle, "Restorative Justice in Native Cultures," *State of Justice 3: A Periodic Publication of Friends Committee on Restorative Justice* (November 2001); Laura Mirsky, "Restorative Justice Practices of Native American, First Nation and Other Indigenous People of North America," parts 1 and 2, International Institute for Restorative Practices, April 27, 2004, May 26, 2004, www.iirp.edu; and Buyi Mbambo and Ann Skelton, "Preparing the South African Community for Implementing a New Restorative Child Justice System," in *Repositioning Restorative Justice*, ed. Lode Walgrave (Portland, OR: Willan, 2003), 271–83.
5 Archbishop Desmond Tutu, *No Future without Forgiveness* (New York: Image, 2000), 31–32.
6 See, for example, Charles Taylor, "Irreducibly Social Goods," in *Philosophical Arguments* (Cambridge: Harvard University Press, 1995), 127–45.
7 As has been demonstrated at length in social psychological studies, prolonged isolation—found most acutely in forms of punitive solitary confinement—drastically increases rates of depression and mental illness, self-harm, and suicide. See, for instance, Craig Haney, "Mental Health Issues in Long-Term Solitary and 'Supermax' Confinement," *Crime and Delinquency* 49, no. 1 (January 2003): 124–56.
8 I have developed and defended accounts that integrate socially instituted personhood and individual freedom in greater detail in both philosophical and theological quarters elsewhere, specifically treating the differing—but, I argue, overlapping—accounts of personhood originating in "I and Thou" encounter in the work of Karl Barth, Martin Buber, Ludwig Feuerbach, Karl Jaspers, G. F. W. Hegel, John Dewey, and Robert Brandom, a list that is far from exhaustive. See Jason A. Springs, "Following at a Distance (Again): Freedom, Equality, and Gender in Karl Barth's Theological Anthropology," *Modern Theology* 28, no. 3 (July 2012): 446–77; and Jason A. Springs, *Healthy Conflict in Contemporary American Society: From Enemy to Adversary* (Cambridge: Cambridge University Press, 2020), chap. 6.
9 Tutu, *No Future without Forgiveness*, 35.
10 King describes these as a form of "cultural homicide." See Martin Luther King Jr., "Where Do We Go from Here?," in *I Have a Dream: Writings and Speeches That Changed the World*, ed. James M. Washington (San Francisco: Harper, 1992), 169–79.

CHAPTER 10. PEACEMAKING CIRCLES AS ETHICAL PRACTICE

1. Father David Kelly, interview by author, Precious Blood Ministry of Reconciliation, Chicago, February 26, 2016.
2. See, for example, Seyla Benhabib, "Toward a Deliberative Model of Democratic Legitimacy," in *Democracy and Difference: Contesting the Boundaries of the Political*, ed. Seyla Benhabib (Princeton: Princeton University Press, 1996), 67–94.
3. This broadly encompassing approach to deliberation differs from the narrow account of deliberative exchange developed by Jürgen Habermas and further developed by Seyla Benhabib. By contrast, I do not think that it conflicts with the related, but more expansive, account of deliberative exchange developed by Robert Brandom and further advanced by Jeffrey Stout. I develop these points in *Healthy Conflict in Contemporary American Society: From Enemy to Adversary* (Cambridge: Cambridge University Press, 2020), chaps. 6 and 8.

CHAPTER 11. JUSTICE THAT HEALS AND TRANSFORMS

1. Joel Kaplan and Andy Martin, "Cops' Neighborhood Finds It Isn't Immune to Violence," *Chicago Tribune*, December 16, 1995, http://articles.chicagotribune.com.
2. Julie Anderson, interview by author, Precious Blood Ministry of Reconciliation, Chicago, March 14, 2016.
3. Anderson, interview.
4. Anderson, interview.
5. Anderson, interview.
6. Anderson, interview.
7. Anderson, interview.
8. Arionne Nettles, "Parents of Teens Convicted of Shootings Find a Common Cause in Prison Reform," *Trace*, November 11, 2019, www.thetrace.org.
9. Anderson, interview. "It's been very humbling for me. Even though it's not easy for me, in some ways it's more difficult. Most of them have another son who is locked up or was lost to violence, gunshot. And no one I knew had any of that. I always felt so alone. [Eric] was in Hartford, and then twelve years [later] he moved to Menard. We visited him, like, five times a month for twenty years. He's now in Cook County since March of [2015], when he moved for resentencing. The law wasn't retroactive—going forward, we won't have [mandatory] juvenile life without parole. Maybe they'll get, like, a hundred years or whatever. So we fought them on that. We passed a bill, which you know I always call my baby [*laughs*], because that was half the bill, because it stopped [mandatory] life without parole—the other half is what we are talking about now."
10. Nettles, "Parents of Chicago Teens."
11. Nettles, "Parents of Chicago Teens."
12. Father David Kelly, discussion Q & A, "Responding to Violence: A Restorative Justice Approach," conference presentation, "Dialogues on Religion and Nonviolence," University of Notre Dame, October 25, 2017.

13 Anderson, interview.
14 Immanuel Kant provides a particularly influential modern philosophical case for a retributive theory of punishment in *The Metaphysics of Morals* (Cambridge: Cambridge University Press, 1996), 104–13. Kant is, in effect, a pure retributivist. He identifies the "law of punishment" as a categorical imperative: "The right to punish is the right a ruler has against a subject to inflict pain upon him because of his having committed a crime" (104). For Kant, deterrence and promoting security can only be secondary and dependent purposes of punishment. To make them primary would be to treat the wrongdoer as a means to an end, rather than an end in himself. Not surprisingly, this point is much debated among Kant scholars. For efforts to establish both punishment and deterrence as a priori features of Kant's account of public law, see B. Sharon Byrd, "Kant's Theory of Punishment: Deterrence in Its Threat, Retribution in Its Execution," *Law and Philosophy* 8, no. 2 (1989): 151–200; see also Thomas E. Hill Jr., "Kant on Punishment: A Coherent Mix of Deterrence and Retribution?," in *Respect, Pluralism, and Justice: Kantian Perspectives* (Oxford: Oxford University Press, 2000); and Arthur Ripstein's discussion in "Public Right IV: Punishment," in *Force and Freedom: Kant's Legal and Political Philosophy* (Cambridge: Harvard University Press, 2009), 300–324.
15 Mariel Alper, Matthew R. Durose, and Joshua Markman, "2018 Update on Prisoner Recidivism: A 9-Year Follow-Up Period (2005-2014)," Bureau of Justice Statistics, May 23, 2018, www.bjs.gov. "The 401,288 state prisoners released in 2005 had 1,994,000 arrests during the 9-year period, an average of 5 arrests per released prisoner. Sixty percent of these arrests occurred during years 4 through 9. An estimated 68% of released prisoners were arrested within 3 years, 79% within 6 years, and 83% within 9 years. Eighty-two percent of prisoners arrested during the 9-year period were arrested within the first 3 years. Almost half (47%) of prisoners who did not have an arrest within 3 years of release were arrested during years 4 through 9. Forty-four percent of released prisoners were arrested during the first year following release, while 24% were arrested during year-9."
16 Jerry Johnstone, "The Teachings of Restorative Justice," *Contemporary Justice Review* 21, no. 6 (March 2018): 1–23.
17 Peter Wagner and Wendy Sawyer, "Mass Incarceration: The Whole Pie 2018," Prison Policy Initiative, March 14, 2018, www.prisonpolicy.org; Emily Yoffe, "Innocence Is Irrelevant," *Atlantic*, September 2017, www.theatlantic.com.
18 Numerous studies indicate that 90–95 percent of federal and state court cases are settled through plea bargaining. Without this practice, the US criminal justice system would grind to a halt and collapse under the weight of its own expansiveness. See Lindsey Devers, "Plea and Charge Bargaining: Research Summary," Bureau of Justice Assistance, Department of Justice, January 24, 2011, 1–4, https://bja.ojp.gov.
19 Howard Zehr, *Changing Lenses: Restorative Justice for Our Times* (Scottsdale, PA: Herald Press, 2005), 45–50.
20 Zehr, *Changing Lenses*, 47.

21 Howard Zehr, *The Little Book of Restorative Justice*, rev. ed. (New York: Good Books, 2014), 8.
22 Marilyn Armour and Mark Umbreit, "The Paradox of Forgiveness in Restorative Justice," in *Handbook of Forgiveness*, ed. Everett L. Worthington Jr. (New York: Routledge, 2005), 491–503.
23 For another powerful argument along these lines, see John Braithwaite, "Redeeming the F-Word in Restorative Justice," *Oxford Journal of Law and Religion* 5, no. 1 (February 2016): 79–93.
24 Equal Justice Initiative, "Miller v. Alabama: EJI Won a Landmark Ruling from the Supreme Court Striking Down Mandatory Death-in-Prison Sentences for Children," n.d., https://eji.org (accessed September 28, 2022).
25 Andy Grimm, "Double-Murder Life Sentence Reduced to 60 Years for Eric Anderson," *Chicago Sun-Times*, May 23, 2017, https://chicago.suntimes.com.
26 She recounts her story in detail in Jeanne Bishop, *Change of Heart: Justice, Mercy, and Making Peace with My Sister's Killer* (Louisville, KY: Westminster-John Knox Press, 2015).
27 Transcript of Record at 155–220, People v. Eric Anderson, 96CR0183802 (2017), quoted in Jeanne Bishop, "Restorative Justice and the Value of Victims, Offenders, and a Cloud of Witnesses," *John Marshall Law Review* 50, no. 3 (Spring 2017): 451–62, 458–59.
28 Danielle Sered, *Until We Reckon: Violence, Mass Incarceration, and a Road to Repair* (New York: New Press, 2018), 111–18.
29 WTTW, "Julie's Son Veers Tragically off Course," *Firsthand: Gun Violence*, 9:40–10:00, n.d., https://interactive.wttw.com/firsthand/gun-violence/stories/julie-anderson.
30 WTTW, "The Supreme Court Changes Everything for the Andersons," *Firsthand: Gun Violence*, 5:48–6:02, n.d., https://interactive.wttw.com/firsthand/gun-violence/stories/julie-anderson.
31 "Double-Murder Life Sentence Reduced to 60 Years for Eric Anderson," *CBS News Chicago*, May 24, 2017, www.cbsnews.com.
32 Sered, *Until We Reckon*, 23–26.
33 Sered, *Until We Reckon*, 33.
34 House Bill 1064 passed in both the Illinois House of Representatives and the Senate with bipartisan support as of January 10, 2023. The bill would ensure that offenders who were under the age of twenty-one when sentenced could apply for consideration for parole after serving forty years. "Senate Passes House Bill 1064," Restore Justice, January 11, 2023, www.restorejustice.org.

CHAPTER 12. #LAQUANMCDONALD

1 Sarah Staudt, used with permission from the author.
2 Mark Agurino and Mark Berman, "Chicago Police Officer Jason Van Dyke Convicted of Second-Degree Murder for Killing Laquan McDonald," *Washington Post*, October 5, 2018.

3   Jamie Kalven, "Sixteen Shots," *Slate*, February 10, 2105, https://slate.com.
4   Kalven, "Sixteen Shots."
5   Kim Janssen, "Some Shoppers Balk at Laquan McDonald Protests on Mag Mile," *Chicago Tribune*, November 28, 2015, www.chicagotribune.com.
6   The consent decree was rescinded by Jeff Sessions, first attorney general for the Trump administration. See Rosemary Sobol, "Attorney General Jeff Sessions Speaks Out against Consent Decree in Chicago Speech: 'Chicago Police Are Not the Problem,'" *Chicago Tribune*, October 19, 2018, www.chicagotribune.com.
7   An especially influential organization in this series of action is Assata's Daughters, a group that Colin Kaepernick raised $25,000 to support. See Resita Cox, "Who Are Assata's Daughters? A Q and A with Founder Page May," *Chicago Defender*, December 14, 2017, https://chicagodefender.com.
8   Ryan Lugalia-Hollon and Daniel Cooper document these conditions in rigorous detail throughout their recent study, *The War on Neighborhoods: Policing, Prison, and Punishment in a Divided City* (Boston: Beacon, 2019).
9   Sarah Staudt, interview by author, Lawndale Christian Legal Center, Chicago, March 4, 2016.
10 Staudt, interview.
11 Staudt, interview.
12 Sarah Conway, "This Chicago Court Uses Peace Circles to Dole Out Justice," WBEZ Chicago, June 19, 2018, www.wbez.org.
13 Yana Kunichoff, "Should Communities Have a Say in How Residents Are Punished for Crime?," *Atlantic*, May 2, 2017, www.theatlantic.com.
14 Jennifer Simeone-Casas, Resita Cox, and Sarah Conway, "Restorative Justice Court Opens in North Lawndale," *Austin Weekly News*, July 26, 2017, www.austin-weeklynews.com.
15 Father David Kelly, interview by author, Precious Blood Ministry of Reconciliation, Chicago, August 6, 2018.
16 Kelly, interview.
17 Patrick Keenan-Devlin, "New Illinois Law Boldly Safeguards and Promotes Restorative Justice Practices," Restorative Justice Project, Catholic Lawyers Guild of Chicago, July 2021, www.clgchicago.org. Pivotal lines from the law read, "c) Anything said or done during or in preparation for a restorative justice practice or as a follow-up to that practice, or the fact that the practice has been planned or convened, is privileged and cannot be referred to, used, or admitted in any civil, criminal, juvenile, or administrative proceeding unless the privilege is waived, during the proceeding or in writing, by the party or parties protected by proceeding or in writing, by the party or parties protected by the privilege." The text of Senate Bill 64 can be found at Illinois General Assembly, "Public Act 102–100, SB0064," https://ilga.gov.

CHAPTER 13. CAN POLICING BE RESTORATIVE TOO?

1   In the remainder of this chapter, I have changed all names in order to preserve the confidentiality of the circle training process.

2 For a more expansive and exhaustive overview of the forms of police brutality Sarah Staudt describes—and how these forms of brutality both presuppose and justify themselves on the basis of false beliefs that Black and Brown youth (especially men, but increasingly women as well) are "dangerous"—see Kristin Henning, *The Rage of Innocence: How America Criminalizes Black Youth* (New York: Pantheon, 2021).

3 Patricia G. Devine et al., "Long-Term Reduction in Implicit Race Bias: A Prejudice Habit-Breaking Intervention," *Journal of Experimental Psychology* 48 (2012): 1267. In the final chapter of *The Rage of Innocence*, Kristin Henning names these practices as opening a workable path forward into challenging and changing the cultural scripts, and ensuing perceptions, by which police stereotype Black and Brown youth and adults. These are practices and habits of "moral imagination" of the kind I developed in chapter 1 of my book *Healthy Conflict in Contemporary American Society: From Enemy to Adversary* (Cambridge: Cambridge University Press, 2020). Such practices must be integrated into training protocols, review and promotion criteria, and general policy. See Marie Pryor, Kim Shayo Buchanan, and Phillip Atiba Goff, "Risky Situations: Sources of Racial Disparity in Police Behavior," *Annual Review of Social Science* 16 (2020): 343–60, citing John F. Dovidio and Samuel L. Gaertner, "Aversive Racism and Selection Decisions: 1989 and 1999," *Psychological Science* 11, no. 4 (2000): 315–19.

4 Officers who respond to calls for service on their beats, especially non-emergency calls. "Beat Officers," Chicago Police Department, n.d., https://home.chicagopolice.org (accessed January 23, 2023).

5 Officers who work undercover, focusing especially on drug-related offenses.

6 Sarah Staudt, interview by author, Lawndale Christian Legal Center, Chicago, March 4, 2016.

7 The officer I identified as John above is an example of this. I encountered him at a citywide restorative justice conference in 2018, nearly three years after the circle training recounted above. At that time, he was incorporating his circle training into his work with juveniles and supporting "officer-only" circles to help his fellow officers both to understand a restorative justice approach to youth and young adults in Chicago and to help them process their own experiences through practices of restorative justice.

CHAPTER 14. THE PRICE OF A POWERFUL SLOGAN IS A CONCRETE, CONSTRUCTIVE ALTERNATIVE

1 For one such framing that positions the spiritual aspects of restorative justice on the "religious" side of the divide, and then seeks to ground restorative justice firmly on the secular side (even as they work to develop "channels of dialogue" between the two), see Erik Klaes and Emilie Van Daele, "Restorative Justice and Volunteering in a Secular Age," in *Religion and Volunteering: Complex, Contested and Ambiguous Relationships*, ed. Lesley Hustinix, Johan von Essen, Jacques Haers, and Sara Mels (Cham, Switzerland: Springer International, 2015), 191–215.

2   Abolitionist scholar-activists and organizations include Angela Davis, Ruth Wilson Gilmore, Mariame Kaba, Critical Resistance, INCITE!, the Movement for Black Lives, the National Lawyers Guild, and Incarcerated Workers Organizing Committee, among many others. For a brief overview, see John Washington, "What Is Prison Abolition?," *Nation*, July 31, 2018, www.thenation.com.

3   For an account that links the contemporary abolition movement to earlier religious movements, see Joshua Dubler and Vincent Lloyd, "Think Prison Abolition in America Is Impossible? It Once Felt Inevitable," *Guardian*, May 19, 2018, www.theguardian.com.

4   For an overview of such positions and exposition of the debates surrounding them, see Jonathan VanAntwerpen, "Reconciliation Reconceived: Religion, Secularism, and the Language of Transition," in *The Politics of Reconciliation in Multicultural Societies*, ed. Will Kymlicka and Bashir Bashir (New York: Oxford University Press, 2008), 25–47. See also Jonathan VanAntwerpen, "Reconciliation as Heterodoxy," in *Restorative Justice, Reconciliation, and Peacebuilding*, ed. Jennifer J. Llewellyn and Daniel Philpott (Oxford: Oxford University Press, 2014), 77–117; and Elizabeth Kiss, "Moral Ambition within and beyond Political Constraints: Reflections on Restorative Justice," in *Truth v. Justice: The Morality of Truth Commissions*, ed. Robert I. Rotberg and Dennis F. Thompson (Princeton: Princeton University Press, 2000), 68–98.

5   Jason Springs, "Tentacles of the Leviathan," *Journal of the American Academy of Religion* 84, no. 4 (December 2016): 903–36; Atalia Omer, "Modernists despite Themselves: The Phenomenology of the Secular and the Limits of Critique as an Instrument of Change," *Journal of the American Academy of Religion* 83, no. 1 (March 2015): 27–71.

6   See Howard Zehr, *Changing Lenses: Restorative Justice for Our Times* (Scottsdale, PA: Herald Press, 2005), chap. 8.

7   Dubler and Lloyd forward such an opposition between "religion" and "the secular" (especially the violence of the secular state) in such terms (e.g., "laws of the gods" versus "laws of the state"). They eschew "strategically" or "pragmatically secular" interventions against US mass incarceration. As they have it, a key reason the prison abolition movement of the 1970s failed (despite having a propitious opportunity at that time) is that it was not explicitly religious in its resistance and intervention in public life. They write, "But in assessing what went wrong last time around, we can't help but notice that 1970s prison reformers—even religious prison abolitionists—made their appeals in overwhelmingly secular, pragmatic terms. . . . They did not sufficiently appeal to the deep veins of the American moral imagination: the abolition movement, the civil rights movement, the suffragettes, all of whom were deeply religious in their politics. . . . When we find our laws enabling barbarism, we must call upon the laws of the gods to abolish them. This cry for divine justice—a justice that rejects state violence, a justice that rolls down like water—is gathering." For a succinct statement of these claims, see Dubler and Lloyd, "Think Prison Abolition in America Is Impossible?"; and

Joshua Dubler and Vincent Lloyd, "The End of Punishment: Restorative Justice, Prison Abolition and the Christian Refusal of State Violence," *ABC Religion and Ethics*, December 18, 2018, www.abc.net.au. For more extensive exposition of this account, and its role within their deeper argument that the US prison abolition movement must claim and embolden an explicitly religious heritage and dimension (i.e., reliance upon the "laws of the gods") in order to finally overcome the violence of the secular state, see Joshua Dubler and Vincent Lloyd, *Break Every Yoke: Religion, Justice, and the Abolition of Prisons* (Oxford: Oxford University Press, 2019), 118–41.

8 See, for example, Dubler and Lloyd, *Break Every Yoke*, 136–41.
9 Daniel Philpott, *Just and Unjust Peace: An Ethic of Political Reconciliation* (New York: Oxford University Press, 2012).
10 Max Weber, "Politics as a Vocation," in *From Max Weber: Essays in Sociology*, trans. H. H. Gerth and C. Wright Mills (Philadelphia: Fortress, 1965), 1–2.
11 Keeanga-Yamahtta Taylor, *From #BlackLivesMatter to Black Liberation* (Chicago: Haymarket Books, 2016), 181.
12 As John Braithwaite helpfully describes the equilibrium to be pursued here, "Our objective can be to keep the benefits of the statist revolution at the same time as we rediscover community-based justice. Community justice is often oppressive of rights, often subjects the vulnerable to the domination of local elites, subordinates women, can be procedurally unfair and tends to neglect structural solutions. Mindful of this, we might reframe the two challenges posed earlier in the paper: 1. Helping indigenous community justice to learn from the virtues of liberal statism: procedural fairness, rights, protecting the vulnerable from domination. 2. Helping liberal state justice to learn from indigenous community justice—learning the restorative community alternatives to individualism." See John Braithwaite, "Restorative Justice," in *The Handbook of Crime and Punishment*, ed. Michael Tonry (Oxford: Oxford University Press, 1988), 337–38.
13 Fay Honey Knopp and Mark Morris, *Instead of Prisons: A Handbook for Abolitionists* (Syracuse, NY: Prison Research Education Action Project, 1976), 11, www.prisonpolicy.org. See also Herman Bianchi and Rene van Swaaningen, eds., *Abolitionism: Towards a Non-Repressive Approach to Crime* (Amsterdam: Free University Press, 1986); and Nils Christie, *Limits to Pain: The Role of Punishment in Penal Policy* (Oxford: M. Robertson, 1982).
14 Paulo Freire, *Pedagogy of the Oppressed*, 30th anniversary ed., trans. Myra Bergman Ramos (New York: Bloomsbury, 2016), chaps. 1–2. I am not alone in using the concept of critical praxis to identify and unpack the significance of lived and everyday religion (or "popular theology," as some scholars term it). For important examples, see Alejandro García-Rivera, *San Martín de Porres: The "Little Stories" and the Semiotics of Culture* (Maryknoll, NY: Orbis, 1995); Nancy Pineda-Madrid, *Suffering and Salvation in Ciudad Juárez* (Minneapolis: Fortress, 2011); and Christopher Tirres, *The Aesthetics and Ethics of Faith: A Dialogue between Liberationist and Pragmatist Thought* (Oxford: Oxford University Press, 2014). I find especially

compelling how Pineda-Madrid and Tirres both ethnographically engage Latinx communities of practice, using resources from American Pragmatist thought to highlight how "critical praxis" is present in communal rituals within Latinx cultural contexts. Pineda-Madrid draws on Josiah Royce to help her unpack the rituals of resistance performed on behalf of the femicides in Ciudad Juárez. Tirres draws on John Dewey in order to elucidate the liberative dimensions of Easter Week rituals at the San Fernando Cathedral.

CHAPTER 15. EVERYDAY RELIGION IN UNEXPECTED PLACES

1 For helpful examples, see Anthony Pinn, "Gathering the Godless: Intentional 'Communities' and Ritualizing Ordinary Life," in *Humanism: Essays on Race, Religion, and Popular Culture* (New York: Bloomsbury Academic, 2015), 93–112. Other sources on lived religion that have influenced the account I offer here include Meredith McGuire, *Lived Religion: Faith and Practice in Everyday Life* (New York: Oxford, 2008); and Nancy Ammerman, *Studying Lived Religion: Contexts and Practices* (New York: New York University Press, 2021). As I noted above, Latinx scholars of theology and religion in the United States have been accompanying indigenous and immigrant communities, and communities of color, for decades and have long been broaching questions of lived religion, everyday religion, and popular religion. For a quick point of entry into this important body of work, see Miguel De La Torre, ed., *Hispanic American Religious Cultures* (Santa Barbara, CA: ABC-CLIO, 2009); and Miguel De La Torre and Edwin David Aponte, eds., *Handbook of Latino/a Theology* (St. Louis, MI: Chalice Press, 2006). Orlando Espín has made vital contributions in this regard, as have Latina feminists such as Ada María Isasi-Díaz, María Pilar Aquino, and Michelle Gonzalez.

2 Robert Orsi, *The Madonna of 115th St.: Faith and Community in Italian Harlem, 1880–1950* (New Haven: Yale University Press, 2010), esp. xv–xvii, xxxi–xlii.

3 Of course, many people account for restorative justice without either invoking a specific religious orientation or explicitly referring to the spiritual dynamics of those practices. My claim is that the relational dynamics of personhood and community at the heart of restorative justice embody its moral elements, and can be illuminated by the array of what people mean when they do use the term "spiritual" (see an array of meanings of "spiritual" below). Some people may prefer not to use the term "spiritual" at all (for example, because they find it irreparably polluted by "religious" connotations, for whatever reasons). If it is not helpful, then other words can work to describe the content and dynamics of "co-creating community" by which restorative justice practices cultivate and sustain relationships that cultivate individual agency and self-reliance and also foster communities that can sustain and nourish the flourishing of those individuals. My fieldwork indicated to me that many people tend to use one or both of these frames, and that people invoking "religion" and "spiritual" and/or the moral character of restorative justice can hold their positions both coherently and transformationally in ways that are helpfully illuminated, and expansively understood, when viewed through the lens of lived religion.

4 Michael Lipka and Claire Gecewicz, "More Americans Now Say They're Spiritual but Not Religious," Pew Research Center, September 6, 2017, www.pewresearch.org; Betsy Cooper, Daniel Cox, Rachel Lienesch, and Robert P. Jones, "Exodus: Why Americans Are Leaving Religion—and Why They're Unlikely to Come Back," Public Religion Research Institute, September 22, 2016, www.prri.org; Jack Jenkins, "'Nones' Now as Big as Evangelicals, Catholics in the US," *Religions News Service*, March 21, 2019, https://religionnews.com.

5 Christian Smith, "On 'Moralistic Therapeutic Deism' as US Teenagers' Actual, Tacit, de Facto Religious Faith," in *Religion and Youth*, ed. Sylvia Collins-Mayo and Pink Dandelion (Farnham: Ashgate, 2010), 41–46.

6 Christian Smith with Melinda Lundquist Denton, *Soul Searching: The Religious and Spiritual Lives of American Teenagers* (Oxford: Oxford University Press, 2005); Kenda Creasy Dean, *Almost Christian: What the Faith of Our Teenagers Is Telling the American Church* (Oxford: Oxford University Press, 2010).

7 Dubler and Lloyd tell the story of the emerging restorative justice movement in the United States in these terms. As they have it, the slippery slope into "spiritualization" is most visible in the first mention of restorative justice in the *New York Times*: Karen de Witt, "Crowded Jails Spur New Look at Punishment," *New York Times*, December 25, 1995. See Joshua Dubler and Vincent Lloyd, *Break Every Yoke: Religion, Justice, and the Abolition of Prisons* (Oxford: Oxford University Press, 2019), chap. 3, esp. 129–32.

8 Gesturing toward an experience of "something more" is one way that people identifying as "spiritual but not religious" re-describe what they mean by "spiritual." See Nancy Ammerman, "Spiritual but Not Religious? Beyond Binary Choices in the Study of Religion," *Journal for the Scientific Study of Religion* 52, no. 2 (June 2013): 258–78.

9 The concept of inclusive nondomination has been most fully developed by John Braithwaite and Philip Pettit in "Republicanism and Restorative Justice: An Explanatory and Normative Connection," in *Restorative Justice: From Philosophy to Practice*, ed. Heather Strang and John Braithwaite (Aldershot: Dartmouth, 2000), 145–63, esp. 150–53; Braithwaite provides more extensive exposition and defense in his *Restorative Justice and Responsive Regulation* (Oxford: Oxford University Press, 2002), 127–34.

10 In my judgment, John Dewey's account of religious sensibilities best describes the kinds of lived religion and moral and spiritual characteristics of restorative justice practices. See John Dewey, *A Common Faith* (New Haven: Yale University Press, 1934), chap. 1. Here Dewey describes "religious" in the adjectival sense as "any activity pursued in behalf of an ideal end, against obstacles and in spite of threats of personal loss because of conviction of its general and enduring value" (27). To engage in a religious activity, in this sense, is "to be conquered in our active nature by an ideal end" in ways that entail acknowledging "its rightful claim over our desires and purposes" (20). Such an adjectival sense of "religious" is further characterized, Dewey argues, by a kind of humbling of one's perspective and rec-

ognition of "our dependence upon forces beyond our control" (24). He continues, "The sense of the dignity of human nature is as religious as is the sense of awe and reverence when it rests upon a sense of human nature as a cooperating part of a larger whole. Natural piety . . . may rest upon a just sense of nature as the whole of which we are parts, while it also recognizes that we are parts that are marked by intelligence and purpose, having the capacity to strive by their aid to bring conditions into greater consonance with what is humanly desirable" (25). In the case of restorative justice, the desired end is a holistic vision of human thriving made possible through the cultivation of just and dignifying relationships of mutual recognition and empowerment, and through that, both resilient communities and individual self-reliance and agency that are nurtured through the practices of restorative justice holistically understood and integratively implemented (20–21). These Deweyan terms help illuminate the "spiritual" dynamics to which many restorative justice practitioners gesture, but need not implicate them in Dewey's anti-clericalism or his suspicion of religious institutions. Finally, it is important to keep in mind that Dewey's "ideal ends" are always what he calls "ends-in-view" rather than "final ends," which separates him fundamentally from what Paul Tillich referred to as "ultimate concern."

11 Ammerman, "Spiritual but Not Religious?"
12 Ammerman, "Spiritual but Not Religious?," 266.
13 Ammerman, "Spiritual but Not Religious?," 267.
14 Ammerman, "Spiritual but Not Religious?," 272.
15 For specific examples of its religious sources and points of intersection across the traditions of Islam, Judaism, Christianity, Buddhism, Hinduism, and Sikhism, see Michael L. Hadley, ed., *The Spiritual Roots of Restorative Justice* (Albany: State University of New York Press, 2001); see also Brian Stevenson, *Just Mercy: A Story of Justice and Redemption* (New York: Spiegel and Grau, 2014).
16 Daniel Philpott demonstrates this (with the examples of Judaism, Christianity, and Islam) in *Just and Unjust Peace: An Ethic of Political Reconciliation* (New York: Oxford University Press, 2012).
17 This is not, after all, Ammerman's purpose in developing this range of understandings and uses.
18 Ammerman's spectrum of everyday uses of "spiritual" corroborates a literature review and exposition of descriptions of the "spiritual" significance of restorative justice by restorative justice researchers Kimberly Bender and Marilyn Armour. These researchers identified nine family resemblances that were frequently described as "spiritual" qualities of restorative justice. They occur in its emphasis on transformation, connectedness/belonging, a common human bond, making right a wrong, pursuit of balance/harmony, the ritualized character of the practices, occasional appeals to "spiritual" phenomena, expressions of contrition, and forgiveness. The authors identify reasons to distinguish these from formal features of "religion" in the restorative justice literature. See Kimberly Bender and Marilyn Armour, "The Spiritual Components of Restorative Justice," *Victims and Offenders* 2, no. 3 (2007): 251–67.

19 Here I am providing ethical exposition of the ideal. In earlier chapters, I examined the ways particular, everyday people strive between the real and the ideal, and how this process unfolds in ways that are at once piecemeal and partial but also unfold and evolve in ways that facilitate resistance, critical liberation, and potentially, transformation.

20 As earlier, here I follow Cornel West's exposition and diagnosis of nihilism in his now classic essay "Nihilism in Black America," in *Race Matters* (1993; Boston: Beacon, 2017), chap. 1, esp. 14–18. It is not the case that such nihilism is unique to marginalized communities, minority communities, or "Black America," West explains. Any person or community can be relationally desolate—suffering from a deficit of care, empathy, compassion, and the substance of meaningful, mutually enriching relationships and broader webs of relationality. West argues elsewhere that forms of such nihilism are as pervasive—in some ways even more insidiously so—amid the materialism, commodification, and distraction of the economically privileged. They are also pervasive in the sicknesses and moral ignorance brought on by the White supremacist ethos of racially advantaged communities.

21 West, *Race Matters*, 13–15.

22 West, *Race Matters*, 19.

23 Helpful here is Jeffrey Stout's exposition of domination as anything that "violates [a person's] dignity, or does them a grave injustice, or arbitrarily exercises power over them." See Jeffrey Stout, *Blessed Are the Organized: Grassroots Democracy in America* (Princeton: Princeton University Press, 2010), 118.

24 Paulo Freire, *Pedagogy of the Oppressed*, 30th anniversary ed., trans. Myra Bergman Ramos (New York: Bloomsbury, 2016), 51–55.

25 Freire, *Pedagogy of the Oppressed*, 79.

26 Annalise Acorn, *Compulsory Compassion: A Critique of Restorative Justice* (Vancouver: University of British Columbia Press, 2004).

CONCLUSION

1 For example, Dubler and Lloyd hold up the Yurok Tribal Court in California as an example of a place outside the state. The tribal court addresses tribal infractions, where the judge allows the convicted defendants to pay their debts in salmon rather than US dollars (salmon being a resource that is more available to them). The authors valorize this as "cultivat[ing] an oppositional sovereignty that refuses the conquerors' claim to the same. Half an hour from Pelican Bay, this is what the Yurok attempt to put into practice: a spiritual revolution in which the carceral logics characteristic of America's settler culture will no longer hold sway." Joshua Dubler and Vincent Lloyd, *Break Every Yoke: Religion, Justice, and the Abolition of Prisons* (Oxford: Oxford University Press, 2019), 137–38. Exoticizing hyperbole aside, this is not sovereignty. It is not "outside"—nor does it stand free from—the state or the (putative) myopic violence that the authors claim saturates the state. Participants are still enmeshed in the system; they are held accountable to its standards; they are still fined and still have to pay their fines. This is, rather, another

form of diversion *that exists insofar as it is granted permission to exist by state prosecutors, and continues at their whim*. Dubler and Lloyd themselves acknowledge that participants are always at risk of being shunted back into the standard criminal court as a "last resort." The fact that they may sometimes be permitted to "pay in salmon" or go to sweat lodges is camouflage for the "carceral logic" of the sovereign state's permission on which they depend in order to practice those exceptions *that the state permits them* (in fact, the "permission/exception" is the very heart of that "sovereign carceral logic"). In short, the exoticized, utopian (i.e., quite literally "no place") rhetoric of absolute "either/or" (either some putatively authentic religio-cultural "outside" the state or captivity to univocally violent conquering state sovereignty and its settler-colonial logic) is an illusory, false dichotomy. In each of these features, the example resembles the diversionary restorative justice courts I describe in chapter 12, and contrasts with the nonnegotiable independence insisted upon, and struggled for, by Precious Blood. Working democratically in neighborhood contexts through holistic self-sufficiency and community formation, and *also* through policy and law for change and reform, to carve out spaces of relative self-determination that are strategically resistant to state control, mediates the real and the ideal in this matter. These practices of restorative justice strive to be free from control by the justice system itself, yet simultaneously remain positioned to work with actors in that system who are willing to engage restoratively, and to recognize and respect the integrity of restorative justice norms and practices. The key difference is that the latter works within the constitutional, liberal-democratic context in order to challenge and transform that context, instead of trying to (somehow) leap outside that context altogether.

2 David Remnick, "10 Years after *The New Jim Crow*," *New Yorker*, January 17, 2020, www.newyorker.com; Rachel Kushner, "Is Prison Necessary?," *New York Times Magazine*, April 17, 2019, www.nytimes.com.
3 Michelle Alexander, *The New Jim Crow: Mass Incarceration in the Age of Colorblindness* (New York: New Press, 2012), 236.

INDEX

accompaniment, at Precious Blood Ministry of Reconciliation, 7, 9; as critical praxis, 101–16; individual agency and, 101; job training and, 102–5; at Precious Blood Ministry of Reconciliation, 40–41, 57; prison abolition and, 189; radical hospitality and, 105, 106; spirituality of, 101–16; trauma discourse and, 98
accountability: of critical participatory action research, 216n20; for destructive conflict, 2; in justice, 130–51; in lived religion, 195, 198; for mass incarceration, 139–41; paradox of, 139–41; in peacemaking circles, 109, 110, 163–64; power in, 71; in restorative justice, 72, 76, 130–51; retribution and, 140–41; in South Africa TRC, 23; for structural violence, 5. *See also* reciprocal accountability
Addams, Jane, 32, 33, 114
Adler University, Institute on Public Safety and Social Justice at, 14, 96, 99–100
agency: community, 3, 104. *See also* individual agency
Alexander, Michelle, 6, 8, 59, 64, 73, 109, 110–12, 207–8, 226m11, 230n26; on empathy, compassion, and meaning making, 150; on fragmentation, 85; on missing black fathers, 230n19; on stigmatization, 82, 84. *See also* New Jim Crow
Alger, Horatio, 60–61
Alinsky, Saul, 29–30, 114
Almighty Popes, 130–31
alternative justice, 5
Alvarez, Anita, 155y

Americanization, 32
Ammerman, Nancy, 195–98, 244n18
amnesty: restorative justice and, 136; in South Africa, 21
amygdala, trauma and, 108
Anderson, Eric, 130–38, 144–48
Anderson, Julie, 14, 130–32, 144, 148
Andre, Emmanuel, 14
Anti-Drug Abuse Act of 1982, 66
apartheid, in South Africa, 21, 22
apology, 156; accountability and, 141; of Anderson, E., 144; New Jim Crow and, 72; in peacemaking circle, 50, 51; in South Africa TRC, 23, 24
Armour, Marilyn, 142, 244n18
Art on 51st, in Back of the Yards, 134, 144
arts and performance, at Precious Blood Ministry of Reconciliation, 7
Assata's Daughters, 238n7
attorney-client privilege. *See* privileged communication
Avondale, restorative justice court in, 160–61

Back of the Yards, 28–39; Art on 51st in, 134, 144; cultural violence in, 82; days in, 87–89; gangs in, 27–28, 41–44, 60; guns in, 87; housing in, 30–36; marginalization in, 59, 82; mass incarceration and, 63; neighborhood council in, 29–30; policing in, 37, 38; racism in, 28, 30–36, 114; religion in, 114; restorative justice in, 114–15; secular in, 114; segregation in, 123; shooting in, 87–91; stigmatization in, 7; trauma discourse in, 87–116;

Back of the Yards (*cont.*)
Union Stock Yards and, 29, 30; urban renewal in, 28, 30; violence in, 56–59; White supremacy in, 114. *See also* Precious Blood Ministry of Reconciliation
Baldwin, James, 31, 84–85
Bender, Kimberly, 244n18
Benhabib, Seyla, 235n3
between-ness, at Precious Blood Ministry of Reconciliation, 113–14
Biehl, Amy, 21–24
Bishop, Jeanne, 144–46, 148
Black codes, 64
Black P. Stones ("Moes"), 41, 223n7
blockbusting, 31, 34
Boyle, Father Greg, 103
Boys Club, 55
Braithwaite, John, 241n12
Brandom, Robert, 234n8, 235n3
Bridging the Divide, 171, 172, 176, 179–80
broken windows policing, 27; Compstat and, 69; in New Jim Crow, 68–69; structural violence and, 56
Brown, AnnMarie, 14
building relationships: in conflict circles, 175; in peacemaking circles, 48, 108; in trauma discourse, 98, 99
Byrne Justice Assistance Grant Program, 69

Campaign for Fair Sentencing for Children, 132
CAPS. *See* community policing
carpentry apprenticeship, at Precious Blood Ministry of Reconciliation, 7, 102, 104, 134
caste system: in New Jim Crow, 67, 69, 80; prison-industrial complex as, 1, 63–64
Catholic Lawyers Guild of Chicago, 164–65
Catholic Worker, 29
Center for Developing Child, at Harvard University, 94
Center for Social Concerns, at Notre Dame, 17
charism, 37, 215n15
checking in, at peacemaking circles, 47, 91, 95
checking out, of peacemaking circles, 47
Chicago. *See specific topics*
Chicago Freedom Movement, 36
Chicago School of Sociology, at University of Chicago, 32–33
child labor, in Back of the Yards, 29
Christianity: on forgiveness, 142; Good Friday to Easter, 112–13; prison abolition and, 184; on restorative justice, 142, 184
Circle for Circle Keepers, 14, 15
circle keepers, 44, 45, 47
Circles and Ciphers, in Rogers Park, 14
Clinton, Bill, 66
closing, at peacemaking circles, 47
cocaine, 66
co-creating community: lived religion and, 194, 197–98; Precious Blood Ministry of Reconciliation as, 97, 101–2, 105, 111, 149; self-reliance and, 242n3
co-creation of community, self-reliance and, 104
coercive force, prison abolition and, 185–86
Communities and Relatives of Illinois' Incarcerated Children (CRIIC), 132, 133, 134, 144, 148
community agency, 3, 104
community-based justice, 71, 241n12; transformative justice and, 204, 205
Community Justice for Youth Institute, 14, 15
community policing (CAPS), 172, 179
Community Renewal Society (CRS), 13–14
compassion, 84, 230n26; forgiveness and, 143; in New Jim Crow, 110–11; in peacemaking circles, 109, 110, 127; at

Precious Blood Ministry of Reconciliation, 112; in restorative justice, 3; in spirituality, 197–98; for structural violence, 5
Compstat, 69
confidentiality: Illinois SB 64 and, 164; at peacemaking circles, 46, 163. *See also* privileged communication
conflict circles, as critical praxis, 173–77
contract sales, 31, 34, 35
COVID-19 pandemic, 14
crack cocaine, 66, 68
craft and skill training, at Precious Blood Ministry of Reconciliation, 7
critical consciousness: of oppression, 8–9; in peacemaking circles, 110, 176
critical participatory action research, for restorative justice, 12–19, 215n15, 216n20
critical praxis, 4, 19; accompaniment as, 101–16; conflict circles as, 173–77; critical participatory action research and, 17, 18; dehumanization and, 77–78; lived religion as, 201, 241n14; of peacemaking circles, 107–10; policing and, 166–80; power in, 78; for prison abolition, 189–90; in restorative justice, 76–78, 84, 148–51; in transformative justice, 76–78, 157
Critical Resistance, 240n2
CRS. *See* Community Renewal Society
cultural homicide, 83, 234n10
cultural violence, 5; in Back of the Yards, 82; defined, 219n8; justice system and, 27; lived religion and, 201; marginalization and, 3, 81; in New Jim Crow, 7–8, 73, 85–86; peacemaking circles and, 110; penetration of, 82–85; prison abolition and, 185; of prison-industrial complex, 6, 187; reciprocal accountability for, 126; relational justice and, 79; in South Africa, 22; stigmatization of, 82; structural violence and, 25; transformative justice and, 85–86, 203, 204; trauma discourse and, 89

Dahl, Roald, 152–53
Dan Ryan Expressway, 35
Davis, Angela, 24, 240n2
Day, Dorothy, 29, 114
The Death and Life of Great American Cities (Jacobs), 30
decriminalization: New Jim Crow and, 69, 80; policing and, 177–78
dehumanization, 2, 117; critical praxis and, 77–78; from retribution, 140; of retribution, 140–41, 188; Tutu on, 122; Ubuntu and, 122, 123, 124; of White supremacy, 83–84
DeMatteo, Matt, 14
Dewey, John, 243n10
drugs, 107; arrests for, 69, 153, 159, 225n7 (chap. 5), 226n11; cocaine, 66; counseling for, at LCLC, 158; crack cocaine, 66, 68; marijuana, 69; policing and, 177. *See also* war on drugs
Dubler, Joshua, 232n20, 245n1

Education Justice Project, at University of Illinois, 54
Eisenhower Expressway, 35
Emanuel, Rahm, 155y
empathy: at CRIIC, 133; critical praxis and, 78; forgiveness and, 143; in restorative justice, 2, 3, 72; in Ubuntu, 123
Englewood: restorative justice court in, 160–61; trauma in, 171–72
epistemic mistake, 121
epistemic values, 215n15
Equal Justice Initiative, 143–44
ethnography: critical participatory action research and, 15; relational, 216n20
everyday religion. *See* lived religion

Fair Housing Act, 35–36
Fair Sentencing Act of 2010, 66

Federal Housing Administration, 34
felon disenfranchisement, 67
Fifteenth Amendment, 64
fight or flight reaction, 108
Fine, Michelle, 16
First Nations, 44, 234n4
forgiveness: Christianity on, 142; in restorative justice, 141–53, 244n18
fragmentation, 82–83, 84; retribution and, 139
Freire, Paulo, 17
Future Leaders Apprentice, 147

Galtung, Johan, 81, 82, 219n8
gangbanger, 107, 126, 131–32
gangs, 223n7; Anderson, E., in, 130–31; in Back of the Yards, 27–28, 41–44, 60; evolution of, 41–42; guns for, 42, 109; peacemaking circles for, 108–9; radical hospitality and, 43–44; in school, 60, 130; war on drugs and, 82
Ganster Disciples ("GDs"), 41, 223n7
Geertz, Clifford, 16
GI Bill, 35
Gilmore, Ruth Wilson, 240n2
Glaude, Eddie, 213n1
grandfather clauses for voting, 64
Great Migration, 31; redlining in, 33
Greektown, 35
guns, 37–38, 153, 224n9; in Back of the Yards, 87; for gangs, 42, 109; trafficking of, 42

Habermas, Jürgen, 235n3
habitual offender statutes, 65
Hansberry, Lorraine, 34–35
harm circles, 48, 49–50, 163
Harvard University, Center for Developing Child at, 94
Hayner, Priscilla, 218n2
Henderson, Charles R., 33
Henning, Kristin, 239n3
Hernon, Francisco, 53–54

historical trauma, 114
Homeboy Industries, of Los Angeles, 103
homelessness: policing and, 177; prison abolition and, 183
housing: in Back of the Yards, 30–36; contract sales for, 31, 34, 35; Fair Housing Act, 35–36; unaffordable, 206. *See also* redlining; restrictive covenants; White flight
Hovel, Carrie, 130–31, 137–38, 144–48
Hoying, Sister Carolyn, 36
Hull House, 32
humanization. *See* dehumanization
Human Rights Watch, 225n7 (chap. 5)
humiliation: in fragmentation, 84; in New Jim Crow, 73; in South Africa, 22, 23; Ubuntu and, 122
hyper-incarceration, 1, 27; self-perpetuation of, 136

icebreakers, at peacemaking circles, at Precious Blood Ministry of Reconciliation, 167–69
Illinois SB 64, 164
impact panels, 97
implicit bias, 27, 178
Incarcerated Workers Organizing Committee, 240n2
INCITE!, 240n2
inclusive nondomination, 124, 195, 243n9
individual agency, 1, 3; accompaniment and, 101; at Education Justice Project, 54; forgiveness and, 143; in relational personhood, 78; in restorative justice, 59–62, 78–82, 119
Industrial Areas Foundation, 30
Institute for Nonviolence of Chicago, 108–9
Institute on Public Safety and Social Justice, at Adler University, 14, 96, 99–100
Institutional Review Board (IRB), at Notre Dame, 215n13

interpersonal neurobiology, 231n6
interracial couples, 64–65
interrelatedness, 121, 139, 195
IRB. *See* Institutional Review Board

Jacobs, Jane, 30
Jim Crow, 63, 64–65; felon disenfranchisement in, 67; marginalization in, 123; oppression in, 123. *See also* New Jim Crow
job placement program, 28
job training: accompaniment and, 102–5; at Precious Blood Ministry of Reconciliation, 39, 102. *See also* carpentry apprenticeship
Johnson, Lyndon, 35–36
The Jungle (Sinclair), 29, 221n4
justice: accountability in, 130–51; in peacemaking circles, 125, 127; power in, 81; relational, 9, 78–80; restorative justice as, 117–24; theory of, 118; transitional, in South Africa, 23–24. *See also* restorative justice; retribution/retributive justice; transformative justice
Justice Equity, and Opportunity Initiative, at University of Chicago, 59
justpeace, 18, 218n24

Kaba, Mariame, 240n2
Kaepernick, Colin, 238n7
Kagan, Elena, 144
Kalven, Jamie, 155y
Kant, Immanuel, 236n14
Kelly, Father David, 14, 37, 39; on accompaniment, 40, 101, 103, 105; on criminal justice system, 115; on Good Friday to Easter, 112–13; on LCLC restorative justice court, 160, 161; Mayorga and, 55; on peacemaking circles, 48, 49–52, 164; on Saturday Sanction, 162–63; on trauma discourse, 98–99
Kewanee Life-Skills Re-entry Center, 147

King, Martin Luther, Jr., 2–3, 35, 114; assassination of, 36; on cultural homicide, 83, 234n10; on segregation, 123–24

Lawndale Christian Legal Center (LCLC), in North Lawndale, 14, 157–59, 172, 178–80; police and, 172; restorative justice court at, 159–61
learning community, 98, 205. *See also* school
legal support: at LCLC, 158; at Precious Blood Ministry of Reconciliation, 7
Liette, Sister Donna, 14, 36, 39; on accompaniment, 40
life sentence with no possibility of parole, 130–32; abolishing of, 150; unconsitutionality of, 143–44
literacy tests for voting, 64
Little, Jonathan, 14, 27–29, 35; on accompaniment, 40–41; on peacemaking circles, 44–45, 48–49; on radical hospitality, 43–44; Saturday Sanction of, 40–41, 44, 95, 161–63
Little Italy, 32
Little Village: gangs in, 42; Urban Life Skills in, 14
lived religion, 4, 12; accountability in, 195, 198; co-creating community and, 194, 197–98; as critical praxis, 201, 241n14; cultural nature of, 192, 195–98; Dewey on, 243n10; meaning making and, 198–99; neoliberalism and, 200; restorative justice and, 191–201; in transformative justice, 203
Lloyd, Vincent, 232n20, 245n1
London, Jack, 29
Los Angeles, Homeboy Industries of, 103
lynchings, 65

mandatory minimum drug sentencing, in war on drugs, 65, 66
Mandela, Nelson, 1
Manquina, Mongesi, 21–24

marginalization, 2; in Back of the Yards, 59, 82; as cultural violence, 81; cultural violence and, 3, 81; in Jim Crow, 123; in New Jim Crow, 123; prison-industrial complex and, 3; racism and, 3; of released prisoners, 57; settlement houses for, 32; in South Africa, 23; as structural violence, 82; trauma discourse and, 90; Ubuntu and, 122
marijuana, 69
Martin, Helena, 130–31, 138, 144–48
Maslow, Abraham, 87
mass incarceration: accountability for, 139–41; Back of the Yards and, 63; fragmentation and, 82; growth of, 24–25; in New Jim Crow, 7–8; nihilism of, 109; oppression of, 213n1; policing and, 3, 6; restorative justice for, 8; secular on, 240n7; size of, 63; social capital and, 2; social control and, 63, 67–68; spirituality of, 2–3; structural features of, 56–57; systemic injustices of, 12, 182. *See also* New Jim Crow; prison abolition
Matilda (Dahl), 152–53
Mayorga, Orlando "Chilly," 14, 53–62
McCarthy, Gary, 154, 155y
McDonald, Laquan, 11, 152–65
McDowell, Mary, 32, 114, 222n14
meaning making, 3; accompaniment and, 104; lived religion and, 198–99; resilience in, 12; restorative justice as, 199
Mennonites, 142
mental health care, 149; at LCLC, 158; prison abolition and, 183; solitary confinement and, 234n7
mentoring: at LCLC, 158; at Precious Blood Ministry of Reconciliation, 7, 39, 55–59
The Metaphysics of Morals (Kant), 236n14
Miller v. Alabama, 143–44
miscegenation, 64–65
Montgomery v. Louisiana, 144

moral dynamics: of forgiveness, 143; of restorative justice, 2, 11–12
Moses, Robert, 30
Movement for Black Lives, 187, 240n2
Moynihan, Daniel Patrick, 33, 222n18
mutual recognition: in moral dynamics, 2; in peacemaking circles, 97, 109; power in, 71; in restorative justice, 3; in South Africa TRC, 23; in transformative justice, 203, 204

NAACP, Addams and, 32
National Lawyers Guild, 240n2
The Negro Family (Moynihan), 33
neoliberalism: lived religion and, 200; prison-industrial complex and, 61
New Age self-help/spiritualism, 9, 201
Newbold, Jayeti, 14
New Jim Crow, 6, 7–8; broken windows policing in, 68–69; caste system in, 67, 69, 80; compassion in, 110–11; cultural violence in, 85–86; decriminalization and, 69, 80; defined, 64–68; fragmentation in, 82–83; marginalization in, 123; oppression in, 123; policing in, 22; restorative justice and, 63–73; retribution in, 69, 80; self-perpetuation of, 136; social control in, 69; stigmatization in, 67, 69, 73, 80; structural violence in, 85–86; transformative justice and, 203; trauma in, 114–15
The New Jim Crow (Alexander), 59, 73, 150, 207–8
Nguni, 83, 119
nihilism, 107, 245n20; lived religion and, 198–99; of mass incarceration, 109; in prison-industrial complex, 3
Nineteenth Amendment, 64
Nixon, Richard, 66
Nofemla, Eazi, 21–24
nondominated consensus, 81, 86
nondomination: inclusive, 124, 195, 243n9; in restorative justice, 135–36

North Lawndale: LCLC in, 14, 157–59, 172, 178–80; restorative justice in, 10–11, 157–59
Notre Dame, 16; Center for Social Concerns at, 17; IRB at, 215n13
Ntamo, Vusumzi, 21–24

Oak Lawn, 167
Oak Park, 35
object-directed inquiry, 18, 218n23
Office of Fair Housing and Equal Opportunity, 36
Okun, Evan, 14
oppression: critical consciousness of, 8–9; critical praxis and, 78; in Jim Crow, 123; of mass incarceration, 213n1; in New Jim Crow, 123

parallel model, 72
parole, 25, 63. *See also* life sentence with no possibility of parole
participatory action, 12–19
Peace Circle for Mothers, 134
peace garden, 36
peacemaking circles, at Precious Blood Ministry of Reconciliation, 7, 9, 15, 38, 44–52, 87–89; accompaniment and, 105; accountability in, 109, 110, 163–64; apology in, 50, 51; building relationships in, 48, 108; checking in at, 47, 91, 95; checking out of, 47; closing at, 47; compassion in, 109, 110, 127; confidentiality at, 46, 163; critical consciousness in, 110, 176; critical praxis of, 107–10; cultural violence and, 110; deliberations in, 128–29; ethics of, 125–29; for gangs, 108–9; guidelines for, 125–29, 169--170; icebreakers at, 167–69; justice in, 125, 127; mothers in, 148–49; mutual recognition in, 97, 109; for personhood, 128; police and, 50–52, 127, 166–76; power in, 126–28; privileged communication in, 163–64; reciprocal accountability in, 97, 125–26; reciprocal respect in, 94, 97, 109, 169; ribbon ceremony at, 46, 51; safe space at, 169; school and, 52; self-reliance in, 94; sharing stories in, 170–73; spirituality of, 107–10, 113; trauma and, 90–96, 107–8; value-based practice of, 169–70
penetration, of cultural violence, 82–85
Peni, Ntobeko, 21–24
personhood: peacemaking circles for, 128; relational, 78–79, 119–23; in restorative justice, 26, 61–62, 118; spirituality and, 198. *See also* individual agency
phenomenological objectivity, 216n20
piety, 191, 213n3, 243n10
Pinn, Anthony, 13
plea bargaining, 141, 236n18
Plessy v. Ferguson, 64
police/policing: in Back of the Yards, 37, 38, 56; Bridging the Divide and, 171, 172, 176, 179–80; brutality of, 11, 152–65, 174, 179, 239n2; CAPS, 172, 179; in conflict circle, 173–77; corruption in, 11; critical praxis and, 166–80; drugs arrests by, 69, 153, 159, 225n7 (chap. 5), 226n11; excesses in, 13; LCLC and, 172; mass incarceration and, 3, 6; McDonald and, 152–65; murder of, 172–73; in New Jim Crow, 7–8; peacemaking circles and, 50–52, 127, 166–76; Precious Blood Ministry of Reconciliation and, 172; prison-industrial complex and, 177; qualified immunity of, 174; racializing of, 91; racism and, 175; restorative justice and, 11, 157, 166–80; suffering by, 173; transformative justice and, 204; trauma and, 172–73; in war on drugs, 127. *See also* broken windows policing
political reconciliation, restorative justice and, 4, 218n3
poll taxes for voting, 64

post-traumatic stress disorder (PTSD), 111, 231n6
power: in critical praxis, 78; in justice, 81; in mutual recognition, 71; in peacemaking circles, 126–28; in reciprocal accountability, 71; in restorative justice, 71, 75, 79, 117–24
Precious Blood Ministry of Reconciliation, 17, 28–29; Art on 51st of, 134, 144; arts and performance at, 7; between-ness at, 113–14; carpentry apprenticeship at, 7, 102, 104, 134; as co-creating community, 97, 101–2, 105, 111, 149; compassion at, 112; craft and skill training at, 7; drive-by shooting at, 91; ethics at, 10; as hub of hubs, 14–15; job training at, 39, 102; justice accountability and, 130–51; legal support at, 7; McDonald and, 156; mentoring at, 7, 39, 55–59; partner initiatives at, 115–16; police and, 172; punishment and, 100; restorative justice at, 37–44, 49–52, 57–59, 99, 100, 111–12; safe space at, 39, 43, 47–48; Saturday Sanction at, 40–41, 44, 95, 161–63; transformative justice at, 207, 208; trauma discourse at, 96–100; tutoring at, 7, 39; urban farming at, 7; violence and conflict at, 43. *See also* accompaniment; peacemaking circles; radical hospitality
prison abolition, 240n2; coercive force and, 185–86; critical praxis for, 189–90; religion and, 183–86; restorative justice and, 181–90; secular and, 184, 185; spirituality and, 184–86; temptations of, 182–87; transformative justice and, 187–90, 206–8
prison-industrial complex: as caste system, 1, 63–64; cultural violence of, 6, 187; marginalization and, 3; mass incarceration in, 25; neoliberalism and, 61; nihilism in, 3; penetration and, 83;

policing and, 177; reform of, 187–90; self-perpetuation of, 136; social control of, 69; structural violence of, 6, 187; systemic injustices of, 4; transformative justice and, 203, 204; violence in, 5. *See also* hyper-incarceration; mass incarceration; New Jim Crow
privileged communication (attorney-client privilege), 163–65; prison reform and, 188
probation, 25, 63; of Mayorga, 57; Saturday Sanction and, 161–62
The Psychology of Science (Maslow), 87
PTSD. *See* post-traumatic stress disorder
punishment, 1; Precious Blood Ministry of Reconciliation and, 100; restorative justice and, 71; right to, 236n14; in tough on crime policies, 67–68; in war on drugs, 67–68. *See also* retribution
Purdie, Pamela, 14; on trauma discourse, 87–89, 91–92
Putnam, Hilary, 215n15, 216n16

qualified immunity, of police, 174
Quintana, Elena, 14, 89, 90, 100, 105, 106, 231n6

race riots, 34
racism: in Back of the Yards, 28, 30–36, 114; marginalization and, 3; passive forms of, 123; police and, 175; restorative justice and, 1; in South Africa, 23. *See also* Jim Crow; New Jim Crow
radical hospitality, at Precious Blood Ministry of Reconciliation, 42–44, 57; accompaniment and, 105, 106; resilience for, 105, 106; trauma and, 98, 106
The Rage of Innocence (Henning), 239n3
Raisin in the Sun (Hansberry), 35
Reagan, Ronald, 66
real estate. *See* housing
reasonable suspicion, 68
recidivism, 140, 236n15

reciprocal accountability: for cultural violence, 126; in peacemaking circles, 97, 125–26; power in, 71; relationality of, 229n15; in relational personhood, 120–21; segregation and, 123; for structural violence, 126; in trauma discourse, 97; Ubuntu and, 124
reciprocal respect: in moral dynamics, 2; in peacemaking circles, 94, 97, 109, 169; in restorative justice, 3; in South Africa TRC, 23; in transformative justice, 204
redlining, 31, 35; Back of the Yards and, 56; in Great Migration, 33
relational ethnography, 216n20
relational justice, 9, 78–80
relational personhood, 78–79, 119–21; reciprocal accountability in, 120–21; Ubuntu and, 122–23
relational restoration and, 79
relentless engagement, trauma discourse and, 98, 99, 100, 105, 106
religion: in Back of the Yards, 114; critical participatory action research and, 18; prison abolition and, 183–85, 186; restorative justice and, 242n3; secular and, 12, 18, 182, 184, 190, 199, 240n7. *See also* Christianity; lived religion
remorse: with life sentence with no possibility of parole, 143–47; in restorative justice, 72
repair of harm agreements, 47, 50, 81, 86, 127–28
reparative model, 228n26
resilience: in meaning making, 12; for radical hospitality, 105, 106; in restorative justice, 139; in transformative justice, 75; in trauma discourse, 94
respect. *See* reciprocal respect
restitution, 23, 72, 139, 156, 159
restorative justice: accountability in, 72, 76, 130–51; amnesty and, 136; becoming concrete, 181–90; Christianity on, 142, 184; critical participatory action research for, 12–19, 215n15, 216n20; critical praxis in, 76–78, 84, 148–51; defined, 4–6; empathy in, 72; ethics of, 9–10, 12, 26–27, 117–24; of First Nations, 234n4; forgiveness in, 141–53, 244n18; greatest temptation for, 19–20; holistic approach to, 1–5; individual agency in, 59–62, 78–82, 119; interpersonal aspects of, 74–86; for interpersonal conflicts, 8–9; as justice, 117–24; lived religion and, 191–201; for mass incarceration, 8; as meaning making, 199; moral dynamics of, 2, 11–12; New Jim Crow and, 63–73; nondomination in, 135–36; in North Lawndale, 10–11, 157–59; parallel model for, 72; personhood in, 26, 61–62, 118; policing and, 11, 157, 166–80; political reconciliation and, 4, 218n3; portability of, 7; power in, 71, 75, 79, 117–24; prison abolition and, 181–90; privileged communication in, 163–65; punishment and, 71; racism and, 1; relationship building in, 80–85; religion and, 242n3; remorse in, 72; for resilience, 139; retribution and, 79–80, 226n19; safety net model for, 72; in South Africa, 24–26; spirituality and, 2, 3–4, 11–12, 110–16, 182, 214n3; stigmatization and, 27, 85; structural violence and, 93, 114, 186; systemic injustices and, 20, 73, 76, 93, 114; transformative justice and, 74–86, 228n4, 229n11; trauma and, 9, 87–116, 231n12; understanding of, 70–73; unitary model for, 72; zero-sum equation and, 137–39. *See also specific topics*
"Restorative Justice and the New Jim Crow" (Springs), 13
restorative justice court, at LCLC, 159–61
Restore Justice Illinois, 132, 147
restoring relationships, 227n21
restrictive covenants, 33, 35

re-traumatization, 93
retribution/retributive justice, 1; accountability and, 140–41; dehumanization of, 140–41, 188; in New Jim Crow, 69, 80; restorative justice and, 79–80, 226n19; South Africa TRC and, 24; as zero-sum equation, 137–39
ribbon ceremony, at peacemaking circles, 46, 51
Rogers Park, Circles and Ciphers in, 14

safe space: at peacemaking circles, 169; at Precious Blood Ministry of Reconciliation, 39, 43, 47–48
safety net model, 72
Saint Agatha Catholic Church, 160
Saturday Sanction, at Precious Blood Ministry of Reconciliation, 40–41, 44, 95, 161–63
school: gangs in, 60, 130; peacemaking circles and, 52; transformative justice and, 206. *See also* zero-tolerance discipline codes
Schub, Ora, 14
Second Chance High School, 37
secular: in Back of the Yards, 114; critical participatory action research and, 18; on mass incarceration, 240n7; prison abolition and, 184, 185; religion and, 12, 18, 182, 184, 190, 199, 240n7
segregation, 123–24; recent high levels in Chicago, 221n9
self-incrimination, 164
self-reliance, 3, 112, 243n10; co-creating community and, 242n3; co-creation of community and, 104; meaning making and, 199; in peacemaking circles, 94; in relational personhood, 78
self-worth, 2, 3, 109
sentencing: Campaign for Fair Sentencing for Children, 132; Fair Sentencing Act of 2010, 66; mandatory minimum drug sentencing, in war on drugs, 65, 66. *See also* life sentence with no possibility of parole
Sentencing Reform Act of 1984, 66
separate but equal, 64
September 11, 2001 terrorist attacks, 231n12
Sered, Danielle, 146, 147
Sessions, Jeff, 238n6
settlement houses, 32
sewage, 33–34
Sharpe, Susan, 229n15
Sinclair, Upton, 29, 114, 221n4
social capital, mass incarceration and, 2
social control: mass incarceration and, 63, 67–68; in New Jim Crow, 69; prison abolition and, 187; of prison-industrial complex, 69
social Darwinism, 32–33
solitary confinement, 234n7
South Africa: amnesty in, 21; apartheid in, 21, 22; Nguni in, 83; restorative justice in, 24–26; transitional justice in, 23–24; TRC in, 6–7, 21–27, 119. *See also* Ubuntu
spirituality/spiritual dynamics: of accompaniment, 101–16; compassion in, 197–98; ethics of, 196; of mass incarceration, 2–3; of peacemaking circles, 107–10, 113; personhood and, 198; prison abolition and, 184–86; restorative justice and, 2–4, 11–12, 110–16, 182, 214n3; systemic injustices and, 12; trauma and, 101–16; varieties of, 195–98. *See also* lived religion
Starr, Ellen Gates, 32
Staudt, Sarah, 14, 152–54, 157–59, 172, 178–80, 239n2
Stevenson, Bryan, 143–44
stigmatization: in Back of the Yards, 7; of cultural violence, 82; with life sentence with no possibility of parole, 131, 149; in New Jim Crow, 67, 69, 73, 80; over-

coming, 204; restorative justice and, 27, 85; in war on drugs, 82
St. John of God, 28, 36, 37
stop-and-frisk, 68
Stout, Jeffrey, 213n2, 218n23, 235n3, 245n23
Stowe, Harriet Beecher, 29, 221n4
St. Raphael the Archangel, 36
Strong, Karen, 226n19, 228n25, 229n11
structural violence, 5; accompaniment and, 103; in Back of the Yards, 56; cultural violence and, 25; defined, 219n8; fragmentation as, 82–83; justice system and, 27; lived religion and, 201; marginalization as, 82; in New Jim Crow, 7–8, 85–86; prison abolition and, 185; of prison-industrial complex, 6, 187; reciprocal accountability for, 126; relational justice and, 79; restorative justice and, 93, 114, 186; in South Africa, 22; South Africa TRC and, 6; transformative justice and, 203, 204; transformative justice for, 85–86; trauma discourse and, 89. *See also* critical praxis
subsidiarity, 115
substance abuse, 205; of parents, 53; policing of, 177; prison abolition and, 183; from trauma, 90. *See also* drugs
systemic injustices: institutional norms for, 100; of mass incarceration, 12, 182; of prison-industrial complex, 4; restorative justice and, 20, 73, 76, 93, 114; South African TRC and, 27; spirituality and, 12

Taylor, Keeanga-Yamahtta, 187
three strikes, 25; New Jim Crow and, 65
Torre, Maria Elena, 216n17
tough on crime policies, 8, 25; fragmentation and, 82; New Jim Crow and, 65; punishment in, 67–68
transcendence, 195–96, 197

transformative justice: critical praxis in, 76–78, 157; interpersonal aspects of, 74–86; for McDonald, 157; prison abolition and, 187–90; restorative justice and, 228n4, 229n11; restorative justice as, 74–86; steps toward, 203–9
transitional justice, in South Africa, 23–24
trauma/trauma discourse, 232n15; amygdala and, 108; as complex or developmental, 232n16; historical, 114; language of, 92–97; at LCLC, 158; in New Jim Crow, 114–15; peacemaking circles and, 90–92, 94–95, 107–8; police and, 172–73; at Precious Blood Ministry of Reconciliation, 96–100; PTSD, 111, 231n6; radical hospitality in, 106; restorative justice and, 9, 87–116, 231n12; spirituality and, 101–16
Truth and Reconciliation Commission (TRC), in South Africa, 6–7, 21–26, 119
truth and reconciliation commissions, 4–5, 218n2
tutoring: at LCLC, 158; at Precious Blood Ministry of Reconciliation, 7, 39
Tutu, Desmond, 119, 122
Twenty-Ninth Street Beach, 34

Ubuntu, 83, 119, 137; ethics of, 122–24
UCan, 160
Ucker, Ethan, 14
Umbreit, Mark, 142
Uncle Tom's Cabin (Stowe), 29, 221n4
Union Stock Yards, 29; closing of, 30
unitary model, 72
University of Chicago: Chicago School of Sociology at, 32–33; Justice Equity, and Opportunity Initiative at, 59
University of Illinois, Education Justice Project at, 54
urban farming, at Precious Blood Ministry of Reconciliation, 7

Urban Life Skills, in Little Village, 14
urban renewal, in Back of the Yards, 28, 30

vagrancy laws, 64, 67
value-free scholarship, 15, 18
Van Dyke, Jason, 152–65
Van Ness, Dan, 226n19, 228n25, 229n11
victim-offender mediation, 5, 97
Violent Crime Control and Law Enforcement Act of 1994, 66
voting rights, in Jim Crow, 64

war on drugs, 8, 25, 27; gangs and, 82; mandatory minimum drug sentencing in, 65, 66; New Jim Crow and, 65–67, 73; Nixon and, 66; policing in, 127; punishment in, 67–68; Reagan and, 66; stigmatization in, 82
Washington, Sylvia Hood, 222n14
Weber, Max, 185, 215n15, 216n16
West, Cornel, 109, 198, 245n20
West Garfield Park, 35
Whiskey Point, 32
White flight, 35, 36; Back of the Yards and, 56
Whiteness: accompaniment and, 40; Americanization and, 32; blurred assimilation of ethnic identities into, 31
White supremacy, 3; in Back of the Yards, 114; dehumanization of, 83–84; penetration and, 83–84; segregation, 123
Williams, Eugene, 34
Wilson, Woodrow, 31
Winfield, Jeremy, 14
Wolterstorff, Nicholas, 233n2

Yukok Tribal Court, 245n1
Zehr, Howard, 142, 226n19, 231n12, 232n15
zero-sum equation, retribution as, 137–39
zero-tolerance discipline codes, 25, 27; New Jim Crow and, 65

ABOUT THE AUTHOR

JASON A. SPRINGS is Professor of Religion, Ethics, and Peace Studies at the University of Notre Dame. He is the author of *Healthy Conflict in Contemporary American Society: From Enemy to Adversary* and *Toward a Generous Orthodoxy: Prospects for Hans Frei's Postliberal Theology*, and coauthor (with Atalia Omer) of *Religious Nationalism: A Reference Handbook*. His articles have appeared in *Journal of Religious Ethics*, *Journal of the American Academy of Religion*, *Journal of Religion*, *Modern Theology*, *Political Theology*, and *Contemporary Pragmatism*, among others.

www.ingramcontent.com/pod-product-compliance
Lightning Source LLC
Chambersburg PA
CBHW020405040426
42333CB00055B/513